D1522421

KANT'S THEORY OF MORALS

KANT'S
THEORY OF MORALS

by Bruce Aune

PRINCETON UNIVERSITY PRESS
PRINCETON, NEW JERSEY

To My Mother

Contents

Preface

THOUGH Kant's views on morals are as important as those of any major philosopher, his writings on the subject are concerned almost exclusively with what he called the "metaphysics" of morals. A metaphysics, for Kant, is a system of "pure" knowledge: it is attained a priori and involves only a priori concepts. Formal logic is also a pure subject, but unlike metaphysics it does not concern "determine objects of the understanding." As Kant conceives of it, metaphysics has two subdivisions: the metaphysics of nature and the metaphysics of morals. The subject of morals, at least as we ordinarily understand it, has, Kant thinks, both a pure and an empirical part. The pure part, which he calls "morals proper," belongs to metaphysics and contains the a priori principles of morality. The empirical part, which he calls "practical anthropology," is concerned with applying these a priori principles to "conditions that can arise in experience."

Kant's first and most famous book on morals is his *Grundlegung zur Metaphysik der Sitten*, known in English translation as the *Groundwork of the Metaphysics of Morals*, the *Foundations of the Metaphysics of Morals*, or the *Fundamental Principles of the Metaphysics of Morals*. As these titles indicate, Kant's book is concerned with the basic principles of the metaphysics of morals, not with the whole subject. These basic principles do not include the distinctive laws of ethics or justice, which he believes can be inferred from the basic principles. Kant develops these distinctive laws in a later work called simply *Metaphysik der Sitten* or, in translation, *The Metaphysics of Morals*. This later work is divided into two parts, *Metaphysische Anfangsgründe der Rechtslehre* (or *Metaphysical Elements of Justice*) and *Metaphysische Anfangsgründe der Tugendlehre* (or *Metaphysical Elements of Virtue*). According to this work, duties of justice are prescribed by juridical laws and duties of virtue (or ethics) are prescribed by ethical laws. These two kinds of duties comprise the system of moral duties that Kant discusses, in a highly abstract way, in the *Grundlegung zur Metaphysik der Sitten*, which from now on I shall refer to as the *Groundwork*.

Although I hope my book will interest specialists in Kant's philosophy, I have written it mainly for students and teachers of moral philosophy who wish to understand and evaluate Kant's contributions to their subject. Nearly every undergraduate course in ethics devotes some attention to Kant's *Groundwork*, but it is difficult to think of any acknowledged philosophical classic that is subject to greater misunderstanding than this one. The fault, I must admit, is partly Kant's. His *Groundwork* is really the visible tip of an intellectual iceberg, and it positively invites misunderstanding because of its misleading terminology, its highly compressed argumentation, and its dependence on ideas developed elsewhere in Kant's writings. To achieve a secure grasp of the system Kant sketches in the *Groundwork* one must not only reflect on his *Metaphysics of Morals*, which works out important details of his moral theory, but also consider certain ideas developed in his *Critique of Pure Reason*, his *Critique of Practical Reason*, his *Critique of Judgment*, and certain minor works. To make my book particularly useful to the student of ethics, I shall focus my attention on the works most commonly studied in ethics courses—namely, the *Groundwork* and the *Metaphysics of Morals*—but I shall introduce material from Kant's other writings in the course of my discussion.

Since this book is not directed specifically to Kant scholars, I have assumed no familiarity with Kant's philosophy. Also, I have rarely referred to other writers on Kant. Many useful books and articles on aspects of Kant's moral philosophy have appeared in recent years, but if I had allowed myself to comment freely on what others have said about my subject, I am sure that I would have ended up writing two books under one cover: a book on Kant, and one on his critics and expositors. Considering the interests of my intended audience, I felt justified in restricting my efforts to the limited but still demanding task of providing a short, clear, unified treatment of Kant's moral theory that takes account of all his principal writings on morality, presents his views in a contemporary idiom, and subjects his arguments to critical scrutiny.

This book grew out of a course on the history of ethics that I have been giving at the University of Massachusetts at Amherst, and it has been improved by discussions with my students there. It has also served as the basis for a seminar in Kant's ethics that I gave at Union College in the spring of 1978. I wish to thank Professor Robert Baker, who attended the seminar and read my manuscript, for many helpful remarks. Several of my friends and colleagues at the University of Massachusetts read parts of my manuscript and offered critical comments for which I am grateful; they include Professors Leonard Ehrlich, John Robison, and Robert Paul Wolff. Two people deserve a special word of thanks: Professor Allen Wood of Cornell University, who supplied several pages of criticism; and my exemplary colleague Gareth Matthews, who has willingly read and criticized everything I have written during the past eight years.

I wish to thank the following publishers for permission to quote from material on which they own the copyright: University of Pennsylvania Press for permission to quote from E. B. Ashton's translation of Kant's *On the Old Saw: That May be Right in Theory, But It Won't Work in Practice*, copyright 1974; Harper and Row, Publishers, Inc., for permission to quote from Mary J. Gregor's translation of Kant's *"Doctrine of Virtue": Part II of the "Metaphysics of Morals,"* copyright 1964; Hutchinson Publishing Group, Ltd., for permission to quote from H. J. Paton's translation of Kant's *Groundwork of the Metaphysics of Morals*, which was included in Paton's *The Moral Law* (London: Hutchinson University Library, 1956); the Bobbs-Merrill Company, Ltd., for permission to quote from L. W. Beck's translation of Kant's *Foundations of the Metaphysics of Morals*, copyright 1959, and John Ladd's translation of Kant's *"Metaphysical Elements of Justice": Part I of the "Metaphysics of Morals,"* copyright 1965.

A Note on References

IN referring to passages in Kant's writings I first give the page number of the appropriate volume in the Royal Prussian Academy edition of *Kants Gesammelte Schriften*, 23 vols. (Berlin, 1900-1956), and then give the corresponding page of an English translation. Since most translations of Kant's works include, typically in the margin of each page, a reference to the corresponding page of the academy edition, the reader relying on an English translation different from the one I use will have no trouble locating the passages to which I refer.

KANT'S THEORY OF MORALS

Chapter I: The First Chapter of the *Groundwork*

As I explained in my preface, the fundamental principles of Kant's theory of morals are set forth in the *Groundwork* and the substantive details of his theory are developed in other works, principally the *Critique of Practical Reason* and the two parts of the *Metaphysics of Morals*. To simplify my exposition and to keep as close as possible to key Kantian texts, I shall build my discussion of Kant's theory around two of these works, focusing my first four chapters on the *Groundwork* and the last two on the *Metaphysics of Morals*. I shall deal with pertinent doctrines of the *Critique of Practical Reason* and other relevant texts *en passant*.

The first chapter of the *Groundwork* is concerned with the nature of our ordinary moral judgment, Kant's chief purpose being to discover the "first principle" of such judgment. In the second chapter Kant will attempt to locate this first principle, the moral law as he calls it, by reference to deeper philosophical considerations, and in the third and final chapter he will try to explain why this law is binding on us as imperfectly rational beings. Although his aim in the first chapter is somewhat limited, he develops important theses in it that underlie his claims in the more philosophical chapters to follow.

1. *The Notion of a Good Will*

Kant begins his first chapter by arguing that if we take our ordinary moral convictions for granted, we shall have to admit, at least on reflection, that the only conceivable thing "in or out of the world" valuable or good without qualification is a good will. His notion of a good will turns out to be complicated and unusual, but we shall not do violence to his theory if we begin by conceiving of such a will as a self-conscious disposition to choose courses of action (and inaction) in a morally commendable way. The first question for us to consider, then, is whether it is reasonable to think that a good will, so understood, is the only conceivable thing in or out of the world that is good without qualification.

Contrary to what one might initially suppose, this question is probably as difficult as any that could be asked in moral philosophy, and it is naive to think that every decent, reflective person would be inclined to answer it in the same way. Kant answers it, in effect, by ruling out plausible alternatives. Most things commonly considered good are easily seen, he thinks, to be qualified goods. Intelligence, wit, judgment, courage, wealth, and health belong to this class. We value them only to the extent that they contribute to other things we value. We want to build a house, learn a language, find our way home: intelligence helps. We want to be amused: wit helps. We want certain luxuries: wealth is indispensable. These goods are qualified because we value them only on the condition that they help bring about other things we value. Unfortunately, they are sometimes put to bad use. An evil man may use his intelligence, judgment, and courage to rob, rape, or murder. Wealth may be used to corrupt morals, start wars, or even destroy civilization. Health, a necessity for many goods, may yet be a bad thing in some cases; as Kant remarks, it may promote a disgusting pride or arrogance, even an aggressiveness, in a bad man. Thus, although most things commonly called good really are good, at least most of the time, they are not good without qualification, and they can be positively bad.

These remarks may not seem to apply to things philosophers often regard as intrinsic goods—namely, pleasure, the absence of pain, and, more generally, happiness. But Kant contends that these states of mind or conditions are good only when they are deserved. As he says, "a rational and impartial spectator can never feel approval in contemplating the uninterrupted prosperity of a being graced by no touch of a pure and good will"[1] and "when someone who delights in annoying and vexing peace-loving folk receives at last a right good beating . . . everyone approves of it and considers it good in itself even if nothing further results from it."[2] Thus, Kant seems to hold that some people may deserve a measure of unhappiness, and that a world in which they actually suffer for the harm they have done to others might be better (other things being equal) than a world in which they are entirely happy and content.

Although philosophers favoring a retributivist conception of punishment would eagerly agree with Kant here, those committed to some form of utilitarianism would remain unmoved. The unconditional value of happiness is perhaps the fundamental point that distinguishes classical utilitarianism from the view Kant accepts, and a utilitarian would certainly not be tempted to abandon his view just because it is widely assumed that certain people may deserve a dose of unhappiness. The dispute between Kant and the utilitarians cannot possibly be resolved in just a few pages, but it can easily be shown that most contemporary philosophers would actually agree, though perhaps only tacitly, that happiness is good only with some qualification.

If happiness were a wholly unqualified good, the more net happiness a world contains the better it would have to be: it would simply contain more units of unqualified goodness. But few philosophers nowadays would be willing to accept this view. In fact, even most latter-day utilitarians would reject it. For them, the moral value of a world is determined not simply by the net amount of happiness in it, but in part by how the happiness is distributed. Some would say that a world A is morally preferable to a world B just when the average net happiness in A is greater than the average net happiness in B. Others would offer more complicated formulas concerning distribution.[3] Though Kant would not agree with any general formula of this kind, he would be pleased with one consequence of every one of them—namely, that happiness itself is not good without qualification. There may be, according to each theory, more net happiness in a world B than in a world A, but A may be morally preferable to, and thus better than, a world B because the happiness it contains may be distributed more satisfactorily than the happiness in B.

To avoid misunderstanding Kant's doctrine we should realize that his distinction between qualified and unqualified good is not the same as the distinction utilitarians commonly draw between instrumental and intrinsic goods. Kant would say that when happiness is good, it is good only with qualification, but he would not say that it is thereby an instrumental good, that is, a mere means to something intrinsically good. If he were to use the term "intrinsic good," he would no doubt apply it to *deserved* happiness, but he would insist that such happiness is good only with the qualification that it is deserved. The same point holds for many other examples of qualified goods: they are good, but they are not, in any normal sense, a *means* to some further good. Since any good that is not a means to some further good is, by definition, an intrinsic good, Kant would have to allow that some things good only "with qualification" may be intrinsically good.

Another point to note here is that when Kant surveys all possible candidates for unqualified goodness, he is considering only things or states that are "in the world or out of it." God, I suppose, is something that, if He exists, would count as out of the world, and Kant would say that God can be considered perfectly good only because He has a perfectly good will. The proviso "in or out of the world" is crucially important in Kant's discussion because he would not deny that a world itself, or at least a certain possible world, could be good without qualification. In fact, he says explicitly that a good will cannot be "the sole and complete good"; and this latter good, which we may call the "summum bonum," is certainly good without qualification.[4] The summum bonum is not a "thing" in or out of the world, however. Roughly speaking, it is a possible state of affairs, or possible world, in which each rational being is both supremely happy and, because he is morally perfect, worthy of being supremely happy. This state of affairs is, for Kant, a moral ideal; and though we may all do our part to realize it, we have no assurance that it will, in fact, be realized at all.

Suppose that Kant is correct in thinking, or at least has very strong grounds for concluding, that with the exception of a good will nothing in or out of the world is good without qualification. Is it reasonable to hold that a good will is actually good without qualification? If a good will is a conscious disposition to make morally commendable choices, it would seem obvious that such a will is good—morally good. But a person who wills to do the right (or moral) thing could easily, in willing to do good, be the source of considerable suffering. In this case a good will could be instrumentally bad. Does this not show that even a good will is good only with qualification? Kant answers no. Even if a good will happens to be the source of a great deal of suffering, it is still good as a will, for its aim is to do good. If one's aim is *fully* good, one cannot be blamed for missing the target or of being negligent in some way. The ill results of one's efforts are not, then, one's fault, and they cannot detract from the moral value of these efforts —or so Kant would argue.

Though plausible, this kind of reasoning does not fully nail down Kant's position. It does seem rational to conclude that if anything in the world is good without qualification, it is a good will or at least a good moral attitude. Yet if we have a moral ideal—Kant's summum bonum, perhaps—we might say that a will is good only with qualifications. If it promotes or helps realize the summum bonum, it really is good; but if it misfires—owing, perhaps, to a false idea of what is good— then it can be considered at least partly nongood. To say this is not to imply that a good will that misses the target is necessarily subject to blame or criticism; on the contrary, if the attitude is moral, nothing more need be required of the agent. Yet it does not follow from this that a morally unobjectionable attitude is necessarily good without qualification.

This last point need not be troublesome to Kant, however. He can preserve the spirit of his claim by drawing a distinction that parallels the distinction "act-utilitarians" sometimes

draw between subjectively and objectively right actions. According to this latter distinction, an act is objectively right just
when, roughly speaking, it maximizes human happiness; it is
subjectively right just when it is performed with the intention
of thus maximizing happiness. Kant would no doubt object
to the terms "objective" and "subjective" applied to moral
value, but he could draw a corresponding distinction between, say, internal and external moral value. He could then
say that a good will is internally good without qualification,
but that it could be externally bad. Being externally bad in
this sense is not morally culpable; it is merely a matter of
bringing about events that happen to be incompatible with
the summum bonum. To be deserving of moral censure, a
will must be internally bad, or internally bad on a particular
occasion.

At the beginning of this section I remarked that we shall
not do violence to Kant's theory if we begin by thinking of a
good will as a self-conscious disposition to make morally
commendable choices. I now want to improve this conception a little by introducing one of Kant's most important
claims about a good will, namely, that a person having such a
will acts (or chooses) "for the sake of duty." It is very easy to
misunderstand Kant on this matter. In answer to the question
"What motives or intentions make the good will good?" a recent commentator has said: "The good will's only motive is
to do its duty for the sake of doing its duty. Whatever it intends to do, it intends because it is its duty."[5] Yet this view is
explicitly rejected by Kant in the *Metaphysics of Morals* as, in
effect, an example of moral fanaticism.[6] He would agree that
a good will (or a person with a good will) is always motivated
by the thought of doing his duty. But this requires only that
such a person always has the intention of doing his duty and
will be moved to do whatever he takes to be his duty, for the
simple reason that it is his duty. Having a good will would
not, therefore, prevent a person from doing, or intending to
do, countless things not required (and not forbidden) by
duty, such as drinking a cool glass of lemonade on a hot day.
Of course, the characteristic acts of a good will—the acts that

show its goodness—will be motivated by the thought of doing his duty, but a good will (that is, a person with such a will) will also have contingent aims or motives, which are not positively required by his character as a good will.

This last conception of a good will is easily related to the conception I began with. Kant believes, as we shall see, that actions or choices are morally commendable when, and only when, they are done or made for the sake of duty. Since the goodness of a person's will is shown by the choices he makes (or the actions he wills), anyone whose will is morally good will be disposed to act (or choose) for the sake of duty. As I have just explained, such a person will also, as a matter of fact, be disposed to make various choices that are not motivated by the thought of duty, but these contingent choices must accord with his view of what duty requires in the sense that they are not contrary to, or forbidden by, that view.

2. Duty and Moral Value

After introducing the concept of a good will Kant proceeds to make several important remarks about duty and moral value. His first remark, which I have anticipated in the preceding paragraph, is as follows:

1. An action has moral value just when it is done for the sake of duty.

This remark will doubtless strike many philosophers as wide of the mark. If an action produces a great deal of happiness in deserving persons, wouldn't it have moral value no matter what the agent's motives were? Kant, of course, would say no. An action not done for the sake of duty might, he admits, "deserve praise and encouragement," but this does not imply that it has *moral* worth.[7] Actually, an act wholly vicious in intention might, by some accident or miscalculation, have fortunate effects, but so might an earthquake; in neither case does the agent or cause have a moral value. Kant says that a morally valuable action deserves our esteem, and it can do so only because it discloses an admirable attitude in its author.[8] Deserved happiness is, of course, morally valuable for Kant, but such happiness is not an action—and its cause, which may be an action (at least partly), is not rendered morally valuable by its mere effects. A vicious will is morally abominable, and an act motivated by such a will is equally abominable, even though it may happen to cause, or bring into being, a morally valuable state of happiness.

Although these reflections do, I believe, add some credibility to Kant's position, they are not really sufficient to establish his claim that actions have moral value just when they are done from a sense of duty. On the face of it, at least, an action done purely from a motive of benevolence—for example, from a feeling of brotherly love—would seem to have moral value and to be deserving of respect and esteem. Saying this is compatible with accepting the Kantian view that a person who does his duty only at the cost of a painful moral struggle may be worthy of greater respect or esteem than a person who, because of a fortunate natural disposition, has never experienced a moral struggle in his entire life. The fact (if it is a fact) that actions done for the sake of duty have a special moral value does not imply that actions done from some other commendable motive never have moral value. Kant's view here thus seems excessively strong and puritanical.

Kant's view of moral action may appear in a more satisfactory light if we consider his second remark, which amounts to the following:

2. The moral value of an action is owing to the maxim on which it is based rather than to its success in realizing some desired end or purpose.

This remark cannot be fully understood until Kant's notion of a maxim is clarified, which is something I intend to do in the next section. But even a superficial understanding of his remark is helpful to us. On the face of it, the criticism I gave to his first remark is consistent with this second remark. If a maxim is a principle on which one acts, then no matter whether it concerns one's duty or the happiness of others, we can still apparently say that the moral value of our action—the feature of it that commands our respect—is the maxim from which it is done.

This last observation is not fully satisfactory, however. Suppose the maxim or principle on which one acts is one prescribing acts of benevolence. Though such a maxim would seem, at first sight, to confer moral value on an action done for its sake, further reflection casts serious doubt on the idea. Kant would certainly want to say that a principle of benevolence could not *itself* confer moral value on actions because benevolent actions are not good without qualification.[9] As he no doubt sees it, there are countless possible conditions in which benevolence is morally objectionable—for example, in fighting just wars or in punishing heinous crimes—and it is not at all evident that this view is untenable. One can, of course, insist that benevolence is generally good, or good nearly all of the time, but insisting on this point is compatible with acknowledging that any principle of benevolence is subject to exceptions or qualifications. In fact, it is compatible with claiming that a benevolent action is morally wrong when it conflicts with one's moral duty. If this last point is correct—and it is far from evident that it is not—both Kant's first and second remarks may be correct (or acceptable) as well.

Kant's third remark is, he says, a consequence of the first two. The remark, in Beck's translation, is this:[10]

3. Duty is the necessity of an action executed from respect for law.

The meaning of this remark, or "principle" as Kant calls it, is far from clear. Since I shall have a lot to say in the following pages about Kant's conception of duty, I shall simply offer a rough paraphrase of it without discussion. As I see it, the principle amounts to something like the following:

3*. A person has a duty to do something A just when he would necessarily do A if he acted out of respect for law.

Kant's reasons for thinking that 3 follows from 1 and 2 are not easy to make out. But any discussion of this matter is unlikely to be fruitful until we have a clearer understanding of Kant's notion of maxims and laws.

3. Maxims, Action, and the Will

The notion of a maxim is fundamental to Kant's entire discussion of morals, and it is thus important to clarify it before proceeding further with his argument. I shall begin with some general reflections on purposive behavior and then show how the idea of such behavior makes it reasonable to introduce the notion of action on a maxim. Having done this, I shall proceed to discuss certain peculiarities in Kant's conception of a maxim. Finally, at the end of the section I shall add some remarks clarifying Kant's conception of volition or will.

The kind of behavior of crucial interest in morals is intentional or purposive behavior. When a person acts purposefully or intentionally, he acts for a reason, and his behavior is somehow based on that reason. A key question in the philosophy of action is, "In what way is an action *based* on a reason?" Though different philosophers have offered different answers to this question, the general answer I regard as correct is this:[11]

> When one does something A for a reason R, one does A as the result of a line of practical reasoning (it may be very short) in which R occurs as a premise.

Thus, if I buy a new pair of shoes for the reason that my old ones are worn out, the idea that my old ones are worn out serves as a key premise in the line of reasoning that leads me to decide to buy a new pair. Needless to say, other premises also occur in this line of reasoning, but the one concerning the old shoes is particularly important.

If a practical inference is a good one, there must be some logical connection between the premises and the conclusion. In fully explicit cases of practical inference the connection between a reason like "Doing A will make me happy" and the conclusion "So, I will do A" is effected by a general premise that Kant calls a "maxim" or "subjective principle"; in the present case it might be:

> For any action A, if doing A will make me happy, I will do A.

Maxims or subjective principles are not the same for all people; they are adopted (consciously or not) because the agent has various desires or purposes. If, for example, one has the purpose of being happy no matter what, one would naturally adopt (or otherwise come to possess) the maxim just given.

In speaking above of a "fully explicit" practical inference, I was deliberately excluding enthymematic inferences—those with missing premises. Outside of logic texts fully explicit inferences are remarkably rare. Thus, instead of reasoning according to the explicit pattern

> All men are mortal.
> Socrates is a man.
> Therefore, Socrates is mortal,

a real person would no doubt reason according to a pattern like this:

> Socrates is a man.
> So, he is mortal.

In conforming to this shorter pattern a person would be reasoning *in accordance with* the premise "All men are mortal," and he would no doubt volunteer this premise if asked to justify his inference. When one reasons in accordance with a premise, I shall say that one reasons with that premise "tacitly" in mind. If Kant's view of practical reasoning is to be plausible, he must allow that many of the maxims on which we act are only tacitly in our minds; we certainly do not repeat them to ourselves every time we act on them.

It is worth observing that a number of different maxims may bear on a particular action. Suppose that I have the maxim of avenging any wrong that might be inflicted upon me. Having received such a wrong, I might then conclude "I will avenge that wrong." To implement this decision I might rely on another maxim, a lower-order one, that prescribes dueling as an appropriate means of avenging a wrong. In accordance with this maxim, I may then conclude "So I will challenge Jones to a duel." But still another maxim may be brought to bear on the case, for I may have a policy of dueling with sabers whenever possible. The reasoning that leads to a particular decision may thus be long and complicated, and a good number of maxims may enter into it.

From what I have just said it might appear that Kant credits us with more maxims than we are apt to possess, and that his view of practical inference (at least as I am presenting it) cannot do justice to cases in which, instead of deriving a decision from various premises, we make a free choice among available means to a given end. I think there is some justice in this charge, but Kant can go a long way toward meeting it. Suppose, for example, that I aim to bring about some state of affairs E and believe that I can bring E about by doing either A or B. Suppose, further, that A and B are incompatible acts and that I have no maxim prescribing a way of realizing E. If, for various reasons, I prefer A to B and choose to do A rather than B, will I not make this choice without reliance on a maxim? I think Kant would say that I do act on a higher-order maxim in this case—one to the effect that, if I have available more than one way of realizing an end, I should choose the means that I happen to prefer. If Kant allows that a maxim of this sort need not be consciously formulated by the agent— that he may merely reason in accordance with it—then Kant's evident view of action on maxims is not undermined by cases of free choice.

Though these remarks help one to understand how maxims enter into practical reasoning, they do not fully explain what a maxim is supposed to be. According to Kant, maxims are practical propositions that "contain a general determination of the will."[12] Thus understood, maxims are general in import and express a volitional attitude. But not all practical principles are maxims. Kant says that maxims are "subjective" practical principles; they express a "general determination" to act under conditions that are, as a contingent matter of fact, of interest or importance to a particular agent. In contrast to subjective practical principles Kant speaks of practical laws, which are, he says, "valid" for the will of every rational being. I shall comment on this notion of validity in due course.

As I initially described them, maxims connect reasons (or motives) with decisions to act. For maxims proper, these reasons or motives are "subjective conditions"; they are acceptable to a particular agent because of contingent facts about him—for example, that he desires this or that. Since a decision to act is commonly expressed in literary English by a sentence of the form "I will do A," we can represent the conditional core of a maxim by the formula

I will do A if p,

where p is understood as expressing an appropriate subjective condition.

I speak of literary English here because, although "I will" is not sharply distinguished, at least in current American speech, from "I shall," there is a literary precedent for distinguishing them. According to this precedent, "I will" is used to express determination or volition whereas "I shall" is used to express mere beliefs, or predictions, about the future. To set matters straight I might say that, in my view, the volitional thought expressed by "I will" differs from the nonvolitional thought, or belief, expressed by the corresponding "I shall" in that the former, but not the latter, plays a distinctive role in bringing about the action.[13] I might add that the implications of "will" and "shall" are reversed in second- and third-person uses. "You shall do A" and "It shall be that p" express the speaker's volitional attitude while "You will do A" and "It will be that p" express mere beliefs or opinions.[14]

Apart from the volitional attitude expressed by the "will" and the conditionality expressed by the "if," maxims also involve, as I pointed out, a significant generality. In some cases this generality is attached wholly to actions; thus, some maxims have the form of

> For any A, if doing A satisfies the condition C, I will do A.

In other cases, however, the generality also attaches to the subjective condition. Recall the maxim of avenging any wrong inflicted upon one. On the face of it, this maxim has the form of

> For any A, if A is an act of wronging me, I will do something B to avenge A.

Here the generality is partly attached to the relevant condition, which happens to be any condition (any act by another) that is of a particular kind—namely, an act of wronging me.

To summarize, we can say that a maxim is a practical proposition that expresses a general determination (or volitional attitude) toward doing something or other that satisfies some specific or general condition in which the agent has some contingent interest. A practical law, as Kant describes it in the *Critique of Practical Reason*, differs from a maxim in expressing a general determination (or volitional attitude) toward doing something that satisfies a "universally valid" condition.[15] I shall discuss Kant's notion of a practical law more fully in the following section, for it raises special problems of interpretation.

In his later *Metaphysics of Morals* Kant draws a distinction between two different kinds of maxims.[16] Maxims of the first kind might be called "maxims of action," for they express a determination to act in a certain way when some condition is met. Kant himself has no special name for such maxims, but he does have a special name for maxims of the second kind: he calls them "maxims of ends." A maxim of ends expresses a determination to *do* a certain thing when some condition is met, but the doing is not an action in any ordinary sense: it is a mental act of "setting an end." To set an end in Kant's sense is to form an intention or purpose, such as that of developing one's talents. In view of this we might say that a maxim of ends expresses a determination (or intention) to form an intention when some condition is met. As far as its logical structure is concerned, a maxim of ends does not seem to differ from that of the maxims of action discussed above.

As I have described them, maxims (whether of actions or of ends) have the logical form of a universal conditional.[17] To avoid misunderstanding later on, it is important to realize that when Kant speaks of the "form" of a maxim he is not (at least for the most part) thinking of logical form. A term he uses in the *Critique of Practical Reason* is "legislative form."[18] As we shall see, he argues that it is morally permissible to act on a maxim only when it has the form of a universal law. Clearly, a maxim like "If I buy a new book, I will write my name in it" does not have the logical form of a universal law. It does, however, have the "legislative form" of a universal law, for it is unquestionably a morally acceptable maxim. I shall attempt to clarify Kant's notion of legislative form in due course; for the moment, it is sufficient merely to indicate that when Kant speaks of the form of a maxim, he generally means legislative form rather than logical form.

Apart from having a certain form, every maxim also has, Kant says, a certain "matter" or "material." Here again it is easy to misunderstand Kant's doctrine. A maxim's matter is not simply its nonformal content; it is the "purpose" or "subjective end" expressed by the maxim. On the whole, it seems reasonable to interpret Kant as holding that the purpose expressed by a maxim is essentially conditional. As far as the maxim considered above is concerned, the matter or purpose expressed would seem to be that of writing one's name in any book x, *if* one buys x. Anyone acting on this maxim has (as Kant would say) a "contingent interest" in any book he buys—an interest by virtue of which he would reasonably have the purpose just described.

Kant's distinction between the form and matter of a maxim is related to an important distinction he draws between formal and material practical principles. Generally speaking, a practical principle is one that "contains" (or expresses) "a general determination of the will"—that is, a volitional attitude toward someone's acting in a certain way. According

to Kant, both maxims and practical laws are practical principles. In the *Groundwork* he says that "practical principles are
formal when they disregard all subjective ends; they are material when they have subjective ends, and thus certain incentives, as their basis."[19] In an earlier paragraph he had remarked in passing that a priori practical principles are formal
and a posteriori practical principles are material.[20] These passages are easy to misunderstand if his distinction between the
matter and legislative form of a maxim is not kept in mind.
His idea is that *if* a practical principle is acceptable (or "valid")
independently of any contingent interest some person may
possess, then it is acceptable a priori by virtue of its legislative
form. If, on the other hand, such a principle is acceptable to
someone only because of a contingent interest that he possesses, then it is acceptable to him a posteriori by virtue of its
matter, which is the purpose (or interest) that it expresses.
The crucial point to keep in mind here is that a practical principle is not formal (and thus acceptable a priori) on account of
its logical form. It is formal on account of what Kant calls its
"legislative form." Exactly what legislative form is and how
it can render a practical proposition acceptable a priori are
matters that we shall investigate in due course.

In discussing maxims Kant constantly speaks of willing to
do something or other. Since the notion of willing (or volition) has been viewed with considerable suspicion by recent
analytical philosophers, I want to end this section with some
remarks on Kant's conception of the will.

As it happens, Kant uses two different expressions in referring to the will; they are *"Die Willkür"* and *"Der Wille."* Generally speaking, *Die Willkür* is the so-called faculty of decision
or choice. To exercise this faculty—to will in the appropriate
way—is just to decide, or perhaps choose, to do something.
Kant seems to conceive of deciding and choosing as mental
activities, but he tells us very little about them. For the limited
purposes of discussing his moral theory, I can see no objection to conceiving of these mental activities in any way that
strikes one as reasonable. In what follows I shall regard them

simply as the kind of volitional thought expressed in literary English by "I will do such and such."[21]

Kant's notion of *Wille* applies to what might be called a "legislating will." When one says "The will of the sovereign is law" or "Thy will be done," presumably one is speaking of the will in the sense of *Der Wille*. Kant interprets *Der Wille* as the will that is expressed in morally commendable choices—that is, the will that, if good, is good without qualification. At the beginning of this section I described such a will as a conscious disposition to make morally commendable choices, and later I qualified this description by saying that a person with a good will is necessarily disposed to act (or choose) for the sake of duty. Having introduced Kant's notion of a legislating will, or *Der Wille*, I can now offer an even more satisfactory description of a will that is good without qualification: it is simply the will to obey moral laws or to do one's duty. Anyone with such a will is necessarily disposed to make morally commendable choices because *Der Wille* is a rational will, and anyone who rationally wills to do his duty would be inconsistent if he made choices not conforming to this will. Also, since any rational being who wills to do his duty and sees that a certain choice is required by his duty will be moved to make that choice, a person with a good will (in the sense of *Der Wille*) is bound to have a conscious disposition to make morally commendable choices.

As we shall see, the reasons Kant will give for regarding *Die Willkür* and *Der Wille* as distinct faculties are highly questionable. Nevertheless, a distinction between legislating and nonlegislating willing is reasonably drawn. Sometimes we *decide to do* something; in such cases we might express our decision in words by saying "I will do such and such." Sometimes, on the other hand, we *decide that* something will occur or, more generally, be the case; in that event we can express our decision in words by saying "It shall be that . . ." or "*X* shall happen." Thus, if a ruler decides that his subjects shall pay taxes according to a certain schedule, he might express his decision by saying "My subjects shall pay taxes according to that schedule" or "It shall be that my subjects pay taxes taxes according to that schedule." (His corresponding belief could be expressed by saying "My subjects will pay taxes according to that schedule.") Conceived this way, the distinction between legislative and nonlegislative willing would be the distinction between *deciding that p* (for some *p*) and *deciding to do A* (for some *A*). If, for certain philosophical purposes, we want to collapse this distinction, we might say that willing-to-do is just a special case of willing-that, for the thought "I will do *A*" could be regarded as equivalent to the thought "It shall be that I do *A*." It turns out that if we do regard these thoughts as logically equivalent, we shall find it much easier to deal with the notion of consistent willing that is crucial for understanding Kant's several versions of the moral law.

4. *Duty and Practical Law*

At the end of section 2 I introduced three important remarks that Kant made about duty and moral value. The remarks were, in effect, these:

1. An action has moral value just when it is done for the sake of duty.
2. The moral value of an action is owing to the maxim on which it is based rather than to its success in satisfying or realizing some desired end or purpose.
3. Duty is the necessity of an action executed from respect for law.

What I propose to do in this section is, first, to offer a fuller account of Kant's reasons for 1 and 2; second, to see whether 3 is, as Kant claims, a consequence of 1 and 2; and, finally, to connect Kant's notion of a good will with the idea of a will that acts out of respect for law. This last task will set the stage for a discussion of the moral law, which I shall undertake in the section to follow.

The reasons Kant gives for 1, at least in his first chapter, rest heavily on his conception of moral value. As we have seen, he makes it clear that, in his opinion, not all value is moral value. Actions may deserve praise and encouragement, he says, without deserving the esteem appropriate to a morally valuable action. Thus, we may justifiably praise an athlete's exploits on the playing field or an actor's efforts on the stage when we know full well that those exploits and efforts do not merit anyone's moral approbation. To be morally estimable—to add luster to the agent's moral character—an action must be done for a morally admirable motive or "principle of the will," for a person's moral character is determined by what he means to do rather than by what he manages to accomplish (or bring about) in the world of experience. We can be assured of this last point because the difference between success and failure in realizing one's intentions is often largely a matter of luck, which does not add luster to anyone's moral character.

The question therefore arises, "What sort of motive, or 'principle of the will,' could possibly confer *moral* value on a persons's actions?" Kant replies that only the motive of doing one's duty could have this character. Any other "purposes we may have for our actions, and also their effects as ends or incentives of the will, cannot give the actions any unconditional and moral worth."[22] Such purposes cannot give our actions an unconditional moral worth because nothing that we can bring about by our actions has an unqualified value. We cannot ourselves bring about the summum bonum, for this requires the happiness as well as the moral perfection of all rational beings; and the only other thing of unqualified value is, as we have seen, a good will. Thus, if our actions ever have an unconditional worth—if their moral value is strict and unqualified—this value cannot be owing to the value of any effect we propose to bring about by our actions: it must depend entirely on the unconditional moral value of our motive. But only the motive of doing our duty can have this kind of moral value.

As I have developed it here, Kant's argument is not very impressive. He is concerned to show that an action has moral value just when it is done for the sake of duty, but his argument seems directed to the more restrictive conclusion that an action has "*unconditional*" moral value just when it is done for the sake of duty. If not all moral value is unconditional, it would appear that an action could have moral value even if it failed to satisfy the condition required for unconditional moral value. Thus, even if we allow that Kant's argument for the more restrictive conclusion is entirely satisfactory, we might contend that the conclusion he is officially concerned to establish remains highly doubtful.

I think, however, that Kant really meant to defend the less restrictive conclusion and that his use of the term "unconditional" (*unbedingt*) is simply misleading. As I have pointed out, the assumption on which he builds his argument is that the moral value of an action depends entirely on the motive or "principle of the will" from which it is done. When he says that nothing we can bring about by our will has "an unconditional and moral worth," he is merely emphasizing, I believe, that nothing we can bring about by our will is certain to be morally valuable in all circumstances. If he is right about this, the motive of bringing about such an effect could not itself ensure that the action has moral value; it would not be an intrinsically admirable motive. The motive of doing one's duty has this feature, however. In fact, it would seem to be the only motive that has it. If this is so, it seems reasonable to conclude that an action has moral value just when it is done for the sake of duty.

It is helpful to consider an example here. Take beneficence. Generally speaking, beneficent actions are morally commendable; in fact, Kant will argue that we have a "duty of virtue" to make the happiness of others one of our principal moral concerns. Yet if, disregarding all thought of duty, I act merely on the principle of making a certain person happy, my action could be morally objectionable. Not only might I be required, as a judge or jurist, to disregard the happiness of a particular person, but by making one person happy, I might be acting unjustly toward another person, and my duty to the latter might be stronger, or more pressing, than my duty to the former. The latter might be my child, my wife, or my aged invalid father whose well-being is my special responsibility. Since action on even the most benevolent of motives might in this way have a morally objectionable outcome, the mere fact that I act on such a motive cannot guarantee that my action is morally commendable. No other motive has this feature—at least no motive not equivalent to that of doing one's duty. This point seems obvious, because no such motive is necessarily incapable of conflicting with the demands of duty. Since Kant is assuming that the moral value of an action is entirely owing to the motive, or "principle of the will," from which it is done, he thus seems warranted in concluding that an action has moral worth just when it is done for the sake of duty. So much for his first claim.

Kant's second claim needs little discussion, because it is closely related to the first one. If an action has moral value just when it is done for the sake of duty, its moral value must be dependent on the motive or, as Kant says, the "principle of the will" from which it is done. But a principle of the will is simply a maxim in Kant's technical sense of the term: it is a "subjective principle" that expresses the agent's purpose and generates the action by a perhaps tacit process of reasoning. Given this, Kant is entitled to say that the moral value of an action is owing to the maxim on which it is based rather than to its success in realizing some desired end or purpose.

As I pointed out earlier, Kant believes that his third claim follows from his first two. Unfortunately, his reasoning is very difficult to understand at this point. One source of difficulty is his use of the term "practical law." As we saw in the last section, Kant characterizes practical laws in a way implying that they could not be (or serve as) maxims. Thus, in his *Critique of Practical Reason* he says that a maxim expresses a volitional attitude toward doing something that satisfies a contingent interest the agent has, but that a practical law expresses an attitude toward doing something that satisfies a "universally valid" condition.[23] Kant does not always distinguish maxims from practical laws in this way, however. In an important footnote in the *Groundwork* he says that a practical law is "an objective principle of volition," one that would "serve all rational beings also subjectively as a principle if reason had full power over the faculty of desire."[24] Since a subjective principle of volition is a maxim, this passage suggests that practical laws are simply "objectively valid" maxims that would be used as subjective principles by perfectly rational beings. It also suggests that the maxim on which morally valuable actions are based must be a practical law, for it is unquestionably "valid" and acceptable to all rational beings.

Though Kant's various remarks on maxims and practical laws are decidedly confusing, his fundamental view seems to be this. A maxim is simply a practical principle on which some agent acts, a principle having the structure described in the last section. For the most part, maxims express a volitional attitude toward doing something that satisfies some contingent interest the agent possesses, that is, an interest that not all rational beings need possess. Sometimes, however, a maxim expresses a volitional attitude toward doing something that satisfies a universally valid condition. In such cases, the maxim may be called "an objective principle of volition" or, less happily, "a practical law." Viewed this way, a practical law is simply a maxim that is universally valid or necessarily acceptable to any fully rational being.

I have just said that a universally valid maxim is not "happily" called a practical law. Kant uses this language, but it is confusing. As Kant conceives of them, laws have two distinguishing features: universality and necessity. Objectively valid maxims have, to be sure, a kind of universality and necessity, for they are necessarily acceptable to (or valid for) all rational beings. But they do not have the *logical* structure of what Kant normally considers a law. A typical maxim has the logical form of

For any action A, if A satisfies the condition C, I will do A,

whereas a typical law has the logical form, for Kant, of

All A's are necessarily B.

The crucial difference here is that a maxim is not a fully general statement; it contains a specific reference to the agent whose maxim it is. But if a given maxim is universally valid, a corresponding, fully general, "lawlike" statement is also "valid," and this corresponding statement seems to be a far better candidate for the relevant law. Thus, corresponding to the maxim "I will help people who cannot help themselves" there is the fully general statement "Any rational being will help people who cannot help themselves"; and if the maxim is universally valid, the corresponding general statement would seem much more appropriate for the relevant practical law.[25]

It is worth observing that Kant himself often speaks of a practical law as a generalized version of a maxim. His basic test for the moral acceptability of acting on a given maxim is that the agent must be able to will that the maxim should be (or become) a universal law. But when he describes the law that a maxim might be willed to be (or become) he describes the law in a fully general way. Thus when, in the *Critique of Practical Reason*, Kant describes his test, he asks whether he could will or "make the law that every man is allowed to deny that a deposit has been made when no one can prove the contrary."[26] Though the maxim he is testing is expressed in the first-person singular, the law he describes is fully general: "Every man is allowed to deny. . . ." It seems fair to say that Kant actually uses the term "practical law" fairly carelessly. Sometimes he applies it to "universally valid" maxims and sometimes he applies it to fully general statements corresponding to such maxims.

For purposes of clarifying some of the intricate arguments Kant presents in his ethical writings, I shall modify his terminology slightly. Specifically, I shall speak of maxims as either subjectively or objectively valid, and I shall generally reserve the term "practical law" for fully general practical statements. If m is a maxim, I shall use the expression $G(m)$ to refer to the generalization of m. I shall then say that if a maxim m is universally valid (or necessarily acceptable to all rational beings) then its corresponding generalization, $G(m)$, is (or expresses) a practical law. As we shall see, significant problems will arise about how certain maxims are to be generalized, but these problems arise for Kant's theory itself; they are not generated by the terminology I shall be using.

With these points of clarification in mind, I can now return to Kant's reasons for thinking that his third remark follows from his first two. Though I have not yet developed the point, Kant is firmly convinced that acting for the sake of duty is fundamentally rational. Given this, we should expect him to claim that the maxim of duty on which morally valuable action is based is unconditionally valid and thus a practical law in his unhappy sense of the term. But this is not what he says. Rather, he says that actions done for the sake of duty are "subjectively determined" by "pure respect for [a certain] practical law." He also says that "this subjective element [in dutiful action] is the maxim that I ought to follow such a law even if it thwarts all my inclinations."[27]

It seems to me that Kant's position here can be clarified as follows. The maxim on which a perfectly rational being would act in performing a morally valuable action is universally valid and thus, as Kant says, a practical law. It is, moreover, a purely formal principle, for its acceptability does not depend on the value of some effect, or proposed result, that can be achieved by acting on it. Such a law is an object of "respect," and accounts for the moral value we attach to dutiful action. But human beings are not perfectly rational, and the universal validity of a maxim (or its character as a law in Kant's misleading sense) is not by itself sufficient to move us to act. Nevertheless, as Kant argues at length in the *Critique of Practical Reason*, when we contemplate a practical law or universally valid maxim, we feel "respect" or "reverence" (*Achtung*) for it, and this feeling induces us to act on it.[28] In acting from this feeling of respect or reverence we are, he adds, responding to the law as a "command" or "imperative," and in doing this we are acting on a "subjective principle," or maxim, that concerns the law. The maxim is to the effect that we should follow the law even if it thwarts our inclinations.

By this route Kant reaches the conclusion that when the action of a man (or an imperfectly rational being) has moral worth, it is done out of "respect" for practical law. Since, as we shall see, he believes that only imperfectly rational beings act for the sake of duty, he can reasonably conclude that

4. An action is done for the sake of duty just when it is done out of respect for practical law.

This conclusion is closely related to Kant's third remark, which he says is a consequence of his assertions 1 and 2. But 4 does not, obviously, follow from 1 and 2 alone; to derive it we need extra premises about the nature of practical laws and the respect they invoke in beings like us. The conclusion, 4, is not, of course, equivalent to Kant's third remark, or to 3★, which I offered as a paraphrase of his third remark in section 3. But it is obvious that his third remark—that is, the assertion 3—does not follow from 1 and 2 alone either. To derive it we need extra premises about practical laws, the respect they inspire in us, and perhaps other matters as well.

Since a good human (or imperfectly rational) will is, for Kant, a will that acts for the sake of duty, we may nevertheless conclude from assertion 4 above that a good will is one that acts out of respect for practical law. The question is, "What is the practical law, or laws, out of respect for which a good human will acts?" I shall discuss Kant's answer to this in the section to follow. To round off this section, I want to add a few observations to what I have said about the reasoning behind Kant's claim that when a human action has moral worth, it is done out of respect for some practical law.

Apart from being highly compressed, Kant's reasoning is complicated by the variety of themes it introduces. One theme concerns the kind of maxim that is by itself sufficient to render an action morally valuable. As we have seen, his fundamental idea is that such a maxim must be, or express respect for, a practical law. Another theme concerns the rational basis for valuing actions based on this kind of maxim. This theme is closely connected with a third one: the explanation of how a maxim that is not based on an intention to bring about some desired effect in the world could move a normal human being to act. The key to his explanation of these points is that human beings are naturally constituted to feel respect or reverence for practical law, and that this feeling of respect or reverence leads them to act on such laws and to esteem others who do so. A final theme concerns the concept of duty or moral obligation. Kant does not develop his view very clearly at this stage, but he seems to think that, as a result of the respect or reverence human beings feel for practical laws, they experience such laws as imperatives or commands and feel "morally constrained," or obligated, to conform to them. Kant will develop these themes more fully as his argument proceeds, but by introducing them all in the two short paragraphs where he supports his third assertion, he makes very heavy demands on his unwary readers.

5. *The Moral Law*

Kant locates the fundamental law on which dutiful human wills act in the following astonishingly brief passage: "Since I have robbed the will of every inducement that might arise for it as the consequence of obeying any particular law, nothing is left but the conformity of action to universal law as such, and this alone must serve the will as its principle."[29] Kant's idea here is that since, as he believes he has shown, a good and dutiful will does not conform to a practical law because the consequences of doing so will satisfy some purpose or "inclination," the only rational basis for conforming to it—the basis that would be sufficient for a purely rational being—must be supplied by the intrinsic character of the law itself. But what is this intrinsic character? Kant's answer, at least at this point, seems to be "the character of being a universal law." In view of this, the "subjective principle of the will" in performing dutiful actions would seem to be

P1: I will conform my actions to universal law

or, better,

P2: I ought to conform my actions to universal law.

P1 has the logical form of a typical maxim or "subjective principle," but P2 is very close to what Kant called the "subjective element" in dutiful action, namely, "the maxim that I ought to follow . . . [practical] law even if it thwarts all my inclinations." Assuming that P2 is the appropriate subjective principle, we can easily identify the relevant practical law by deleting the "I ought," which expresses a human being's reaction to such a law. Formulated as an imperative directed to imperfectly rational beings generally, the law would be

L: Conform your actions to universal law.

Although L is the obvious choice for the fundamental law Kant has in mind, he surprises us by continuing the passage quoted above with the words: "That is to say, I ought never to act except in such a way *that I can also will that my maxim should become a universal law*. Here bare conformity to law as such (without having at its base any law prescribing particular actions) is what serves the will as its principle, and it must so serve if duty is not to be everywhere an empty delusion. . . ."[30] Later on Kant gives his first formulation of the practical law that he will call "the moral law" and "the categorical imperative." His law has the logical form of an imperative, and it is addressed to imperfectly rational beings generally:

C1: Act only on that maxim through which you can at the same time will that it should become [or be] a universal law.[31]

The question is, "Which is really the fundamental practical law, L or C1—or are these just different formulations of the same principle?"

Unfortunately, Kant makes no attempt, at least explicitly, to deal with this important question. His exposition clearly suggests that he would view L and C1 as the same basic principle, for after saying that "the will's principle" in dutiful action is that of conforming to universal law as such, he introduces C1 by a mere "that is to say" and then adds: "Here bare conformity to law as such . . . is what serves the will as its principle. . . ." But C1 differs significantly from L in practical import, at least, and the line of thought leading naturally to L does not seem adequate to render C1 credible. Since these differences between L and C1 should be as apparent to Kant as they are to us, it is difficult to believe that he would actually regard L and C1 as different versions of the same principle.

By saying that *C1* differs from *L* in practical import, I mean
that *C1* is useful in a way that *L* is not. As I have formulated
it, *L* is a higher-order principle telling us to conform to certain lower-order laws. But if we do not know what these
lower-order laws are, we shall not find *L* a very useful principle. *C1* does not seem to possess this limitation. Even if I do
not know what principles are properly considered universal
laws, I know they are practical principles that, being universal, are binding on all rational beings. Knowing just this
much, I could no doubt decide whether I could will that the
maxims of many possible actions should be (or become) such
laws. If, respecting a maxim *m*, I could not will such a thing,
C1 would show me that I ought not to act on that maxim, or
that doing so is morally forbidden. *C1* would thus have practical value for me even though I had no idea how to comply
with *L*.

Kant emphasizes the practical significance of *C1* by calling
it "the general canon for all moral judgment of action,"[32] and
later on he uses it as a basic principle to derive a whole system
of moral laws that prescribe what he calls duties of virtue and
justice. Since these moral laws are unquestionably the universal laws to which *L* refers, a plausible conception of the relation between *L* and *C1* would seem to be this: *L* formulates
the basic requirement of moral action, and *C1* formulates the
fundamental principle to be followed in complying with this
basic requirement. The underlying assumption, which Kant
clearly accepts, is that we conform to universal law (and so
satisfy *L*) just when we obey *C1* and act only on maxims that
we *can* will to be universal laws.

It is worth observing that if this last assumption is accepted,
L and *C1* must be regarded as at least equivalent principles in
spite of their differing practical import. This may be seen as
follows. *L* and *C1* have the *logical* form of

   $L^\star$: Act on *m* only if action on *m* conforms to universal
       law.
   $C1^\star$: Act on *m* only if you can will that *m*, or its gen-
       eralization *G(m)*, should be a universal law.

If, according to the assumption, the clauses following the "only if" in these formulas are equivalent in the sense of implying one another, the same must be true of the formulas themselves. Given this, any action forbidden by L is also forbidden by C1, and vice versa. Furthermore, if C1 can be used to identify morally permissible actions (as Kant seems to imply in several places)[33] then any action permitted by C1 is also permitted by L, and vice versa. Thus, even though L and C1 differ significantly in practical import, they must be regarded as equivalent if the above assumption is made. Since Kant clearly accepts this assumption and since, as we shall see, he sometimes treats equivalent but distinguishable principles as "different formulations" of the same law, it is *possible* that he also views L and C1 this way. As I have pointed out, however, this does not seem to be the best way of viewing them. The most reasonable view of L and C1 would be that L formulates the basic moral requirement while C1 shows us what must be done to comply with this requirement.

In the last section we saw that an action has moral worth, for Kant, just when it is done for the sake of duty. We also saw that, to be done for the sake of duty, an action must be done out of respect for universal law. But if C1 is the basic moral law, or the fundamental principle showing us how to comply with our basic moral requirement, it would appear that our moral duties must consist entirely of omissions, of not doing certain things, and that a person who acts for the sake of duty must be one who *refrains* from doing something because he believes that duty requires him *not* to do it. This view seems inevitable because C1 merely tells us *not* to act on any maxim that we cannot will to be a universal law; it does not tell us that we ought positively to act on some maxim or other. Though I shall contend that C1 actually has this consequence, Kant will argue to the contrary. In his view certain lower-level moral laws may be inferred from C1, and some of these laws do obligate us to act on particular maxims. Laws having this feature are sometimes conditional, such as "If you make a promise, keep it," and sometimes (at least on the face of it) categorical, such as "Be beneficent." By virtue of the close connection Kant sees between L and $C1$, it seems reasonable to say that a person who acts out of respect for a law inferred from $C1$ is acting "for the sake of duty" and is therefore performing a morally estimable action.

I have pointed out that Kant unquestionably assumes that we conform to universal law when and only when we act on maxims that we can will to be universal laws. Though Kant offers no explicit defense for this assumption, it is by no means an obvious truth. We may, as he says, commonly believe that it is morally wrong to act on maxims that we are not willing to have others act on. Yet the mere acceptance of this belief, however widespread it may be, is not sufficient to guarantee that a person who acts on maxims that he *can* will to be universal laws is, in fact, conforming to universal law. If Kant is to make a credible case for $C1$ as a fundamental moral principle, he must, therefore, provide a compelling argument for the assumption that underlies his move from what is in effect L to $C1$.

The philosophical importance of such an argument stands out sharply if we look at the reasoning by which Kant introduces $C1$. As we have seen, he begins with the assertion that an action has moral value just when it is done for the sake of duty. He then claims that an action's moral value is owing to the maxim on which it is based rather than to any effect that may be brought about by the action. From here on his argument is very highly compressed, but his thought seems to continue as follows. On account of the objective rationality of morals, any maxim giving moral worth to an action must be (or express respect for) a practical law. Since such a maxim is intrinsically acceptable rather than acceptable as a mere instrument for realizing some desired effect, a virtuous being would conform to it just because it is (or expresses respect for) a practical law. Such a being thus has a fundamental propensity to conform to practical laws as such, and a fundamental principle of his will is "I will conform my actions to universal law." This subjective principle, being thoroughly rational, "constrains" the will of an imperfectly rational being, and for such a being it could be expressed as "I ought to

conform my actions to universal law." Since this last formulation reflects an imperfect being's attitude to an objective law,
we can identify the relevant higher-order law by deleting the
"I ought" and changing the "my" to "your." The result is L:
"Conform your actions to universal law."

Though Kant's reasoning here is somewhat convoluted, its
basic thrust is relatively clear and highly plausible. If the
moral value of an action is entirely owing to the maxim on
which it is based, and if a maxim can render an action morally
estimable only when it is (or expresses respect for) a practical
law that is not a mere instrument for producing some desired
effect, then a morally estimable action must be rationally
motivated by respect for practical law as such. If this is so, the
basic requirement for morally estimable action could be reasonably expressed by the command "Conform your actions
to practical law as such." Though Kant's language is somewhat unusual, the view he is expressing is tacitly accepted by
every philosopher who holds a deontological rather than a
teleological conception of moral obligation.

According to such writers as W. D. Ross, the moral rules
(or lower-level laws) that define our basic obligations cannot
be justified by their tendency to realize some *telos* or end, because obeying them is, at least ideally, intrinsically meritorious.[34] Of course, if everyone obeyed these rules, the result
would be extremely desirable. But from a moral point of
view the desirability of this result would depend on the fact
that the rules are obeyed—that lies are not told, that promises
are kept, that justice is done. Since our obligation to conform
to moral laws (or principles or rules) is morally fundamental
and not justifiable by reference to the results of conforming to
them, Ross would have to allow that the ultimate, higher-
order principle of morality could be formulated by the command "Conform to the rules (or 'laws') of morality." Obviously, this command is tantamount to the law L.

Though this deontological approach to moral obligation is
extremely common in contemporary moral philosophy, it
faces several well-known problems, one of which is epis-
temological: How can we identify the moral laws to which

we ought to conform our actions? As I have suggested, Kant seems to think that *C1* can be used to resolve this problem: the lower-level principles derivable from *C1* are precisely the laws to which we ought morally to conform. If Kant is right, one of the basic problems of deontological ethics has a solution. But an argument is clearly required for this view. The principle *C1* is by no means a trivial consequence of *L*; as we have seen, it goes beyond *L* in an extremely important way. The reasoning by which Kant introduces *C1* thus contains a crucial gap: it moves to *L* by plausible steps, but it then jumps to *C1* by a puzzling and highly dubious "that is to say."

I suspect that Kant has an argument, at least at the back of his mind, by which he would attempt to defend the transition from *L* to *C1*. I shall discuss this possibility in a later chapter where I discuss Kant's principle of autonomy, which he calls "the sole principle of ethics."[35] At the moment I simply want to emphasize that Kant owes us an argument for *C1* and that, if he cannot supply it, his claim to have established *C1* as the first principle of morality must be rejected.

Chapter II: Two Forms of the Moral Law, C1 and C2

In Chapter 2 of the *Groundwork* Kant subjects the notion of a moral law to philosophical analysis. As the result of his analysis, he claims that the moral law can be formulated in at least five different ways. I shall begin by discussing various matters associated with Kant's analysis, but my principal subject in this chapter will be the clarification and evaluation of his first two versions of the moral law, which I shall label *C1* and *C2*. I shall discuss his other versions of the law in the chapters to follow.

1. *Laws and Imperatives*

Like most people, Kant was convinced that there is a basic moral law that provides a norm or principle for correct moral judgment. This basic law is binding, Kant thought, on all rational beings, that is, on all beings capable of thought and reasoning. There is no doubt that human beings are subject to the moral law, but Kant would insist that if gods, angels, or even devils exist, they are bound by the law as well. If they do not conform to it, they must be viewed as immoral or possibly even wicked. The moral law would even be binding on intelligent agents from another planet, whether they have feathers, fins, or purple leaves; but it is not binding on birds, fish, dogs, or cats. These familiar creatures may be gentle or dangerous, but they are never morally good or bad. They are not rational beings, and they have no moral obligations.

If there really is a moral law, it must have the distinctive features of a law. For Kant, these distinctive features are universality and necessity. Whatever exactly it may be, the moral law is clearly universal in scope, for it is applicable to *all* rational beings. It also has, at least on the face of it, a kind of necessity, for it *requires* all rational beings to behave in certain ways. The relevant kind of necessity here is that of moral requiredness or obligation, and it might be termed "moral necessity." An important feature of Kant's treatment of the moral law is the analysis of moral necessity that he provides. He argues, or at least claims, that moral necessity is reducible to the familiar kind of necessity expressed by a descriptive law.

The formulation of the moral law that I have discussed in the last chapter—namely, *C1*—had the character of an imperative:

> *C1*: Act only on that maxim through which you can at the same time will that it should become a universal law.

Since Kant says that all imperatives can be expressed with an "ought" (*Sollen*), it should be possible to emphasize the imperatival character of *C1* by fitting an "ought" into it in some suitable place.[1] (I shall consider this possibility a little later.) An imperative, Kant says, is always addressed to a partially rational being, one who does not necessarily act in a rational way. Instead of thinking "I ought to do *A*," a fully rational or "holy" being would think "I will do *A*." Thus, *C1* is addressed to imperfect beings such as ourselves; it enjoins us to do something that we do not do "by a necessity of nature."

Since what an imperfectly rational being must do is just what a perfectly rational being necessarily does do according to rational laws, it would seem that the moral "ought" can be interpreted according to the schema:

> *S* ought to do *A* if and only if a fully rational being would necessarily do *A*.

As it happens, this schema is a little too simple for Kant. Although fully rational beings necessarily pursue their own happiness, we have, Kant thinks, no actual obligation to pursue our own happiness. He holds this view because we pursue our own happiness by a necessity of nature, and we cannot be obligated to do what we necessarily do. To accommodate this view, we must modify the schema given above. The following would appear to be satisfactory:

S ought to do *A* just when (*a*) *S* does not do *A* by a necessity of nature and (*b*) a fully rational being would necessarily do *A*.

By virtue of this schema we can say that the notion of moral necessity is reducible to (or explicable in terms of) the kind of necessity expressed by a purely descriptive law—specifically, by a descriptive law concerning the behavior of perfectly rational beings.

It is worth observing that the schema just given is instructive for another reason: it shows us how Kant can reasonably say that the moral law is a synthetic a priori proposition. As Kant formulates it, the moral law is a command or imperative, and it is puzzling to think of an imperative as logically synthetic and capable of being known a priori. But there is nothing puzzling in the claim that a descriptive law can have this character. It seems to me that when Kant speaks of the moral law as being a synthetic a priori proposition, he has in mind what he regards as the descriptive equivalent of the moral law—namely, the law about the behavior of perfectly rational beings. This descriptive equivalent does not include the qualification that imperfectly rational beings do not conform to the moral law by a necessity of nature, but Kant often overlooks this qualification when he talks about the relation between moral necessity (or obligation) and the behavior of perfectly rational beings.

Before proceeding, we should probably stop and ask ourselves just how plausible Kant's reduction of moral necessity (or moral obligation) to descriptive necessity really is. For my part, the reduction does not seem very promising. Apart from having a general doubt about the existence of any objective moral law, I find it very doubtful that basic moral requirements can be understood as requirements of rationality itself. On the other hand, it does not seem very helpful to debate this kind of question in the abstract. The best way of evaluating Kant's analysis of moral necessity is to see what he is able to do with it. If he can construct a moral theory on the basis of it that seems, on the whole, defensible, then his analysis may be regarded as successful, no matter how dubious it may initially appear.

Kant thinks he can show that *C1* is the fundamental moral law merely by analyzing the notion of a categorical imperative. To provide this analysis he begins by claiming that all imperatives command either hypothetically or categorically. The former, he says, "present the practical necessity of a possible action as a means to achieving something else which one desires (or which one may possibly desire). The categorical imperative would be one which presented an action as of itself objectively necessary [i.e., necessary for all purely rational beings], without regard to any possible end."[2] By speaking of an action as practically necessary, Kant means that, given the way of the world, if the action is not done, the desired end cannot be realized. A hypothetical imperative thus tells one to do something that must be done *if* a certain purpose is to be satisfied. If the purpose is merely a possible one that the agent need not have, the hypothetical imperative is a "problematic" or "technical" one; if the purpose is one that the agent actually has, the hypothetical is called "assertoric." Since categorical imperatives do not "command" an action as the means of satisfying some purpose, they are neither problematic nor technical; Kant calls them "apodeictic practical principles."[3]

Kant's classification of imperatives is not really satisfactory. For one thing, in addition to being categorical or hypothetical, imperatives may be disjunctive ("Be quiet or leave the room") as well as conjunctive ("Go home and take a nap"). For another thing, not all hypothetical imperatives prescribe actions as means to some end; an example is "If you make a promise, keep it." These drawbacks to Kant's classification do not affect his ethical doctrine, however, and I shall ignore them—except for a comment, later on, about the example of "If you make a promise, keep it."

After distinguishing the three kinds of imperatives mentioned above—namely, the technical, the assertoric, and the apodeictic—Kant points out that they may be distinguished by, among other things, the "constraint to which they subject the will."[4] He says that technical imperatives amount to "rules of skill," assertoric imperatives to "counsels of prudence," and apodeictic imperatives to "commands (laws) of morality." Concerning imperatives of the first two kinds, Kant says that if we could form a "definite" concept of happiness, counsels of prudence would be similar to rules of skill: they would disclose necessary means to a determinate end, and any partly rational being who willed the end would feel a very strong constraint to obey the counsel and adopt the prescribed means. But "it is a misfortune," Kant remarks, "that the concept of happiness is so indefinite that, although each person wishes to attain it, he can never definitely and self-consistently state what it is he really wishes and wills."[5]

Kant's claim about the concept of happiness is very important, for it implies that we cannot hope to base a practical *law* on our admitted desire for happiness. If we cannot really say in advance and with full confidence what will make us happy or unhappy, we shall not be able, obviously, to specify any necessary means to our happiness. In support of his view Kant describes the plight of even the most clearheaded and capable person who tries to form a definite concept of what would make him happy:

> If he wills riches, how much anxiety, envy, and intrigue might he not thereby draw upon his shoulders? If he wills much knowledge and vision, perhaps it might become only an eye that much sharper to show him as more dreadful the evils which are now hidden from him and which are yet unavoidable, or to burden his desires—which already sufficiently engage him—with even more needs! If he wills a long life, who guarantees that it will not be a long misery? If he wills at least health, how often has not the discomfort of the body restrained him from excesses into which perfect health would have led him?[6]

Kant concludes that one would have to be omniscient to know what would make one truly happy.

The difficulty of forming a determinate concept of what would make one happy does not show that counsels of prudence are impossible; it only shows that such counsels cannot be definite laws or principles that can *command* us to behave in a certain way. According to Kant, the only reasonable counsels of prudence concern such things as diet, economy, courtesy, and restraint, "which are shown by experience best to promote welfare on the average."[7] It seems to me that Kant is right on this matter, though the indeterminacy applies not to the concept of happiness, as he initially says, but to the concept of what will make us happy, where this concerns not the available means to our happiness but the various desires, hopes, and so forth whose satisfaction or realization will make us happy. A callow youth, obsessed with a trio of pressing desires, may claim to have a clear idea of what will make him happy, but experience will show him that his clear idea is largely an illusion. An older, wiser person will not only acknowledge that his idea of what will make him happy is vague and indeterminate, but like Rasselas he may harbor serious doubts about whether, apart from fleeting moments, he is actually capable of achieving happiness at all.

Before proceeding with Kant's attempt to identify the categorical imperative, we should note that Kant's distinction between categorical and hypothetical imperatives is not based on the grammatical structure of sentences expressing them. As a sentence, "Close the door!" is correctly classified as an unqualified imperative, but it does not thereby express an imperative that "commands unconditionally." As Kant puts it, many imperatives that appear to be categorical are yet hypothetical "in a hidden way."[8] Although he does not give fully explicit directions for distinguishing categorical from hypothetical imperatives, his thought seems to be this. Every imperative presents an action as practically good or valuable and in some way necessary for a being whose actions are rationally motivated. If the action is presented as instrumentally good, the imperative must be hypothetical; if the action is presented as good without qualification, the imperative is categorical. In the case of "Shut the door!" the relevant action is no doubt commanded as a means to an end—perhaps that of staying in the good graces of the speaker. If we are to determine whether a given imperative is categorical or hypothetical, we must, then, attend to the manner in which the relevant action is being "presented."

Kant emphasizes that it is often extremely difficult to tell how an imperative is presenting an action. This difficulty leads Kant to say that, by appealing to examples, we cannot expect to prove that there are any genuine categorical imperatives at all. We might naturally think that "Thou shalt not make a false promise" is a clear case of a categorical imperative, but we really cannot be sure that the person uttering it (whether this person is ourself or someone else) is not offering a mere counsel of prudence based on a "secret fear of disgrace, and perhaps also [an] obscure apprehension of other dangers. . . ."[9] As Kant points out explicitly at the beginning of the chapter, our true motives in action are often extremely difficult to appreciate.

In view of this difficulty Kant claims that "we have to investigate purely a priori the possibility of a categorical imperative."[10] This investigation is crucially important, he says, because "the categorical imperative can alone be taken as a practical *law*, while all the others [are at best] principles of the will. . . . This is because what is necessary for the attainment of an arbitrary purpose can be regarded as itself contingent, and we get rid of the precept once we give up the purpose, whereas the unconditional command leaves the will no freedom to choose the opposite. Thus it alone implies the necessity we require of a law."[11] This argument may seem highly questionable since not all our purposes are arbitrary; in fact, Kant himself insists that we have the purpose of being happy by a necessity of nature. As we have seen, however, this purpose is too indefinite to yield a practical *law*. It happens that, to the extent that we are rational, we necessarily have other purposes as well (at least in Kant's opinion), but I shall consider the consequences of this possibility a little later.

Kant thinks that the categorical imperative can be identified merely by reflecting on the concept of a categorical imperative. As he puts it:

If I think of a categorical imperative, I know immediately what it contains. For since the imperative contains besides the law only the necessity that the maxim should accord with the law, while the law contains no condition to which it is restricted, there is nothing remaining in it except the universality of law as such to which the maxim of the action should conform; and in effect this conformity alone is represented as necessary by the imperative.

There is, therefore, only one categorical imperative. It is: Act only according to that maxim by which you can at the same time will that it should become a universal law.[12]

Though this passage is highly condensed and, in consequence, extremely difficult to follow, Kant does not elaborate upon the argument it contains. Yet if we attend to the points of Kantian doctrine developed thus far, we can work out a plausible reconstruction of the line of thought Kant probably has in mind.

As we have seen, a valid imperative commands us to do something that a perfectly rational being necessarily does. When such an imperative is categorical, the command is unconditional: we are required to do something that a rational being necessarily does, but we are not required to do it as a means of realizing some further end or purpose. To discover what can be contained in a valid categorical imperative, we might therefore begin by asking ourselves what a rational being necessarily does. The general answer is that such a being necessarily acts on maxims that are (or correspond to) practical laws. There are, of course, many laws of this kind; an example that Kant formulates as an imperative is "Thou shalt not make a false promise." Yet a truly categorical imperative could not be focused on acts as specific as promise keeping, for the reasonableness of these acts is always based on some further purpose or condition. As Kant in effect points out, a scoundrel might reasonably adopt the maxim of keeping promises as a means of winning friends and influencing people, and a person of good will would reasonably adopt it as a means of doing his moral duty. A perfectly rational being would not, of course, adopt such a maxim for either of these reasons (only imperfect beings have moral duties) but he would have a distinctive motive for adopting it—namely, his commitment to the higher-order maxim (or law) of conforming his actions to universal law as such. As we saw in Chapter I, this higher-order maxim is the fundamental principle of a rational being's will; and since it is fundamental, it and only it can support an imperative that is both valid and absolutely categorical: "Conform your actions to universal law as such" For reasons that remain as obscure at this point as they were in his first chapter, Kant seems to think that this higher-order imperative is either equivalent to or can be alternatively formulated as "Act only on maxims that you can will to become universal laws."

According to Kant's argument here, precepts like "Never make a false promise" do not count as categorical imperatives. This is surprising, for in his *Critique of Practical Reason* he says that the rule not to make deceitful promises "is a law, because it is a categorical imperative."[13] To render Kant's doctrine consistent, it would seem advisable to distinguish a stricter from a looser sense of the term "categorical imperative." If rational beings conform to the laws of promise keeping because of a more fundamental commitment to conform to universal law as such, we can say that, in the strict sense of the term, there is only one categorical imperative, namely, the moral law *C1*. On the other hand, since Kant holds that "all imperatives of duty can be derived from this one imperative as a principle,"[14] we can reasonably add that laws like "Never make a false promise" or "If you make a promise, keep it" are derivative imperatives whose validity depends only on the rational acceptability of the moral law. Though these imperatives are not categorical in the strict sense, their validity does not depend on some merely contingent condition: they are genuine laws that are necessarily binding on all rational beings. In this regard they clearly differ from hypothetical imperatives, which "present the practical necessity of a possible action as a means of achieving something that one desires (or that one may possibly desire)." Since Kant commonly speaks of imperatives as either hypothetical or categorical, it would seem reasonable to call such derivative imperatives "categorical" in a looser sense of the word.

Though the point is not evident from my exposition, Kant does not believe that the reasoning he has offered thus far actually proves that *C1* is valid, or binding on all partly rational beings. His aim has merely been to show what is "contained in the concept" of a valid categorical imperative. If this concept is justifiable—if it actually applies to a valid principle—it applies to the principle *C1*. Later on, in the third chapter of the *Groundwork*, he will argue that the concept of a truly categorical imperative is, in fact, justifiable or rationally acceptable and that *C1* expresses a genuine law. His arguments thus far are therefore provisional in an important sense: they are concerned with locating a basic practical principle that he will attempt to justify later on.

Before concluding this section I want to consider how an "ought" can be fitted into *C1*. As I pointed out earlier, Kant says that all imperatives can be expressed with an "ought"; yet the appropriate position for an "ought" in *C1* is not immediately obvious. We might observe, to begin with, that we cannot reasonably reformulate *C1* as

You ought to act on a maxim *m* only if you can will that *m* should become a universal law.

This would be unsatisfactory, because if one has the premise "I cannot will that *m* should become a universal law," one could conclude only " ~ (I ought to act on *m*)" and not "I ought not to act on *m*," as Kant's view requires. A more promising approach is to reformulate *C1* this way:

You ought not to act on a maxim *m* if you cannot will that *m* should become a moral law.

If we view *C1* as merely telling us what maxims we should not act on, then this last formulation seems all right. But in his *Metaphysics of Morals* and later in the *Groundwork* Kant claims that the categorical imperative also shows us what is permitted.[15] His idea seems to be that if one *can* will that a maxim should become a universal law, then one is morally permitted to act on it. If we want to formulate $C1$ so that this last idea is clearly implied by it, we might say the following:

> You ought not to act on a maxim m when and only when you cannot will that m should become a universal law.

If, given this principle, you have the premise " $\sim$ (I cannot will that m should become a universal law)" or in English, "I *can* will that m should become a universal law," you may then infer " $\sim$ (I ought not to act on m)" or "It is not the case that I ought not to act on m." But, clearly, this conclusion is equivalent to "I may (am permitted to) act on m." If we take full account of the logical relations between the "may" of permission and the "ought" of moral obligation, we can thus reformulate $C1$ in a positive way by saying:

> You may (are morally permitted to) act on a maxim m when and only when you can will that m should become a universal law.

To make the universality of $C1$ fully explicit, we might render it, finally, as follows:

> For any imperfectly rational being s, s may (is morally permitted to) act on m if, and only if, s can will that m shall become a universal law.

This last formulation of the law $C1$ is based on the idea that $C1$ is supposed to show us what we are permitted to do as well as what we are obligated to do. I remarked above that in several passages Kant clearly implies that the moral law shows us what we are permitted to do, but the fact remains that all his formulations of the moral law (even those to be discussed in the chapters to follow) are explicitly concerned only with what we are obligated to do. The question therefore arises, "If Kant really holds that the moral law tells us both what we are permitted to do and what we are obligated to, why does he formulate $C1$ in the words 'Act only according to that maxim by which you can at the same time will that it should become a universal law'?"

I am afraid that I don't know the answer to this question. On the other hand, it is not difficult to see why Kant might have thought that his formulation of the moral law could provide a satisfactory principle by which we can determine both what we are permitted to do and what we are obligated to do. As we have seen, Kant views the moral law as *the* fundamental principle of morals, the principle from which *all* our moral duties are derivable. Given this view, he might naturally have reasoned as follows. As formulated, *C1* explicitly lays down a general condition under which we are morally forbidden to act on a maxim: If we can't will that *m* should become a universal law, then we ought not to act on it. But suppose that this general condition is not satisfied for a particular maxim. In this case *C1* (or the moral law) does not forbid us to act on the maxim. Yet if the moral law does not forbid us to act on the maxim, no other law forbids us to do so either, for the moral law is the principle from which all our duties are derivable. (If we are morally forbidden to do something, we have a duty not to do it.) Yet if no law forbids us to act on a maxim, we are not forbidden to act on it at all. But anything we are not forbidden to do is, by definition, something that we are permitted to do. Thus, if the moral law is the basic principle of morals—the principle on which *all* our duties are ultimately based—we may regard it as showing both what we are obligated and what we are permitted to do.

If the reasoning just given accurately represents Kant's view of the moral law, he must acknowledge that, strictly speaking, his system of morals has two basic principles rather than one. The first principle amounts to a strict reading of his categorical imperative, namely:

> You ought not to act on a maxim if you cannot will that it should become a universal law.

The second principle is to the effect that you may (are morally permitted to) do anything not forbidden by the first principle. Since a strict reading of the first principle in the form of *C1* specifies just one condition under which one ought not to do something, the second principle can alternatively be formulated as

> If you can will that a maxim should become a universal law, you may (are morally permitted to) act on that maxim.

These two principles entail the version of the moral law that I proposed earlier, namely:

> You may (are morally permitted to) act on a maxim *m* when and only when you can will that *m* should become a universal law.

There is no doubt that Kant accepts this last principle; the question at issue is how we should view its role in Kant's system. If we give his first version of the moral law a strict reading, we shall have to say that Kant's system is really based on two fundamental laws and that the principle is a logical consequence of them. But if we give his version of the moral law a looser reading and regard it as Kant's only basic moral principle, we can say that it is equivalent to the principle given above. It seems to me that either alternative yields a plausible reconstruction of Kant's system, but for purposes of convenience, I shall adopt the latter one. When I refer to Kant's law *C1*, I shall therefore be referring to the principle containing the "when and only when."

2. *C1 and the Notion of Consistent Willing*

If we are to make use of *C1* in resolving moral problems, we must understand what Kant means when he speaks of being able to will that a maxim should become a universal law. It will turn out that there is some doubt about this matter, but one point, at least, is relatively clear: the relevant willing must be *consistent* willing. I shall work my way toward an interpretation of *C1* by considering what consistent willing is best understood to be.

In line with a suggestion I made in section 4 of the last chapter, I shall conceive of all willing as having the "legislating" form of *willing-that*. I remarked that a sovereign who wills that his subjects shall pay taxes according to a certain schedule might think: "My subjects *shall* pay taxes according to that schedule." The "shall" here, in contrast to its use in the first person "I shall pay taxes," expresses volition, and the sovereign's thought may be taken as an example of willing-that. Corresponding to every willing-that is a thinking-that. If the sovereign merely thinks, in the sense of believes, that his subjects will pay certain taxes, he might express his belief by saying "They will pay those taxes." It is very convenient, in discussing Kant's notion of consistent willing, to have a special symbol for representing volitional thoughts. The sovereign who willed that his subjects shall pay certain taxes could have expressed his will by using the volitional prefix "It shall be that. . . ." In place of this prefix I shall use the letter S. When this letter is prefixed to an indicative sentence P, the result, which I shall express by $S(P)$, represents a legislative willing-that.[16] If the sovereign I have been talking about used my special prefix to express his will, he would say "S(my subjects will pay taxes according to that schedule)."

A fully clarified notion of consistent willing would require a theory of practical or volitional consistency, but Kant provides only a few hints on the subject. One of his hints is this:

> Whoever wills an end, so far as reason has decisive influence on his action, wills also the indispensably necessary means to it that lie in his power.[17]

This hint is not correct, however. Even a fully rational being who wills to realize an end E may fail to will an indispensably necessary means to E if he does not know that this means exists. To be correct, Kant should have said this: A fully rational being—at least one who draws the conclusions implied by his premises—would, if he willed $S(E$ is realized) and believed that E would be realized if and only if A is done, conclude $S(A$ is done). Of course, even fully rational beings do not actually draw all the countless conclusions that are implied by their premises. Nevertheless, we can say that the premises "$S(E$ is realized)" and "E is realized if and only if A

is done" warrant the conclusion "$S(A$ is done)." We can express this fact by saying that the following is a valid principle of practical reasoning:

1. If $S(E)$ and E is necessary and sufficient for A, then $S(A)$.[18]

Another principle bearing on our subject is this:

2. $S(P)$ is inconsistent with $S(Q)$ just in case P is inconsistent with Q.

According to this principle, "S(Mary goes to college)" is inconsistent with "S(Mary does not go to college)" just because "Mary goes to college" is inconsistent with "Mary does not go to college." Intuitively, the idea here is that volitions (or volitional thoughts) are inconsistent just when they are directed to inconsistent states of affairs.

A further principle, which I accept but which is controversial among students of volitional consistency, is this:

3. $S(E)$ is inconsistent with $\sim E$.[19]

According to this principle, if you have the premise $\sim E$, you would be inconsistent if you willed $S(E)$. Finally, a weaker principle than Kant's principle 1 seems acceptable:

4. If $S(E)$ and E requires A, then $S(A)$.

Other principles could be added to this list, but the four just given will be sufficient for our purposes in discussing Kant's several versions of the moral law.

To assess the moral significance of Kant's imperative $C1$, we might begin by considering how an agent who is tempted to act on a maxim m might be unable consistently to will that m should become a universal law. As we have seen, a universal law is (or corresponds to) a practical principle on which fully rational beings necessarily act. Thus, to will that m shall become a universal law is, presumably, to will that all rational beings necessarily have m as a maxim so that $G(m)$ truly describes their behavior. Now, one way in which the agent could be inconsistent in willing that the maxim m should be-

come a universal law is this. Let m be "S(I do A if I want B)."
To will that m become a universal law would involve willing
that S(all rational beings necessarily adopt the maxim of
doing A if they want B). But suppose this latter volition implies a conclusion C. If the agent in question could not, for
some reason, consistently accept C, then he could not consistently will that S(all rational beings necessarily adopt the
maxim of doing A if they want B). He could not consistently
will this, because it has a consequence that he cannot consistently accept.

An important possibility should be considered at this point.
It does not seem unreasonable to suppose that ordinary
human beings can consistently will many things that could
not be consistently willed by a perfectly rational being. Yet if
this supposition is sound, Kant's formula $C1$ is subject to an
obvious counterexample. It is unquestionably morally wrong
to inflict pain on another person merely for the sake of the
pleasure it gives you. Thus, action on the following maxim
should be disallowed by $C1$:

m: I will inflict pain on another if it pleases me to do so.

But consider the case of Maxwell Jones, a sadomasochist. On
the face of it, Maxwell Jones *could* consistently will that m become a universal law, for if others acted on m and thereby inflicted pain on him for their pleasure, Maxwell Jones would
also be pleased; receiving pain from others is as acceptable, as
pleasing, to him as giving it to others. But, according to Kant
in his "Doctrine of Virtue," a rational being necessarily wills
the happiness of others.[20] Consequently, since inflicting pain
on some others (who are not masochists) would conflict with
the volition of promoting their happiness, the maxim m could
not be consistently adopted by a rational being and could not
accord with universal law, whether Maxwell-Jones could
consistently will it to be such or not.

This last example discloses an obvious inadequacy in the
imperatival version of the principle $C1$, particularly if that
principle allows us to infer that actions satisfying the universalization condition are morally permissible. The key difficulty is that the formula

You may act on a maxim *m* just when you can consistently will that *m* should become a universal law

does not take account of the fact that what *you* can consistently will must be determined (if the Maxwell-Jones case is to be avoided) by your supposed nature as a *rational* being, or by your nature to the extent that it is rational. Kant assumes and will eventually argue that even the most irrational of people may justifiedly be viewed as rational "in themselves." But an imperative is addressed to us as imperfectly rational beings whose wills may be seriously at odds with our nature as things in themselves.

In view of this difficulty it might occur to us to qualify Kant's formula by saying:

You may act on a maxim *m* just when, to the extent that you are rational, you can consistently will that *m* should become a universal law.

This qualified formula may accord with Kant's intentions, but to apply it with any confidence we shall have to have more information about what rational beings, or imperfect beings to the extent that they are rational, do or do not will. Lacking this information, we shall find *C1* of little use in identifying specific moral obligations and permissions.

Though Kant does not seem to worry about possible sadomasochists, he does recognize that there are serious difficulties in the way of applying *C1* to the imperfect world of our experience. His view of these difficulties and his strategy for avoiding them are not clearly presented in the *Groundwork*, but they can be inferred from his other formulations of the moral law and from certain remarks he makes in his *Critique of Practical Reason*. I shall discuss these matters in the section to follow.

3. *The "Typic" of the Moral Law*, C2

Shortly after introducing *C1* Kant says that "the universal imperative of duty can also be expressed" as follows:

C2: Act as though the maxim of your action were by your will to become a universal law of nature.

If we compare *C2* with *C1*, we shall naturally wonder about the difference between the sort of universal law mentioned in *C1* and a "universal law of nature." Kant's view of the distinction is this: A universal law in the sense of *C1* is a universal and necessary principle describing the behavior of perfectly rational beings. By contrast, a universal law of nature is a universal and necessary principle describing the imperfect world of our experience: the world of partly rational beings, nonrational animals, plants, ponds, sticks, and stones. Though *C2* is obscurely formulated, it seems to tell us that we may (are morally permitted to) act on a maxim *m* just when we can consistently think of ourselves as having *m* and as willing that a generalized version of *m* should hold as a law for the world of our experience. The question is, "Why did Kant offer this peculiar formula as a version of the moral law?"

Kant does not attempt to answer this question in the *Groundwork*, but he outlines an answer in his *Critique of Practical Reason*.[21] In this latter work he says that since *C1*, his first formulation of the moral law, is specifically concerned with universal laws that concern the behavior of perfectly rational beings, we cannot, as members of a morally imperfect world, apply it to our experience in any direct way. We can, however, apply *C1* to our experience in an indirect way by directly applying a related law, namely *C2*, that represents *C1* for us. This related law represents *C1* in the sense that it serves as a "typic," "type," or analogue of it.

We should consider, in less abstract terms, why Kant should see a special problem in applying *C1* to the world of our experience. Viewed concretely, the problem is not obvious—at least if, like Kant, we are not worried about cases like that of Maxwell-Jones. To consider whether a maxim *m* could be willed to be a universal law, it would seem that we need only consider whether one could consistently will that all rational beings should have *m* as one of their maxims. But what is problematic about this, particularly if we think we understand what consistent willing is?

Kant's reply to this last question would, I think, be this. To determine whether we could consistently will that *m* should

become a universal law, we must consider whether the consequences of *m*'s being a universal law are consistent with
other things that we will. Recall the principle:

If $S(E)$ and E requires G, then $S(G)$.

If we knew that *m*'s being a universal law had a consequence
G, then if we also willed $S(\sim G)$, we should be inconsistent in
willing $S(m$ is a universal law). Kant seems to think that the
consequences of a maxim's being a universal law could not be
ascertained in the morally imperfect world of our experience;
in fact, he seems to think that we have no direct way of ascertaining these consequences at all. Given this, we could not
reasonably apply *C1* to the world as we know it in experience: the universal laws it mentions govern a domain to
which we lack experiential access.

Kant's concern with the consequences of a maxim's being
universalized and his conviction that we must take account of
such consequences in determining whether it is permissible to
act on that maxim can be illustrated by his treatment of
four examples. These examples all show us how *C2* is to be
used; significantly enough, Kant does not attempt to apply
C1 at all. For convenience, I shall begin with Kant's second
example.

KANT'S SECOND EXAMPLE.

The maxim to be tested in this example is

m: Whenever I believe myself short of money, I will borrow money and promise to pay it back, though I know
I will never, in fact, repay it.

To test this maxim for moral permissibility Kant says we
should ask: "How would things stand if my maxim became a
universal law (of nature)?" His answer is that "promising,
and the very purpose of promising, [would be] . . . impossible, since no one would believe [if $G(m)$ were a law of nature]
that he was promised anything, but would laugh at all utterances of this kind as empty shams."[22] Obviously, if this were
so, the generalization of *m*, $G(m)$, would not be a law of na

ture: people who need money would not attempt to borrow it with the promise of paying it back. The supposition that $G(m)$ is a universal law of nature thus leads to the conclusion that $G(m)$ is not a law of nature. This shows us, Kant thinks, $G(m)$ could not possibly be a law of nature: it "necessarily contradict[s] itself." On the assumption that one cannot consistently will what one recognizes to be impossible, Kant concludes that anyone who considers "how things would stand" if everyone acts on m could not consistently will that $G(m)$ should be a universal law of nature.

Though Kant says that the generalization of m "necessarily contradicts itself," he should not be interpreted as holding that $G(m)$ is logically inconsistent or self-contradictory. When he asks "How would things stand if my maxim became a universal law [of nature]?" he makes it clear that he is considering what might be called the "natural consequences" of his maxim's being a law of nature, and these consequences are to be determined in large part by our knowledge of natural things, including morally imperfect human beings. Thus, it is only by reference to what we know about human behavior that we are entitled to conclude that, if everyone began to act on the maxim m, utterances of "I promise . . ." would come to be regarded as empty shams.

These last observations bring out an important point about the way Kant intends his principle $C2$ to be applied. The point is that, in applying $C2$ to cases that might arise in experience, we are allowed to make assumptions (or draw conclusions) about what *would* happen in nature *if* a certain maxim were universally acted upon so that its generalization became a law of nature. In making these assumptions (or in drawing these conclusions) we are entitled to take into account what we know about the way nature works, or the laws governing natural occurrences. When we test a maxim for moral acceptability, we thus have to ask ourselves whether we could consistently think of ourselves as actually willing that the maxim be ours and also be a law of nature, where thinking this requires us to consider the "natural consequences" of the maxim's having this double character.

Here the maxim to be tested is, as Kant puts it:

> From self-love I make it my principle to shorten my life if its continued existence threatens more evil than it promises pleasure.[23]

To determine whether this maxim could be willed to be a law of nature Kant again considers whether it could *be* a law of nature—whether, more exactly, its universalized form is consistent with what we know of natural law. Kant concludes that the maxim could not be such a law on the ground that self-love has a particular "function" in nature—that of stimulating the "furtherance" of life. His reasoning here depends on a conception of nature that he elaborates in his *Critique of Judgment*. In that work he says that we are rationally entitled to view nature teleologically: to regard things in it as directed to certain ends and as having distinctive natural functions.[24] In line with this view he thinks we are entitled to assume that "self-love" is directed to (or has as its natural function) the stimulation or furtherance of life. If we must accept this assumption as expressing a teleological law of nature, we cannot consistently will that the maxim being tested (or its generalization) should be a natural law, for we should then be willing something that we acknowledge to be contrary to natural law and, therefore, impossible.

Kant does not clearly formulate the maxim to be tested in this example, but it would appear to be something like the following:[25]

> I will neglect to develop a talent if I find it agreeable to do so.

Kant's argument in connection with the example seems to be this. A rational being belonging to the world of nature would realize that in such a system his talents, if developed, would serve many possible ends. Since he necessarily wills to realize all his ends, he cannot consistently will to neglect something that is necessary for realizing those ends. Consequently, he cannot consistently will that his maxim (or its generalization) should be a universal law—that every person, including himself, "should let his talents rust" if he finds it agreeable to do so.

Kant's argument here is not very impressive. If the agent is supposed to reason as follows, the argument is a non sequitur:

1. I will realize all my ends.
2. Developing talent t is necessary for some possible end e.
3. Therefore, I will (because I must) develop talent t.

This argument is a non sequitur because the assumption that the agent wills to realize all his ends does not warrant the conclusion that he should realize a merely possible end, that is, an end that he *might* have. If Kant's argument is not to be viewed as patently fallacious in this way, he must introduce some further premise showing that if a person does not will to develop all his talents, he is certain not to develop some end he actually has. But it is hard to imagine that a plausible premise of this kind can be found. I shall have more to say about this matter in Chapter VI when I discuss Kant's use of essentially the same argument in his *Metaphysics of Morals*.[26]

KANT'S FOURTH EXAMPLE.

Here the relevant maxim is very hard to identify; I assume, though, that the following would conform to Kant's intention:[27]

I won't help others in distress unless doing so promotes my selfish interests.

The kernel of Kant's argument here, which he will develop more fully in his *Metaphysics of Morals*, seems to be this. In a system of nature each person might easily require the unselfish help of others from time to time. Since every person, to the extent that he is rational, necessarily wills to be helped when in distress, he cannot, if he is aware of the assumption we are making about nature, consistently will that the maxim in question be a law of nature, for this would require that no one helps anyone else in distress if doing so is not in his selfish interest.

Here again Kant's argument does not quite work. To be sound his argument needs the premise that a rational being (or person to the extent that he is rational) *knows* that, in the system of nature, he will sometime need the unselfish help of someone else. It also needs the premise that, if a maxim m is "I (Jones) won't help others unless doing so promotes my (Jones's) interests," then the corresponding law is "For any person s, s will not help another person unless doing so promotes s's interests." As we shall see in a later chapter, this last premise is problematic. Suppose, to anticipate a little, that D is a description in fully general terms that is applicable, as it happens, only to me. The law of nature corresponding to the maxim "I won't help another unless doing so promotes D's selfish interests" is then "For any s, s will not help another unless doing so promotes D's interests." Yet if my selfish maxim is expressed in this latter way, Kant's argument against a policy of utter selfishness does not succeed.

Apart from showing how the law $C2$ can be used, in Kant's opinion, to derive specific moral duties, the examples just discussed illustrate two ways in which a person may be unable to will that a maxim (or its generalization) shall be a universal law of nature. The first way is illustrated by the first two examples: one may be unable to will that a principle $G(m)$ shall be a law of nature because one sees that $G(m)$ could not possibly be such a law, and one cannot, at least rationally, will what one views as impossible. Viewing a principle $G(m)$ in this way does not, as I pointed out, amount to viewing it as self-contradictory or internally inconsistent, though Kant unfortunately uses language that suggests this interpretation. As his examples clearly show, a general principle can be viewed as incapable of being a natural law when one sees that its "natural consequences" are in some way inconsistent or when, more generally, one sees that its consequences are incompatible with what one knows (or is justified in assuming) about the teleological character of nature. The second way is illustrated by the third and fourth examples. Here one is unable to will that $G(m)$ shall be a law of nature because one sees that, given the way nature works, the natural consequences of $G(m)$'s being such a law are inconsistent with something that one *must* will either insofar as one is rational (such as one's own happiness) or insofar as one acts on the maxim m.

As it happens, Kant regards these two ways of being unable to will that a principle shall be a natural law as having great theoretical importance. In the *Groundwork* he merely observes that the first way allows us to identify "perfect" moral duties and the second way "imperfect" moral duties,[28] but in the *Metaphysics of Morals* he draws far-reaching consequences from the two ways, arguing that perfect moral duties yield a well-defined system of juridical duties (or duties of justice) and imperfect duties yield a well-defined system of ethical duties (or duties of virtue). Since Kant's distinction between these systems of duties raises important problems that deserve detailed treatment, I shall reserve my discussion of these duties for Chapters V and VI, where I concentrate on the two major parts of his *Metaphysics of Morals*.

4. *General Remarks on the Law* C2

As I pointed out above, Kant tells us in the *Critique of Practical Reason* that C2 is not the moral law but only a type or typic for it. Strictly speaking, C2 seems to be a "rule of judgment" by which we can estimate or determine whether a certain case "in experience" does or does not fall under the law C1.[29] Concerning a type or typic for the moral law Kant says, "Happiness and the infinite useful consequences of a will determined only by [the maxim of] helping itself could, if this will be made itself into a universal law, certainly serve as a very adequate type for the morally good but still not be identical to it."[30] But if C2 is not, then, just another formulation of the law expressed by C1, how can an application of C2 throw light on what the moral law requires?

Kant's answer seems to be this. The laws of freedom define a possible "order" of rational wills. As imperfectly rational natural beings, our only available *model* for such a rational order is nature "as regards its form," that is, as a system of natural laws. These natural laws are to be understood teleologically: they describe a world in which each element has a natural place or function and in which everything that happens contributes to some supreme end. What we assume in applying $C2$ is that if the order-in-nature specified by the universalization of a maxim is *not* consistently willable in the appropriate sense (that is, if it is inconsistent with the conjunction of what we will and what we may assume about nature conceived of in teleological terms), then the corresponding order of rational wills is not possible either, and vice versa. Viewed this way, Kant's idea would seem to be an application of the abstract principle that if M is a model of a system S, then if a certain order is not possible in M, the corresponding order is not possible in S, and vice versa.

Kant's reasoning here needs development to be persuasive. We may be able to conceive of or otherwise represent a rational order of wills only on the basis of a model M, but we have to be assured that M is an *adequate* model if we are to conclude that, if something cannot hold in it, a corresponding thing cannot hold in the rational order. Whether a model is adequate for this purpose depends, of course, on how the relation of *correspondence* is to be determined. But Kant is not explicit about this; we have to speculate.

Although it is tempting to suppose that Kant would claim that the world of nature is an acceptable model for a rational order because the world of nature (at least the human part of it) may justifiably be regarded as a spatiotemporal appearance of a world of rational intelligences existing "in themselves," I think Kant would give a different answer. He would say, I believe, that the system of natural laws applying to dogs and cats as well as human beings is to be understood as defining a *teleological* system—one in which events occur for the sake of realizing natural ends. In conceiving of nature this way we are imposing a rational order on it; we are conceiving of it as a fundamentally rational system. As so conceived, the formal structure of natural laws is not just analogous to the formal structure of rational laws: the formal structure is the *same* in both cases. Given this, the system of nature is *necessarily* an adequate model for a system of rational wills.[31]

I think it is fair to say that if the use of *C2* requires us to adopt a teleological view of nature, then *C2* must be considered as obsolete as a teleological view of nature clearly is at the present time. A defender of Kant might wish to reply that using *C2* does not require us actually to assume that nature is a teleological system; it merely requires us to view nature *as if* it were such a system. Although this reply no doubt expresses Kant's actual view of the matter, it prompts another charge that Kant has no way of avoiding—namely, that if we are merely to view nature *as if* it were governed by teleological laws, we could have no rational way of settling disputes about nature's supposed purposes, or about what function a natural thing is supposed to have. Consider, for example, the supposed function of self-love. Kant views self-love *as if* it had the function of "stimulating the furtherance of life." But suppose I view its function as that of stimulating the furtherance of a life in which pleasure outweighs pain. What could Kant possibly say to prove my view erroneous? After all, many people do commit suicide because they find life intolerable. Could they not say that, through love of self, they are just putting themselves out of their misery? If we are merely viewing nature *as if* it operated according to purposes, there seems to be no limit on the variety of purposes we could credit it with.

If we reject a teleological conception of the whole of nature even in an "as if" sense (as most contemporary philosophers no doubt do) we could still accept a teleological conception of that part of nature consisting of imperfectly rational beings. This limitation on the scope of teleological laws might allow us to retain *C2* as a basic moral principle. The question is, "How good is *C2* as a basic principle for identifying moral permissions and obligations?"

If we are restricting the scope of teleological laws to the behavior of imperfectly rational beings (that is, to the behavior of beings in the world of experience that are significantly rational) then to will that a maxim m, or its generalization $G(m)$, holds as a law of nature is to will that all imperfectly rational beings have m as their maxim. An important point to consider here is what must be required of a being that has m as a maxim.

To appreciate the importance of this matter, consider the following maxim:

> m: If the life of a professional philosopher seems more attractive to me than any other way of life open to me, I will become a professional philosopher.

Suppose everyone (every partly rational being) has this maxim. If having this maxim required acting on it, and if acting on it required the agent actually to become a professional philosopher, then, since no one in his right mind could consistently will that everyone should become a professional philosopher, we would have to conclude that action on m is morally impermissible. But clearly this would be absurd: any reasonable criterion of moral permissibility ought to allow action on this innocent maxim. A different conception of having a maxim thus seems in order here. I suggest the following: To have a maxim requires only that one accept its provisions and be prepared to act on them should the occasion arise. Since the antecedent of m above is simply not satisfied for most people (the life of a professional philosopher is not that attractive to them) the idea of everyone's *having* m does not seem problematic.

It is worth observing that if acting on a maxim does not require the agent to succeed in his aim, there is really some doubt about whether the consequences of everyone's acting on the maxim we are considering would be objectionable. A person acting on m would have the intention of becoming a professional philosopher and would act in a way that he believes will at least contribute toward realizing his intention. If, for example, he is a college student, he may declare himself a philosophy major; and if he is a business executive, he may attempt to enroll in some philosophy program, and so on. It is not entirely evident that activities of this kind add up to an impossible totality: it is not as if we are faced with the prospect of everyone actually being, at the same time, a professional philosopher. On the other hand, it is not entirely clear that the consequences of everyone's *intending* to become a professional philosopher would be acceptable. It is true that not everyone's intention could possibly be realized, but then a lot of other socially useful intentions would probably not be formed—for example, the intention to continue farming one's land, tending one's children, or running for public office. I am inclined to believe that the consequences of everyone's actually intending to become a philosopher (to the extent that this is even possible) really would be objectionable, but it is not easy to show that this belief is true.

I indicated, by a parenthetical remark, that it may not be possible for everyone to act on the maxim *m*. Actually, it does not seem possible for everyone even to have this maxim. How could a person who is a practicing philosopher have the maxim of *becoming* one if he admires the philosopher's life? Also, if in applying *C2* we are to consider "how things would stand" in nature if a certain maxim were universalized, we generate all the familiar problems of contrary-to-fact suppositions.[32] We are faced with a world full of widely differing people attempting to realize an enormous variety of purposes. But then we are asked to consider how things would stand if they all had (or possibly acted on) one and the same maxim. If they all had this maxim, no doubt they would not have all kinds of maxims that, in point of fact, they do have. But exactly what maxims are we entitled to suppose they give up? And if they do give up certain maxims, how has their situation in life been affected? No doubt we can evaluate the consequences of everyone acting on *m* only by abstracting greatly from the actual character of men and nature, but the allowable limits of this abstraction are extremely difficult to determine. If we apply Kant's formula *C2* with great care and full attention to logical subtleties, we shall find that we are faced with questions incomparably more difficult than the proverbial "What if Napoleon had won the battle of Waterloo?"

Kant might, of course, offer the following response to the

remarks I have just made: The formula $C2$ should not be pressed too hard, for it is merely a "rule of judgment" for applying the moral law, which is properly expressed by $C1$. The point in using $C2$ is to form a rational *estimate* of what the law requires under various conditions that can arise in experience, and the basis for such an estimate may sometimes be fairly rough and ready.[33] It is, admittedly, difficult to be fully confident about the consequences of many counterfactual suppositions, but this does not mean that the consequences of such suppositions are not well worth considering. In fact, we have no alternative to considering such consequences; we do so every time we deliberate about our future conduct. Thus, although we may sometimes encounter considerable uncertainty in applying $C2$, this does not mean that we cannot use it to make a reasonable (though perhaps not infallibly true) *estimate* about the moral acceptability of acting on all sorts of possible maxims. No doubt cases will occasionally arise in which we cannot apply $C2$ with a high degree of confidence. If we have available no other rule to which we can appeal, we may then be in serious doubt about what the moral law, $C1$, actually requires. But this does not show that $C2$ is an objectionable rule of moral judgment. It may not be a perfect rule, but is perhaps the best we can reasonably hope for.[34]

Before considering any further objections that might reasonably be raised against Kant's principle $C2$ I want to make some remarks about an important matter that I have thus far been neglecting—namely, the significance of Kant's strategy in applying the predicate "is morally permissible" not to actions *simpliciter* but to actions *on* some maxim or other. If, as Kant seems to be doing, we include actions among the metaphysical furniture of our world, we shall be forced to acknowledge that the very same action may be described or conceived of in more than one way. Sometimes we describe an action in relation to the agent's purpose: for example, we might describe a patently dull remark as "Jones's attempt to be interesting." Sometimes we describe an action in relation to its effects: Jones's act of frightening Smith may have been an act of saying "Boo!" that was successful in causing Smith to be frightened. The different descriptions applicable to a particular action may be extremely numerous; indeed, there seems to be no end to variety of ways in which an action can be described.

The fact that a particular action may be described in many different ways is very important for moral philosophy. Suppose Jones frightens Smith thinking him to be Harris. As it happens, Smith has a very bad heart and dies as the result of his fright. Harris, however, is a healthy young person who does not mind being frightened; in fact, he enjoys playing tricks on other people and does not mind having other people play tricks on him. Jones intended to frighten Harris with a trick cigar, one that would explode when lighted. Considered as *an attempt to frighten Harris*, Jones's act would seem to be innocent and morally permissible. But considered as *an act of frightening Smith to death*, Jones's act would not seem to be morally permissible at all. To avoid the conclusion that one and the same action could be both morally permissible and morally impermissible, some philosophers would say that actions should be considered morally permissible or impermissible only "under certain descriptions."[35] By saying this, they do not mean that, under a certain description, an action is morally permissible or impermissible. They mean that an action is morally-permissible-under-a-description. Their idea is that "morally permissible" is an incomplete predicate that is not applicable by itself to an action.

As I understand him, Kant adopts a similar strategy in dealing with moral permissibility. Instead of saying that an action is morally permissible or impermissible, he says that it is morally permissible or impermissible for a person to act on a certain maxim. Saying this does not commit him to the view that things called "actions-on-maxims" are morally permissible or impermissible, for this would be an odd view to hold. Rather, he could say that the expression "morally permissible" should be viewed as part of a prefix, "It is morally permissible that," which is applicable to indicative sentences of the form "*s* acts on the maxim *m*." The result of appending this prefix to a sentence has a truth-value that is determined,

Kant says, by *C1*, for as Kant says in the *Metaphysics of Morals*, the categorical imperative "expresses what obligation [and therefore permission] is."[36] If we can specify the conditions under which sentences containing the moral prefix (as I shall call it) are true, we can justifiably claim to understand what moral permissibility is even though we deny that it is a property that actions (or anything else for that matter) can possess.

I now want to make some final remarks about the acceptability of Kant's principle *C2*, which is the principal subject of this section. A natural objection to it can be built on the contention that actions morally permissible in some circumstances are not always permissible in others. I may have the maxim of laughing for a minute whenever I feel tense; but although action on this maxim may be morally permissible in most circumstances, it is certainly not permissible at funerals where people would be seriously offended by an outburst of laughter. Since the principle *C2* makes no provision for the moral significance of the circumstances in which one acts on a certain maxim, it would appear to be seriously defective as a basic moral principle.

This objection is actually more serious than it might initially appear. One might think that Kant could easily meet it by qualifying *C2* as follows:

> It is morally permissible for *s* to act on *m* in circumstances *C* if and only if *s* can consistently think of himself as having *m* as his maxim in *C* and as willing that *G(m)* holds as a natural law for all significantly rational beings in circumstances relevantly similar to *C*.

Unfortunately, it is extremely doubtful that Kant could accept this kind of qualification. For one thing, he unquestionably holds the principle expressed early in the *Groundwork* that the moral value of an action is determined by the maxim on which it is based and not by anything external to the maxim—as the circumstances clearly are. For another thing, if it is really wrong (as a matter of moral principle) to laugh at funerals, Kant would say that no rational being could have the maxim of laughing at funerals. But this means, according to Kant's theory, that it is morally impermissible for imperfectly rational beings to act on the maxim of laughing at funerals —not that it is wrong, at funerals, to act on some maxim that requires laughing. Both of these points make it fairly clear, I think, that the circumstances of action have moral significance, for Kant, only to the extent that they are represented in the maxim on which the action is done.

There is another, perhaps subtler reason why Kant's law cannot be revised in the suggested way. As I remarked earlier, there is virtually no limit to the variety of ways in which an action can be described or conceived of. The same is true, obviously, of the circumstances in which an action is done. Since Kant constantly emphasizes the central significance of the agent's motive (or maxim) in acting, he would no doubt insist that the manner in which a person conceives of his circumstances is more important, morally, than the actual character of those circumstances. The need for insisting on this point stands out sharply when we consider the question of what some person could consistently will. If I am to decide whether I can will that everyone in certain circumstances could act on a certain maxim, my decision must be based on *my conception* of those circumstances. Yet my conception need not agree with those of other people. This possibility undermines the objectivity of the revised version of *C2* because if I conceive of funerals as happy occasions in which to celebrate someone's passing on to a more fortunate mode of existence, I might have absolutely no trouble willing that people at funerals should always act on maxims requiring laughter, whereas someone who conceives of funerals as solemn ceremonies may be utterly incapable of willing such a thing.

If all this is right, Kant must reject the suggested revision of his law *C2*. But how, then, would he deal with the fact *we* should express by saying that actions permissible in some circumstances may be impermissible in others? The answer to this question is not evident from what Kant says in the *Groundwork*, but he introduces a short section toward the end of his *Metaphysics of Morals* that provides an important indication of how he would respond to the question.[37] Though Kant's remarks in this section are somewhat obscure, he seems to be saying that the duties derivable from the categorical imperative (or moral law) are "principles of obligation for men as such to one another" and that "the duties of men to one another with regard to their circumstances" do not "comprise" such principles. To discover our duties in specific circumstances, we must consider, he says, how our principles of obligation "apply" to those circumstances.

Kant's thinking here can be clarified, I believe, as follows. As we have seen, Kant thinks that the categorical imperative either involves or amounts to the requirement that we conform our behavior to universal laws. Viewed from the perspective of imperfectly rational beings, these laws are seen as moral laws of two kinds, laws of justice and laws of virtue (or ethics). As the four examples Kant gives in the *Groundwork* indicate, such laws are highly general and concern such things as developing one's talents, helping others in distress, not making false promises, and not committing suicide. Since these laws are "universally valid," they hold for all circumstances, but they do not refer to particular circumstances such as funerals or cocktail parties. Nevertheless, to ascertain what we ought to do in specific circumstances, we must consider what these general laws require and how they apply to such circumstances. As an example of how we might ascertain such a thing, consider a tense person at a funeral who has the maxim of laughing for a minute whenever he feels tense. Though there is, as we may suppose, no moral law or principle specifically concerned with laughter at funerals, there is an ethical law requiring us to "show respect for every other man." It is not unreasonable to suppose that this ethical law applies to the case in point. If acting on the maxim of laughter while at the funeral amounts to showing disrespect for some mourner (or for his feelings, as we should say nowadays), it would be natural to conclude that it is morally impermissible, in the circumstances, to act on that maxim.

It is important to realize that, in adopting this strategy, Kant is not guilty of an inconsistency. It might appear that since there is pretty clearly no "formal" difficulty in willing that everyone should have the maxim of laughing for a minute when he feels tense, Kant is committed to the view that it is morally permissible to act on this maxim—a view inconsistent with the idea expressed in the last paragraph. I think it cannot be denied that the maxim of laughing when you feel tense does satisfy the test of $C2$ and that action on this maxim is, in a sense, permissible. But to be guilty of an inconsistency Kant must be committed to the view that it both is and is not morally permissible to act on this maxim in the same sense of the term "morally permissible," and I can see no reason to suppose that Kant is actually committed to this view. To clarify his actual position, we might adapt the terminology of W. D. Ross and say that action on any maxim satisfying the general test of $C2$ (or some other version of the moral law) is "*prima facie* permissible," for it is not explicitly contrary to some universal law of justice or virtue. On the other hand, we can say that when an action on some maxim is rendered morally unacceptable by the way universal moral laws apply in the circumstances, it is "absolutely" impermissible.[38] Since Ross put his terminology to a purpose somewhat different from this, we might alternatively say that, for Kant, any action based on a maxim satisfying $C2$ or its equivalent is "in principle permissible" but that an action rendered objectionable by the way a moral law applies to its circumstances is "contingently impermissible." The word "contingent" is particularly appropriate here, because it helps remind us that the action is morally objectionable by virtue of contingent facts about the circumstances in which it occurs.

If, as I am claiming, Kant conceives of the kind of permissions and obligations directly inferable from $C2$ as essentially general in import, then objections to $C2$ based on special circumstances of action are reasonably viewed as irrelevant. This conclusion accords well with the spirit of Kant's discussion even in the *Groundwork*, for he constantly speaks of the moral law as providing a "formal" test for morally acceptable action, and such a test could not be expected to account for moral requirements that depend on the contingent character of specific circumstances. Though Kant did not himself draw a distinction between what is contingently permissible (or forbidden) and what is in principle permissible (or forbidden) such a distinction is clearly required by the structure of his theory.

Given the limitations of Kant's evident aim in introducing his moral law (or its typic, $C2$) we thus see that the law provides a more satisfactory principle than one might initially suppose. Nevertheless, $C2$ faces some general difficulties that are not easy to resolve. One was mentioned in connection with the pure law $C1$: How can $C2$ possibly prove that it is morally impermissible to act on the sadomasochist's maxim, "I will inflict pain on another whenever it pleases me to do so"? I shall conclude the present section by commenting on the problem.

When I discussed Kant's treatment of his fourth example, I pointed out that, for purposes of $C2$, the question of what a person can consistently will must be determined, in part, by his nature as a rational being.[39] If, as Kant will argue, a rational being (or an imperfect being to the extent that he is rational) necessarily wills the deserved happiness of others, it would appear that even a sadomasochist could not rationally will that the generalization of his favorite maxim should become a universal law. This result would be sufficient to avoid a serious counterexample except for one stubborn fact. The only grounds Kant seems to have, at least at this stage of his argument, for any claim about what a rational being necessarily wills is provided by $C1$ or $C2$; yet to draw conclusions from these principles he must apparently make assumptions about rational willing and therefore about what rational beings (or humans to the extent that they are rational) necessarily will. As a result of this stubborn fact, Kant is open to the charge of establishing moral conclusions by circular reasoning. As it happens, Kant does have a strategy for avoiding this kind of circularity, but I shall discuss it only after I have introduced other formulations of his moral law, which add significant content to his notion of rational willing.

Chapter III: Rational Ends and Moral Autonomy

IN this chapter I shall be concerned with the third and fourth formulations of the moral law that Kant gives in the *Groundwork*. These formulations, which I shall refer to as *C3* and *C4*, involve the ideas of humanity as an end in itself and the moral autonomy of rational beings. To clarify these difficult Kantian ideas, I shall have to discuss three complicated matters: the account of "natural ends" that Kant presents in his *Critique of Judgment*, his distinction between the sensible and the intelligible world, and his metaphysical view of human freedom.

1. *Kant's Derivation of the Formula* C3

Kant introduces this formula at the conclusion of a very difficult and, for most readers, highly confusing discussion of means, ends, and rational motivation. His aim is to show that there is a rational motive for accepting the moral law, that this motive concerns rational beings as ends in themselves, and that, by virtue of this motive, the moral law can be expressed in the form of

> *C3*: Act in such a way that you always treat humanity, whether in your own person or in the person of any other, never simply as a means but always at the same time as an end.

I shall work my way toward this form of the moral law by analyzing his remarks about rational motivation.

Kant begins with the assertion that "the will is conceived of as a power of determining itself to action *in accordance with the idea of certain laws*."[1] On the face of it, this assertion does not make sense. How can a power "determine" a power (namely, itself) to action? But Kant's thought is perhaps this: Instead of being determined to action by some urge or desire, the will can be determined to action by a willed principle of action. Put in familiar language, the idea would be that we are capable of willing to do something, not because we feel some urge or desire to do so, but because we accept some maxim or principle that requires us to do so. Suppose that we have the principle:

I will act on a maxim *m* only if *m* is K-universalizable,

where "K-universalizable" means "satisfies the test implicit in Kant's principle *C2*." If we also have the premise,

m★ is not K-universalizable,

we may then will (or decide):

I will not act on *m*★.

Here we will to do something (not act on *m*★) because we will to act on a general principle that could be formulated as a universal law.

Kant says that the "objective ground" of the will's self-determination is an *end*. Whenever we will to do something, or will that something is the case, we have some end in mind. Some ends are merely "subjective"; they depend, Kant says, on impulses or urges. But some ends are "objective"; these depend on "motives valid for every rational being." A motive is presumably some kind of thought that moves us to will something; the objective end, since it is distinguished from the motive, is no doubt the object or state of affairs that the motive concerns, represents, or is directed to. If the motive for the volition "I will do *A*" is the thought "Doing *A* would be fun," then the end I pursue in doing *A* could be described, I should think, as "the fun in doing *A*."

Kant proceeds to argue that the categorical imperative has an "objective ground"; it is adopted because of a motive valid for every rational being. This claim might seem surprising, for when Kant first introduced the categorical imperative in the first chapter of the *Groundwork*, he said, "Since I have robbed the will of every inducement that might arise for it as the consequence of obeying any particular law, nothing is left but the conformity of actions to universal law as such, and this alone must serve the law as its principle."[2] At first sight this remark suggests that the will (or rational being) does not adopt the categorical imperative for any *motive* at all: it has been "robbed of every inducement." This suggestion is not supported, however, if we read Kant carefully: what he says is that the will is robbed of every inducement "that might arise as the consequence of obeying any particular law." If we interpret this remark strictly, we can say that there can be a valid motive for adopting the moral law *if* that motive is not focused on some end that would "arise" or be realized as the consequence of obeying the moral law.

What is the motive in question? Unfortunately, Kant does not describe it clearly. He does say, however, that the motive concerns something that has an "absolute value"—something that is not valued because something else is valued. This thing having an absolute value is, he says, an "end in itself," and the "objective ground" of the categorical imperative concerns its existence. Though the point is by no means certain, Kant might be identifying this objective ground when he says that "rational nature exists as an end in itself."[3] His general argument seems to be that, since (*a*) every rational being exists as an end in itself and (*b*) all such ends have an absolute value for every rational being, there is an "objectively valid" motive for adopting the categorical imperative. A purely rational being would adopt it *because* he necessarily values rational beings as "ends in themselves."

If we are to understand what Kant is saying here, we must understand what he means in saying that a rational being exists as an end in itself. His terminology is highly confusing, for although we naturally conceive of an end as something that is to be realized or brought into being by an action, Kant has made it clear (as we have seen) that the end associated with the motive for adopting the moral law *cannot* be viewed in this way.

A clue to Kant's meaning can be found in his discussion of "natural ends" in the *Critique of Judgment*.[4] He says there that a thing exists as a natural end if "it is both cause and effect of itself." The notion of causation appropriate here is, he says, "ideal or teleological causation": a thing is caused to be what it is by an idea of its end. Even without further details about natural ends, it seems reasonable to think of rational beings as possible ends in this sense of being things that are "both causes and effects of themselves." Specifically, we can say that

x is a rational end = df x is a rational being and x's idea of itself causes (in the "ideal" way) x to be what x is.

The term "causes" makes sense here, because rational beings (at least the imperfect ones we know as men) change over time: young ones become older and wiser. Thus, we may express the idea as follows:

To the extent that a being is rational, it is what it is at least partly because of its conception of its rational nature.

As an illustration of this, we can imagine Kant saying that a rational being will develop its talents *because* it views the development of its talents as required by its nature as a rational being.

In the *Critique of Judgment* Kant conceives of nature as a system of natural ends: one natural end may be subordinate to another in the sense that it contributes to, or exists for the sake of, another.[5] For example, grass exists as food for animals, and animals exist as food for (or slaves of) man. Kant also seems to think the value of a thing's existence is determined by the extent to which it serves its function in the total system. Thus, grass is valuable as food for animals that are valuable as food and so forth for man. But this natural hierarchy ends with man, Kant thinks. To the extent that he is rational, man does not exist for the sake of anything else, and he does not possess value in relation to anything else. As an end, man possesses a supreme value, for all other ends exist and have value for the sake of man. As Kant puts it: "Man is the final end of creation. Without man the chain of mutually subordinated ends would have no ultimate point of attachment."[6] This is an astonishing, even extravagant view to take of a perverse creature such as man,[7] but Kant would no doubt attempt to account for its extravagance by saying that the teleological view of nature is bound to be anthropocentric since it is the one that we, as men (= human beings), naturally take. It is surely not surprising that human beings should view themselves as the most valuable things in the world.[8]

With this understanding of what Kant means in speaking of rational nature as an end in itself, we can now return to the line of reasoning that leads him to a third form of what he calls the moral law. As we saw, Kant argued that if there were a valid motive for adopting the moral law, it could not concern some end that is to be realized as the consequence of obeying that law. Having located an end that, because it is an end in itself, is objectively valuable and not something to be realized or brought into existence as the effect of our conformity to a principle, Kant thinks that he has located an appropriate motive for adopting the moral law. Unfortunately, his argumentation is confusing at this point, and he does not clearly formulate the motive.

It might appear that the motive is just the "ground" mentioned earlier—namely, that rational nature exists as an end in itself. But this ground does not seem to be the motive for the categorical imperative. Beck translates the crucial passage as follows: "If there is to be a . . . categorical imperative for the human will, it must be one that forms an objective principle of the will from the conception of that which is necessarily an end for everyone because it is an end in itself. Hence this objective principle can serve as a universal practical law. The ground of this principle is: rational nature exists as an end in itself."[9] Here we are told that the categorical imperative *forms* an objective principle (which, as objective, is a law) *from* the conception of a certain end. The objective principle thus formed seems different from the categorical imperative, and the fact that rational nature exists as an end in itself seems to be the ground of the principle formed. If this is so, we have not located the ground, in the sense of motive, for accepting the categorical imperative itself. In fact, the ground just mentioned seems to be an ingredient of the categorical imperative, for later in the paragraph Kant seems to be saying that "it must be possible to derive all laws of the will" from this "supreme practical ground."[10]

The difficulty of interpreting Kant on this matter is increased by his careless use of the term "ground." Early in his discussion he tells us that the "objective ground of a volition" is a *motive* that is valid for all rational beings. But later he says that "if there is something whose existence has itself absolute value, then this thing could be the ground of the categorical imperative." This is very confusing, because a practical principle or law is a principle of volition, whose ground should be a motive rather than a thing, or end. But perhaps Kant's thought can be clarified by a double use of "ground": he might be saying that the ground of (= the basis for accepting) the categorical imperative is an objectively valid motive that is grounded on (based on the conception of) a thing that, because it is an end in itself, has absolute value for every rational being.

This suggestion seems supported by the following reasoning. If a certain sort of thing is of value to me, I may form some motive concerning it, which may move me to act. For example, Mary's happiness is of value to me, and in thinking about it I form the motive of doing something that will make her happy. Her happiness is thus my end, and my motive of making her happy is directed to that end. Since my motive was generated by the fact that I valued her happiness, we can say that my motive was *based* (or grounded) on the value to me of her happiness. Now consider rational nature. As an end in itself, rational nature has value to me and to every rational being. (I shall consider Kant's argument for this claim a little later.) The awareness of this absolute value may generate (be the basis or ground for) a motive concerning it. What this motive is we do not yet know, but it concerns rational nature as an end in itself, and it can serve as a rational basis (or ground) for accepting the moral law.

This line of thought seems to be supported by several remarks Kant makes. In the paragraph preceding the last passage I quoted Kant says that ends in themselves are "objects of respect" that "restrict all arbitrary choice." This remark may be viewed as suggesting that the motive for adopting the moral law (or categorical imperative) is *respect for rational nature as an end in itself*. This suggestion is supported, I believe, by some remarks Kant makes later on, when he summarizes the argument of his entire second chapter. After noting that "in the idea of an absolutely good will there must be abstraction from every end that is to be produced [or realized]," he says that the end appropriate to such a will must "be conceived, not as an end to be produced, but as a self-existent end."[11] As such, he says, the end must "be conceived only negatively—that is, as an end against which we should never act, and consequently one which in all our willing we must never rate *merely* as a means, but always at the same time as an end."[12]

In view of these considerations I suggest the following interpretation. We are aware that rational nature exists as an end in itself and is, in consequence, absolutely valuable to every rational being. This awareness generates an objectively valid motive concerning such valuable ends—namely, the motive of respecting rational nature as an end in itself. Since an end in itself is a "self-existent" end, it is not something that a rational being can "produce or realize." The motive of respecting it can therefore justify (or "ground") only a negative principle—one requiring us not to "act against" rational nature: to treat it always as an end and never merely as a means. Since a principle of this kind does not require us to produce, bring about, or realize some valued end, it can be a valid categorical imperative.

Kant claims, as we have seen, that there is just one categorical imperative—namely, the moral law. Since the principle just described is a valid categorical imperative, it must be equivalent to (or be another way of formulating) the moral law. Kant supports this claim by the following remarks:

> The principle "So act in relation to every rational being (both to yourself and others) that he may at the same time count in your maxim as an end in himself" is thus at bottom the same as the principle "Act on a maxim which at the

same time contains its only universal validity for every rational being." For to say that in using means to every end I ought to restrict my maxim by the condition that it should also be universally valid as a law for every subject is just the same as to say this—that a subject of ends, namely a rational being himself, must be made the ground for all maxims of action, never merely as a means, but as a supreme condition restricting the use of every means—that is, always as an end.[13]

Thus, Kant's view of the relation between *C1* and *C3* amounts to this: to adopt only those maxims that can be K-universalized is just to adopt only those maxims that, in effect, treat rational beings as ends rather than as mere means to ends.

2. On Treating Rational Beings as Ends

If we are to understand the formula *C3* we must, of course, know what is involved in treating humanity, or rational nature, as an end. Kant makes two important remarks on this matter when he shows us how *C3* applies to the four examples we discussed in section 3 of the last chapter. His first remark is this:

The violator of the rights of man intends to use the person of others merely as a means without taking into consideration that, as rational beings, they ought always at the same time to be rated as ends—that is, only as beings who must themselves be able to share in the end of the very same action.[14]

His second remark is this:

Humanity could no doubt subsist if everybody contributed nothing to the happiness of others but at the same time refrained from deliberately impairing their happiness. This is, however, merely to agree negatively and not positively with *humanity as an end in itself* unless everyone endeavors also, so far as in him lies, to further the ends of others. For the ends of a subject who is an end in himself must, if this conception is to have its *full* effect on me, be also, as far as possible, *my* ends.[15]

These two remarks add significant content to the idea of treating rational beings as ends, but they raise problems of interpretation.

Take the second remark first. On the face of it, one would think that if *C3* were an essentially negative principle having the same content as *C1*, the following would be both necessary and sufficient for treating rational beings as ends:

> Always act in such a way that you do not thwart the permissible or legitimate ends of others,

where a permissible or legitimate end is presumably one whose corresponding maxim is K-universalizable.[16] But the second remark clearly indicates that a stronger condition is needed: we treat others as ends just when

> we act in such a way that we not only do not thwart their permissible ends but endeavor, so far as possible, to realize (or help them realize) those permissible ends.

It is obvious that Kant's second remark is logically stronger than the first one. According to the first, you treat another as an end only when the other "may share" in the end you are trying to realize by your action. As we might expect from Kant's words about agreeing negatively with humanity as an end, another person *may* share your end, for Kant, just when your end is compatible with his end—just when he could consistently adopt your end (e.g., your realizing *E*) as his own. This amounts to the idea, which Kant will develop in the *Metaphysics of Morals*, that you treat another negatively as an end just when your pursuit of your end does not necessarily interfere with his freedom to pursue his allowable ends. Obviously, this condition is much weaker than that implied by Kant's second remark: the latter requires me not just to use others in ways consistent with the realization of their ends but in ways that positively further their ends.

In view of Kant's second remark one might naturally suppose that the principle *C3* is significantly stronger than his original principle, *C1*. On the face of it, *C1* places a mere negative restriction on permissible actions: I act in a morally permissible way when and only when I can consistently will that a generalized form of my maxim should be a universal law. This gives me a motive for *not* doing certain things—specifically, for not acting on maxims that are not K-universalizable—but it does not, at least in any obvious way, give me a motive for doing something positive, that is, for acting on some maxim or other. I certainly have no motive for doing everything I am morally permitted to do; in fact, I may have the policy of not doing many things that are morally permissible, such as writing my name in my own books. But Kant's remarks about what is involved in treating rational beings as ends in themselves suggest that *C3* does give us a motive for doing positive things. If, as a rational being, I must "endeavor, so far as in me lies, to further the ends of others," then if doing *A* is morally permissible, not incompatible with the pursuit of a legitimate end I have, and the means to someone else's legitimate end, do I not then (at least if I am aware of these facts about *A*) have a motive for performing it?

As we shall see in Chapter VII, the answer to this particular question is somewhat problematic.[17] But there is no doubt that Kant thinks we have some kind of duty to further the ends of others, at least when those ends are not immoral; and he assuredly thinks that this duty is inferable from *C1* (or *C2*) as well as from *C3*. His view on this matter was explicit in his remarks on the fourth example that he introduced in connection with *C2*. When I discussed those remarks in section 3 of the last chapter, I claimed that Kant's argument for a duty of helping others in distress does not succeed, and in Chapter VI I shall contend that his arguments for related duties do not succeed either. Thus, though *C1* and *C3* do not actually have the same consequences, at least if I am right, Kant unquestionably thought they do.

When I summarized my discussion of how *C2* applies to Kant's four examples, I pointed out that those examples illustrate two ways in which one may be unable to will that a maxim should become a universal law: either one sees that it could not possibly be such a law or one sees (roughly) that its becoming such a law is incompatible with something else that one wills. It turns out that, in Kant's view, these two ways of being unable to will that one's maxim shall become a universal law yield two distinct tests for morally permissible action, and these tests coincide with the tests associated with the negative and positive treatment of humanity as an end in itself. As we shall see in Chapters V and VI, Kant views the impossibility of one's maxim becoming a universal law as equivalent to the idea that action on that maxim will necessarily limit another person's allowable freedom, and he views the incompatibility between willing that the maxim shall be a universal law and willing certain other things (which one must will either insofar as one acts on the maxim or insofar as one is rational) as equivalent to the idea that action on the maxim will amount to not treating humanity positively as an end in itself. He also contends that these two distinct tests for morally permissible action yield two systems of moral duties: duties of justice and duties of virtue. These points are important in the present context, because they make it clear that, although Kant's principles $C1$ (or $C2$) and $C3$ do not appear to be equivalent or different formulations of the same law, Kant has deep-seated reasons for viewing them this way. I shall have a lot to say about those reasons in the chapters to follow.

For the sake of shedding some possible light on the notion of consistent willing appropriate to the categorical imperative, we might attend to one of the assumptions Kant is no doubt making when he says that $C1$ and $C3$ are at bottom the same principle. The assumption is that rational beings necessarily will the happiness of others. When he discussed the use of $C2$ as a means of applying $C1$, he remarked that rational beings necessarily will their own happiness and the development of their talents. By virtue of what he says about the importance of "agreeing positively" with humanity (or rational nature) as an end in itself, it seems reasonable to add that rational beings also necessarily will the happiness of others. Given this, we can analyze the notion of consistent willing appropriate to a rational being as follows:

> A rational being can consistently will that *p* just when willing that *p* is consistent with other things that he wills, including his own happiness, the happiness of others, and the development of his talents.

Though the point is by no means certain, Kant may hold that if, according to this conception, a rational being cannot consistently will that *p*, then we, to the extent that we are rational, cannot consistently will that *p*, and vice versa. Perhaps the "can will" in *C1* should be understood in this way.

In the paragraphs above I have commented on the plausibility of Kant's view that *C3* is just another formulation of the categorical imperative, *C1*. Actually, as is clear from its reference to humanity, *C3* cannot possibly be *identified* with the categorical imperative, that is, the moral law *C1*. At best, *C3* is an alternative formulation of *C2*, which is a typic for, or analogue of, the moral law. When Kant applied *C3* to his four examples, he made it clear that he views *C3* as a counterpart to *C2*. In asking whether an action can be "compatible with the Idea of humanity *as an end in itself*," Kant expects us to consider "how things would stand" in nature if the action were universally performed under similar circumstances. Thus, his use of "humanity" rather than "rational being" in *C3* is not the result of any carelessness on his part. He clearly views *C3* as another typic for the moral law. Saying this is compatible with admitting, of course, that the moral law could be formulated by an analogue of *C3* in which "humanity" is replaced by "rational being." In fact, Kant clearly seems to introduce such an analogue in the passage I have quoted at the end of the last section, though he does not explicitly distinguish it from the principle *C3*.

Before concluding this section I want to make some final remarks about Kant's notion of rational nature as an end. As we saw, Kant introduced this notion in the course of seeking a motive, or "objective ground," for the moral law. Motives concern ends, and the end appropriate to the motive of morality turns out to be rational nature. To speak of rational nature as an end in this context seems confusing. When we are discussing the subject of rational motivation, we naturally think of an end as something that could be realized or made actual by a possible course of action. But rational nature cannot be viewed this way: we must conceive of it, Kant says, as "self-existent." The questions therefore arise: "What does it mean to say that rational nature is 'self-existent'?" and "Does it really make sense, in a discussion of motivation, to speak of rational nature as an *end* at all?"

It is relatively easy to answer the first question. Rational nature is self-existent in the sense that it exists, but does not exist for the sake of something else. According to Kant's teleological view of nature, grass exists for the sake of nourishing animals (at least among other things), and some animals exist for the sake of feeding man and assisting his labors. But rational beings do not exist for the sake of anything else. Their existence does not satisfy some higher end or purpose, and it is not valuable to the degree that it does so. Kant seems to draw the following conclusions from these points. First, since rational nature already exists, our basic motive concerning it cannot be that of bringing it into existence or realizing it. Second, since it is self-existent, our motive must be ultimate in the sense that, whatever exactly the motive is, we do not have it because rational nature serves some further end that we value. For us, the value of rational nature is absolute, not relative. Consequently, in concerning rational nature, our motive concerns something that both exists and has absolute value to us.

The second question is more difficult to answer. Even if rational nature is not an end for us, it is still an end in a crucially important sense: it is something for the sake of which everything in nature ultimately exists. As such, it is an object of ultimate or absolute value. To the extent that our motive concerns it, our motive concerns something that, because it is the final end of nature, is an object of absolute, nonrelative value. This justifies calling it an "end," even though, as the object of a rational motive, it is not something that we endeavor to realize or bring into existence.

It might be suggested that, contrary to what Kant says, there is a significant sense in which rational nature can be an end that creatures like us might endeavor to realize. If we take lessons in logic or morals, are we not endeavoring to realize (or make actual) rational nature *in us*? And if we are, does this not imply that rational nature can be a human end in just the way that Mary's happiness can be John's end? I think Kant might reply to these questions as follows. To the extent that we are capable of taking any lessons at all, we are already significantly rational, so that rational nature is already realized in us to a significant degree. On the other hand, if "realizing rational nature in us" means "becoming fully rational," then we may indeed seek to realize rational nature in us, but the motive for doing so would not be "objectively valid" and so would not undermine the reasoning leading to *C3*. The reason this motive would not be objectively valid is that some rational beings would certainly not have it—those beings who, like God and the angels, are perfectly rational already. Apart from all this, the questions raised are based on a confusion. It is not simply rational nature, or the existence of rational nature, that imperfect beings might seek to realize: it is the perfect (or almost perfect) rationality of this or that being. But the possibility of a human end of this kind was never put in doubt by the line of reasoning leading to *C3*.

3. *The Formula of Autonomy*, C4

Kant calls his next formulation of the categorical imperative "the principle of autonomy." As we shall see, he does not formulate this principle very clearly, but there is no doubt that the idea behind it is extremely important; in fact, Kant claims that the principle of autonomy is "the sole principle of ethics."[18]

As far as I can see, the line of argument by which Kant introduces his new principle is something like this.[19] From the "mere fact" that the moral law is a *categorical* imperative we can infer that its acceptability for a rational being cannot depend on any "interest" that such a being might satisfy as the result of accepting it. Consequently, its acceptability to a rational being must be intrinsic to it. Now, as we saw when we first introduced $C1$,[20] what the moral law fundamentally requires is "conformity to universal law as such." If the principle requiring this kind of conformity is to be intrinsically acceptable, then, it would seem, the universal laws it concerns should be equally acceptable. Since these universal laws are practical laws—that is, objectively valid principles of volition—they can be intrinsically acceptable to rational beings only by being principles that rational beings freely accept or "legislate." But if this is so, the will of a rational being is not just subject to practical law, but subject in such a way that it can "be considered as also *making the law* for itself." The idea behind the principle of autonomy is thus "the Idea *of the will of every rational being as a will which makes universal law*."[21]

Before trying to formulate the principle associated with this idea of autonomy, I want to comment on the line of argument just given. The first part of the argument is not new; it was at least implicit in the arguments Kant gave for other formulations of the moral law. The key line of argument can be elaborated as follows. If there is, as we have been assuming, a fundamental moral law, it must be intrinsically acceptable to a rational being. To be convinced of this fact, we need only consider the reasoning by which a rational being would decide to adopt an extrinsically acceptable practical principle. Viewed abstractly, the reasoning would have this structure:

1. Conforming to principle P is a necessary means of satisfying the interest i.
2. I will satisfy the interest i.
3. Therefore, I will conform to the principle P.

But if P is to be a practical law acceptable to all rational beings, the premise 2 must also be acceptable to all rational beings. Yet if this is so, premise 2 expresses a practical law itself, for a practical law is simply a universally valid practical principle. But if a rational being conforms to P on the basis of a premise that is a practical law, P cannot be a fundamental law. If a law is genuinely fundamental, its acceptability cannot, therefore, be extrinsic: it must be acceptable in and of itself, without regard to the interests that might be satisfied by conforming to it.

The second part of Kant's argument, at least as I have represented it above, can be reconstructed as follows:

4. Certain universal laws are intrinsically acceptable to rational beings.
5. Therefore, those universal laws are freely accepted, legislated, or "made" by rational beings.

Although the cogency of this argument is certainly open to doubt, Kant unquestionably accepts it. As he says in one of his clearer passages, "When they [that is, previous philosophers] thought of man merely as subject to a law (whatever it might be), the law had to carry with it some interest in order to attract or compel, because it did not spring as a law from *his own* will: in order to conform with the law his will had to be necessitated by *something else* to act in a certain way."[22] The implication here seems plain: If the law does not have to carry with it some interest in order to attract or compel a man's obedience, it does spring as a law from his own will.

As I mentioned earlier, Kant does not formulate the principle of autonomy in the clearest possible way. At one place he says this: "If there is a categorical imperative . . . it can command us to act always on the maxim of a will in us as can at the same time look upon itself as making universal law."[23] A little later he speaks of every rational being as one who "must regard himself as making universal law by all the maxims of his will."[24] Finally, he says that the principle of autonomy is:

"Never to choose except in such a way that in the same volition the maxims of your choice are also present as universal law."[25]

None of these remarks renders his principle very clear. Paton, in his analysis of the *Groundwork*, suggests this formulation:

"So act that your will can regard itself at the same time as making universal law through its maxim."[26]

Since Kant explicitly says that an action "compatible with the autonomy of the will is *permitted*,"[27] we are clearly entitled to formulate his principle as a biconditional. I suggest the following:

> C4: It is morally permissible for s to act on m just when s can consistently view himself as laying down a generalized version of m as a universal law.

To be plausible, this principle should, of course, be qualified in ways that we have discussed in the last chapter. In particular, the "viewing himself" in C4 should be rational viewing, and the permissions established by C4 should be understood as things "permissible in principle."[28]

As I have formulated it, C4 comes very close to C1: the difference is just that C4 requires the agent to be able to view himself as making or laying down a universal law whereas C1 requires him to be able to will that something should be a universal law. This difference is really not great, for willing that something be a universal law seems to be an act of legislation itself. This stands out sharply if we consider the legislative form of willing. To think (or will) "It shall be that L is a universal law" is no doubt to perform a legislative act. If this is right, C1 and C4 differ only in emphasis: their content is really the same. Kant would agree with this claim, for he contends that there is really only one categorical imperative. His various formulas, at least when pure, are supposed to provide different ways of stating the same general principle.

Having introduced the subject of universal legislation, I can now come to terms with an important problem that I broached in Chapter I. When I discussed the passage in which Kant attempts to derive his first formulation of the moral law, I remarked that he *seems* to regard C1 as just a variant formulation of the principle

> L: Conform your actions to universal law.

Although I confessed some uncertainty about Kant's actual view of the relation between C1 and L, I pointed out that his derivation of *C1* is unquestionably based on the assumption that we conform to universal law when and only when we act on maxims that we "can will" to be universal laws.[29] As far as I know, Kant never provides an explicit defense for this assumption, but his remarks on autonomy suggest a means of defending it that might very well have been at the back of his mind.

As a first step in developing the argument, we might observe that since any action subject to moral evaluation must be based on some maxim, we can reasonably say that we conform to universal law just when we act on a maxim that is consistent with universal law. Given this way of speaking, we can express the assumption to be defended in the more explicit form of *A*:

> *A*: The maxim *m* on which *s* acts is consistent with universal law just when *s* can will that *m* should be a universal law.

If we consider that the phrase "can will" in *A* refers to what *s* can consistently will and that willing something to be a universal law amounts, in view of Kant's views on autonomy, to an act of rational legislation, we can see that Kant would accept the premise:

> 1. *s* can consistently will that *m* is a universal law just when, as a rational legislator, *s* can consistently adopt *m* as a universal law.

But the following premise seems equally acceptable for Kant:

> 2. As a rational legislator, *s* can consistently adopt *m* as a universal law just when *m* is consistent with what, as a rational being, *s* freely legislates.

Since Kant holds that what a person freely legislates as a rational being is identical with the system of universal law, we can infer from 1 and 2 that

> 3. *s* can consistently will that *m* is a universal law just when *m* is consistent with universal law.

But 3 is logically equivalent to A, the assumption to be defended.

Since the argument just given accords very nicely with Kant's characteristic claims about practical laws and moral legislation, there is a good chance that he may have tacitly employed it in moving from L to $C1$. Since it is also a very simple argument, there is even a good chance that he may have thought it too obvious to require formal statement. Nevertheless, it is not a good argument. The difficulty lies in the notion of willing that a maxim shall be a law. As I pointed out in Chapter I, a maxim lacks the logical form of a proper law; what one can will to be a practical law is, at best, the *generalization* of a maxim.[30] Given this, premise 1 in the argument should be reformulated as

   1*. s can consistently will that $G(m)$ is a universal law just when, as a rational legislator, s can consistently adopt $G(m)$ as a universal law.

Premise 2 should be similarly revised, with $G(m)$ in place of m. As a consequence of these revisions, the conclusion Kant is entitled to draw is only:

   3*. s can consistently will that $G(m)$ is a universal law just when $G(m)$ is consistent with universal law.

But 3* is not adequate for Kant's purposes, for it does not allow us to say that a *maxim* (or action on a maxim) is consistent with universal law when and only when *its generalization* could be willed to be a universal law.

It may be helpful to explain exactly why the desired conclusion cannot be inferred from 3*. To infer A from 3* we must prove that:

   4. m (or action on m) is consistent with universal law just when $G(m)$ is consistent with universal law.

But this formula is not a logical truth. It is a logical truth that if $G(m)$ is consistent with universal law, m (or action on m) is consistent with that law, for $G(m)$ logically implies m. Yet the converse does not hold: there is no logical absurdity in the supposition that *m* (or action on *m*) is consistent with universal law when $G(m)$ is not. To see this, note that, for all we know, the only universal law bearing on the maxim *m* might be to the effect that if a person *x* acts on *m*, at least one person *y* must not do so. In this case *m* itself (or a particular action on *m*) may be perfectly consistent with universal law even though $G(m)$ is patently incompatible with it.

Since 4 is not a logical truth, we cannot deduce *A* from 3★. Of course, if we could show that 4 is warranted by certain a priori facts about universal laws, then, even though 4 is not a logical truth, we could use it to defend *A*. But Kant provides us with no facts of this kind. Apart from telling us that universal laws are freely legislated by rational beings, he tells us very little about them until he has *C1* in hand—at which time he uses *C1* to draw conclusions about them. Since he needs assumption *A* to derive *C1* from *L*, he cannot, without begging the question, use any conclusions inferred from *C1* to show that 4—and therefore *A*—is acceptable. Yet if there is no available means of defending 4, the argument for assumption *A* that I have been considering must be counted a failure.

If Kant cannot support assumption *A*, his derivation of *C1* must be viewed as unsuccessful. According to his derivation, "the will's principle" in conforming to *C1* is "bare conformity to law as such."[31] In the terminology I have been using, "bare conformity" to universal law is what is explicitly required by the law *L*, and we now see that this law is not logically equivalent to *C1*. If Kant could provide a compelling argument for assumption *A*, he could reasonably maintain that *L* and *C1* are equivalent in a nonlogical sense, but no such argument seems to be available. Consequently, Kant's derivation of *C1* from a principle of "bare conformity to law as such" is highly questionable at best. There is every reason to believe that it simply does not succeed.

Before concluding this section I want to comment on some of the language Kant uses in speaking of the moral law. As I remarked in Chapter I, Kant often speaks of the categorical imperative as providing a purely "formal" test for morally permissible action.[32] In a line with this he sometimes says, notably in the *Critique of Practical Reason*, that it is morally permissible to act on any maxim having the "form" of a universal law.[33] When Kant speaks of form in this connection, he is not, obviously, speaking of logical form, because a morally innocent maxim like "If I buy a new book, I will write my name in it" certainly does not have the logical form of a universal law. As I pointed out, his view is that we are morally entitled to act on a maxim just when it has the "legislative form" of a universal law. His notion of legislative form is no doubt based on his view of moral autonomy. It seems fair to say that a maxim *m* has the legislative form of a universal law just when a rational legislator could consistently include *G(m)* among the laws he freely accepts. Though *consistency* is a purely formal notion, the notion of legislative form appears to be significantly nonformal, since a maxim can have this kind of form only if it is consistent with the laws that a rational being actually adopts. Kant believes and will attempt to show that these laws can be identified by reference to *C1*, but this law seems to have a significantly richer content than the abstract, uninformative principle *L*, which, in requiring bare conformity to law as such, has a better (but not really good) title to the term "formal."

Though I have been highly critical of Kant's derivation of *C1*, I should add that his derivation of *C3* is a good deal more promising. In specifying a motive for universal legislation (namely, respecting rational nature as such) it shows us that such legislation, though freely adopted, is not pointless. It also provides a reasonable basis for identifying moral principles, one that does not pretend to be purely formal. I shall have more to say about this matter in the section to follow.

4. *Autonomy, Freedom, and Moral Value*

Kant's third and fourth formulations of the moral law—that is, his formulas *C3* and *C4*—are introduced by importantly different lines of thought, but Kant relates them to one another by saying that "a rational being must always be regarded as *making universal law*, because otherwise he could not be conceived as *an end in himself*."[34] In what follows I shall

attempt to clarify this remark and spell out some of its implications for Kant's conception of moral value.

In earlier sections I explained what Kant meant in speaking
of man as an end in himself: he (or his existence) is an end for
other things, such as animals, but he is not, in turn, a mere
means to anything else. In explaining Kant's meaning here I
called attention to his remark in the *Critique of Judgment* that
"man is the final end of creation." The passage in which he
makes this remark continues as follows: "Without man the
chain of mutually subordinated ends [in nature] would have
no ultimate point of attachment. Only in man, and only in
him as the individual being to whom the moral law applies,
do we find unconditional legislation in respect of ends. This
legislation, therefore, is what alone qualifies him to be the
final end to which nature is teleologically subordinated."[35]
Here we see the connection between man's autonomy and his
character as an end in himself. Although he—or, more
properly, his existence—is an end for other things, he does
not exist, in turn, for the sake of anything else: his end is self-
imposed, determined by practical laws that, because they are
unconditional, promote no further end.

If we recall that Kant's teleological view of nature is supposed to be the view that human beings naturally take, the
idea that "man is the final end of creation" is at least understandable, if no longer credible. But why, exactly, does Kant
think that basic practical laws must be understood as *self-
imposed* by rational beings? In the remark I quoted at the beginning of this section Kant says that if man is not regarded as
making universal law, he cannot be conceived of as an end in
himself. Yet what is the basis for this claim? Why can't we
suppose that man is an end in himself because, first, his existence is (at least as he views the world) an end for various
plants and animals, and, second, his existence furthers no
higher end? Supposing this does not seem inconsistent with
saying that the practical laws to which, as a man, he should
conform are simply descriptive of the nature of a perfectly
rational being and not self-imposed in any sense at all.

In the last section I outlined Kant's official argument for the principle of autonomy. The key line of reasoning was as follows. Fundamentally, the moral law enjoins conforming to universal law as such, without regard to any end or ends that might be realized as a consequence of conforming to them. If a fully rational being necessarily conforms to these laws without intending to realize any further end that his conformity to them might promote, then they must be (as I put it) intrinsically acceptable to him. But (Kant seems to conclude) any practical law intrinsically acceptable to a rational being must be a law that he makes himself.

The concluding inference here certainly seems questionable. Why could rational beings not be born (or created) with a built-in respect for practical laws? Or again, why could practical laws not be the laws governing a rational being's reasoning in just the way that Newton's laws are the laws governing the motions of natural bodies? In either case practical laws could be said to be valid for rational beings without being understood as something a rational being "makes for himself." Though Kant did not, so far as I know, explicitly address himself to either of these questions, the text of the *Groundwork* leaves no doubt about the kinds of answer he would want to give. As I see it, his answers would be based on moral as well as metaphysical considerations. I shall begin with the moral considerations and work my way into the metaphysical ones.

Perhaps the basic moral consideration is this: To the extent that we are moral, we view human beings as having an absolute value or "dignity" and as being worthy of a certain reverence or respect. What is the basis for this? Why do we view a human being, even a criminal, as having a value incomparably greater than a dog, horse, or even a herd of elephants? To answer these questions we have to consider what is special about, or distinctive of, human beings. As Kant sees it, human beings are distinguished from other natural beings by their ability to act on principle. They are not, he believes, at the mercy of their desires, urges, or impulses; they are capable of acting for disinterested motives, and they may deliberately sacrifice their own happiness for the sake of various ideals. In viewing human beings this way we are viewing them, Kant believes, as free agents—as creatures with a free will who are not determined to act (or will certain things) by natural laws. The capacity of man to rise above "the law of his own needs" and to act on principles he has freely adopted is the source of his dignity and value.

As my last sentence suggests, Kant thinks that men are genuinely free only if they are autonomous in his sense. To be free only in the sense of doing what you want is to be subject to the law of your own needs;[36] this is not genuine freedom, for it is in essence no better than "the freedom of a turnspit, which when wound up also carries out its motions of itself."[37] For Kant, genuine freedom has both a positive and a negative aspect. Negatively, it is the property of being able to act (to will) "independently of determination by alien causes"; a genuinely free agent is thus not determined to act by "the law" of its own desires, urges, or inclinations. Positively, however, freedom of the will is "the property which a will has of being a law to itself"—and this property is what he has called autonomy.[38]

Kant's conception of genuine freedom deserves further elaboration, which I shall attempt to provide shortly. Yet if we assume that human beings, the only things in nature that possess unconditional or absolute moral value and deserve reverence or respect on account of their humanity, are distinguished from other creatures by their capacity for genuine freedom, and if this freedom requires autonomy in Kant's sense, then we can see why Kant might say that "the principle of autonomy is the sole basis of ethics."[39] If, furthermore, we consider the disinterested character of moral behavior as particularly admirable (as Kant seems to do)[40] then any principle that enjoins moral disinterestedness (as C1 clearly does) and emphasizes the value of human autonomy (as C4 does) should impress us as providing a key to the value of a rational will. Like Kant, we might say "it is just this freedom from dependence on interested motives which constitutes the sublimity of [the moral law]" and "the dignity of man consists precisely in his capacity to make universal law, although only on condition of being himself also subject to the law he makes."[41]

These last remarks recall Kant's first words in the *Groundwork*: "It is impossible to conceive of anything at all in the world, or even out of it, which can be taken as good without qualification, except a *good will*."[42] A good will, he went on to tell us, is one that acts out of respect for universal law; and now we learn that one who acts out of respect for universal law acts out of respect for a law that he has in some sense made or legislated. Of course, not all men (at least on the face of it) act out of respect for law all the time, so their wills are not good without qualification. Yet they still have "an intrinsic value—that is, *dignity*"—because they are *capable* of making and acting on universal laws. This capacity for making universal law is fully actualized in a perfectly rational being, whose will is good without qualification. The morally proper aim of a partly rational being is thus to become as rational as he can. Since Kant seems to believe that a genuinely (or completely) free human being acts according to universal law, he no doubt believes that imperfectly rational beings are imperfectly free: they are *capable* of genuine freedom, but this capability is not fully realized in them. I shall have more to say about this matter later.

To get a deeper understanding of Kant's view of the relation between freedom and moral autonomy, we have to dwell a little longer on his conception of the positive aspect of freedom. Genuine freedom, for Kant, is freedom of the will; and he regards will, or willing, as "a kind of causality belonging to living beings so far as they are rational."[43] Viewed negatively, freedom of the will is thus the property this causality has of being able to "work" independently of "determination by alien causes." But freedom must have a positive aspect, since any kind of causality involves a law according to which causes have particular kinds of effects. Thus Kant says: "The freedom of the will, although it is not the property of conforming to laws of nature, is not for this reason lawless: it must rather be a causality conforming to immutable laws, though of a special kind."[44] But then he asks rhetorically: "What else [given the foregoing] . . . can freedom of the will be but autonomy—that is, the property which a will has of being a law to itself?" Since a will having this property is one that acts on no maxim other than one that could be (and thus conforms to) a universal law, "a free will and a will under moral laws are one and the same."[45]

Kant's reasoning here is extremely ingenious but difficult to understand; some clarifying remarks are therefore in order. To begin with, it seems undeniable that whenever we can justifiably speak of causes, we must assume that there are laws in accordance with which effects are produced. It also seems undeniable, at least to anyone prepared to countenance acts of will, that willing is a way, form, or mode of causing—one distinctive of rational beings. Since causes always operate according to laws, willing must also operate according to laws, whether it is free or not. Kant claims that the peculiarity of free willing is that it operates according to special, nonnatural laws, the "laws of freedom." When a person wills in accordance with these laws, his willing is not "determined by alien causes": desires, urges, and so forth do not cause him to will one thing rather than another. Evidently, his will is moved by rational motives rather than urges, yens, or desires. For a distinctively rational form of causation, anything nonrational is "alien" to its sphere of operations.

Unlike most philosophers who believe that we have a free will undetermined by alien causes, Kant is not claiming that a free willing (or choice) must be totally uncaused. In fact, he insists that a free choice may be nonnaturally caused by a rational motive.[46] The peculiarity of his view is that the universal laws governing genuinely free willing must be understood as self-imposed or self-legislated and that the genuine freedom of a human choice is ultimately owing to this legislation. Kant's conception of self-legislation is not entirely clear, but he seems to be saying that rational beings (or human beings, to the extent that they are rational) conform to certain laws *because they will to do so*. Since these laws are conceived of as strictly universal and valid for all self-legislators, the will to conform to them yields a higher-order test for rationally acceptable maxims: It is permissible to act on a maxim m just when an appropriately generalized version of m could consistently be enacted as a universal law. As we saw at the end of the last section, Kant holds that any maxim whose generalized form could consistently be willed to be a universal law must be consistent with universal law; consequently, he would say that action on such a maxim is bound to conform to universal law. Since free willing presupposes universal laws that, because they are totally unconditional, are valid for all rational beings, the will to conform to them is equivalent, for Kant, to an acceptance of the moral law—that is, of willing to act on a maxim just when one can consistently will that it should be enacted as a universal law.

Kant's understandable emphasis, in a work devoted to the principles of morals, on the moral law as a higher-order principle for ensuring conforming to universal law has the consequence that his notion of a lower-order universal law is not developed as fully as we might wish. It is worth emphasizing, therefore, that universal laws are supposed to be practical laws, which are objectively valid principles of volition. An obvious example of a nonmoral practical law would be this: A rational being who wills to do A if p and believes that p necessarily wills to do A. This example is instructive because it locates a "cause" that, by virtue of a law of freedom, has a particular effect. The cause is the complex of willing to do A if p and believing that p; the effect is willing to do A. The grounds for supposing that this example counts as a nonmoral practical law is that the corresponding hypothetical imperative seems clearly valid: If you will to do A if p and believe that p, then you ought to (will to) do A. An obvious example of a moral practical law is this: A rational being who realizes that he has an undeveloped talent necessarily wills to develop that talent. In the sections to follow I shall discuss other examples of universal laws; the ones just given may help, however, to bring Kant's highly abstract discussion a little closer to the ground.

To put Kant's discussion of freedom in full perspective, I

must say something about the "two standpoints" from which
Kant views human beings. In the *Groundwork* Kant develops
these two standpoints from an observation that is "possible
without any need for subtle reflection." The observation is
this: "All ideas coming to us apart from our own volition (as
do those of the senses) enable us to know objects only as they
affect ourselves: what they may be in themselves remains unknown."[47] This observation allows us to draw a distinction
between things as they appear to us and things as they are in
themselves, or between the *sensible world* and the *intelligible
world*. Kant claims that the first world "can vary a great deal
according to differences in the sensibility of sundry observers,
while the second, which is its ground, always remains the
same."[48] Each person, Kant thinks, knows himself as he appears to himself, not as he really is. Since he is aware of himself as capable of reasoning, he may infer that he belongs to
the intelligible world as an "intelligence," but this is all he
actually *knows* about himself as a member of that world.

Kant thinks that morality requires us to view ourselves
from both standpoints. We cannot help thinking of ourselves
as free—as having a free will—but "when we think of ourselves as free we transfer ourselves into the intelligible world
as members and recognize the autonomy of the will together
with its consequence—morality; whereas when we think of
ourselves as under obligation, we look upon ourselves as belonging to the sensible world and yet to the intelligible world
at the same time."[49] Thus, it is as members of the intelligible
world that we may regard ourselves as rational makers of
universal law, and it is as members of the sensible world that
we are obligated to obey that law. Since we have no "direct
insight" into our nature as intelligible beings, we are not directly aware of ourselves as makers of universal laws. Our
role as moral legislators has to be inferred from the moral law
or, more exactly, from our justifiable conviction that we have
free will.

Kant's argument in the first two chapters of the *Groundwork*
was essentially hypothetical: If there is a moral law to which
we are subject as imperfectly rational beings, then, he argued,

it is a categorical imperative that can be formulated in a number of specific ways. His principal aim in the third chapter is to show that we are justified in believing that the antecedent of this hypothetical is true—that is, that there is a moral law to which we are subject as imperfectly rational beings. His attempt to show this is based directly on his distinction between the sensible and the intelligible world. Although, as he thought he proved in his famous *Critique of Pure Reason*,[50] the sensible world must be viewed as a deterministic system in which even sensible human behavior is determined by antecedent causes ("by desires and inclinations," as he says in the *Groundwork*)[51] there is no reason to believe that things in themselves are thus determined. For all we can actually know, it is thus possible that we are free as things in themselves. Since we are aware of a power of reason within us, which seems to involve a "pure spontaneity," and since we cannot act "except *under the Idea of freedom*," we are justified in supposing that, as things in themselves, we are free—even if we cannot actually prove that we are. But freedom, Kant argues, is "a property of the will of a rational being."[52] Since we are justified in believing that we are free as things in themselves, we are justified in believing that, as things in themselves, we are *rational* wills or intelligences and thus makers of universal law. But if we are justified in believing this, we are justified in believing that the moral law accords with our rational will and is binding on us as partly rational beings in the world of sense.[53]

Kant's account of how his two standpoints are brought together in the concept of morality raises a barrage of difficult problems for his theory of moral action. I shall not attempt to survey these problems here, since doing so would take me too far from his theory of morals, which is my subject in this book. I might say, however, that his conception of the two standpoints seems seriously defective from the very beginning. The key consideration is this. Although we may reasonably draw a distinction between the way the world appears to creatures with sense organs and nervous systems like ours and the way it is "in itself," there is no good reason to suppose that we cannot have scientific knowledge of the latter. Kant's reason for denying that such knowledge is possible seems to be based largely (though not entirely) on an obsolete conception of the limits of inductive reasoning. Thinking of induction as essentially generalization from experience, he did not consider that we can legitimately achieve by what C. S. Peirce was later to call "the method of hypotheses." The peculiarities of this method are still open to dispute, but it seems clear that we can use this method to confirm hypotheses about the world as it exists in itself—the world of photons, mesons, and the like. There is no possibility of perceiving such things, but we can nevertheless have scientific knowledge of them.[54]

If, as I am prepared to do, we reject Kant's conception of the intelligible world as a domain of scientifically unknowable entities, we shall have to develop some alternative treatment of his distinction between the causal order of nature and the rational order of purposive action. Kant developed this distinction along the following lines. When we are concerned to explain rational behavior, we seek reasons for the agent's decision (or volition) to perform it. But the relation between reasons and decisions (the latter being practical conclusions) is not causal, in the sense involving natural laws; rather, it is rational in some sense. Of course, if a person decided to do A because of some reason R, the relation between his reason and his decision, though "rational," cannot be purely formal; it must have some factual character. This factual character cannot be known if rational connections belong only to the intelligible world; as sensible beings we can conceive of it only in attenuated formal terms as some exemplification of the ground-consequent relation—a relation that we can represent by "if . . . , then . . ." and ". . . because. . . ." (If we use the word "causation" here we must acknowledge that it has a special attenuated meaning; it too can refer only to some unknown exemplification of the ground-consequent relation.)[55] On the other hand, we do know that things in nature are subject to natural laws; consequently, if a person does A, there are natural causes for his action. These natural causes cannot be reasons, for reasons are not related to actions by *natural* law. We are left, therefore, with two distinct orders according to which human actions are produced: one involving natural causes, which we can fully understand; the other involves rational causes, which, because they do not belong to the natural order, must concern things in themselves and be conceived of only in attenuated formal terms.

Although we do, I believe, view human beings from both a rational and a natural standpoint, these views are not directed to different worlds; they are both directed to the world we know in experience. There is, to be sure, a rational or, I should prefer to say, logical connection between premises and conclusions or between reasons and decisions, but there is also a natural (or causal) relation between the mental act of entertaining a certain premise or reason and the act of drawing an appropriate conclusion or making a reasonable decision. From a purely logical (or rational) point of view, no one conclusion or decision is ever positively required by a given premise or reason: infinitely many conclusions can be drawn with equal validity. Thus, from the premise p we can infer $q \vee \sim q$, $p \vee q$, $\sim p \supset r$, and countless other things. As I see it, the conclusions we actually draw from certain premises, or the decisions we actually make on the basis of certain reasons, are determined (generally speaking) by our particular mental habits.[56] These habits may be more or less sophisticated, depending on our logical training and native intelligence; but they lead us to draw a given conclusion or make a particular decision by a process that is as natural (or causal) as the process of reading words on a printed page or of salivating at the sound of a bell. Thus, however rational we may be in drawing conclusions and making decisions, we do not possess two minds, one natural and the other rational. We are natural creatures through and through, and we perform logical operations only because we have developed logical habits of an appropriate sort.

These observations have an obvious application to Kant's conception of our will. In Chapter I, I remarked that Kant uses two terms for our will, *Der Wille* and *Die Willkür*. The first refers to what he calls our rational will, the will we possess as members of the intelligible world. The second refers to what might be called our natural will, the will we possess as members of the sensible world. If, as I have claimed, we do not really have two minds or selves—a transcendentally rational one and an empirical, imperfectly rational one—we do not really have two wills either, and Kant's distinction between *Der Wille* and *Die Willkür* must be rejected. Of course, it is possible, as I pointed out in Chapter I, to draw a distinction between legislating and nonlegislating willing, and Kant's two terms might be used to mark this distinction. But this distinction is not the same as Kant's, and its theoretical importance may be negligible.

If we reduce Kant's two worlds to one, in the way I have suggested, we shall have to reject a key element in his resolution of the freedom–determinism issue. Though an alternative resolution of this issue would require a book by itself, it is worth pointing out that Kant's resolution is really far from clear and that a one-world theorist can do as good a job of resolving the issue as Kant did.

As I pointed out, Kant thinks that freedom of the will has both a positive and a negative aspect. Positively, it is, he says, "a causality conforming to immutable laws, though of a special kind."[57] This claim can be acknowledged by a one-world theorist: he can say that decisions are made according to special laws concerning the nature of human reasoning or inference. Negatively, freedom of the will is not compatible, Kant insists, with "determination by alien causes."[58] Since Kant acknowledges that even the decision to conform to universal law may be "determined" by a motive, it is by no means obvious that a one-world theorist must reject the possibility of such negative freedom. If he can reasonably maintain that certain volitions result, according to appropriate psychological laws, from rational motives and not mere "desires and inclinations," he can claim that they are not determined by causes that are alien. Kant believes, of course, that no matter what a free being actually wills on a certain occasion, he could have willed something else instead. But if a certain motive is a rational ground for a particular volition, then if the agent had willed something else, he would have had a different motive.[59] Though Kant would insist that the agent's having a different motive and thus willing something else is a genuine possibility, he has to admit that he cannot explain how this is possible.[60] His claim is that the determinism of the natural order does not show that this is impossible and that, practically speaking, we must assume that it is possible because we must assume that we have free will. But a one-world theorist could make a similar claim—though he would have to argue, as philosophers in our time have argued, that the lawful character of his one world does not imply that the state of the world could not *possibly* be different from the way it actually is.[61]

By way of concluding this section, I want to point out that if we reject Kant's conception of the intelligible world as an actually existing but largely unknowable domain of rational intelligences, we can preserve a large portion of his moral theory by conceiving of rational beings as ideal beings rather than transcendentally real ones. We can say that, although we ourselves are nothing more than imperfectly rational creatures, we can strive to be as rational as possible. If we were fully rational, we should behave as Kant's perfectly rational beings do behave: we should freely make universal law and thus conform to the moral law. Since conforming to the universal law is something that a purely rational being would necessarily do, we, who will never actually succeed in becoming perfectly rational beings, *ought* to conform to that law.

I cannot pretend that, if we conceive of Kant's intelligible world as a mere ideal, we can salvage all his moral theory. One part that we cannot salvage is his account of why the existence of rational nature as an end in itself yields an objective principle of volition. Kant's argument for this point, which I did not comment on when I discussed his derivation of *C3*, is as follows: "*Rational nature exists as an end in itself*. This is the way a man necessarily conceives his own existence; it is therefore so far a *subjective* principle of human actions. But it is also the way in which every other rational being conceives his existence on the same rational ground which is valid also for me; hence it is at the same time an *objective* principle, from which, as a supreme practical ground, it must be possible to derive all laws for the will."[62] Kant's idea is that each person, conceiving of himself as an autonomous member of the intelligible world, conceives of himself as the subject of universal self-legislation; in this sense he conceives of himself as an end in himself and wills in accordance with this conception. But since each rational being conceives of himself as an end in himself on this same ground—that is, as a maker and subject of universal legislation—each rational being must conceive of every other rational being as such an end; for as makers and subjects of universal law, rational beings are indistinguishable. Consequently, the conception of rational *nature* as an end in itself is an objective principle of volition—that is, one valid for every rational being.

If we reject Kant's view that each of us is, in himself, a rational self-legislator, we must reject Kant's argument for the principle that rational nature exists as an end in itself. On the other hand, we can still value rational nature as an *ideal* end in itself and, to the extent that we are rational, we can act on the principle that rational nature is an end in itself. Of course, the question can arise, "Why should we, as imperfectly rational beings, value rational nature in this way?" If we have trouble answering this question, we can take comfort from the fact that Kant himself cannot answer it. As he says: "The subjective impossibility of *explaining* freedom of the will is the same as the impossibility of finding out and making comprehensible what *interest* man can take in moral laws; and yet he does take such an interest."[63] If it is impossible to find out and make comprehensible the interest we have in the moral law, it is equally impossible to find out and make comprehensible why we value a rational nature that is the "rational ground" of the moral law.

Chapter IV: Concluding Remarks on the *Groundwork*

THIS chapter concludes my discussion of the *Groundwork*. I begin by examining Kant's final version of the moral law, his kingdom-of-ends formula, and then, after commenting on a distinction he must draw between permissible and impermissible "subjective ends," I compare his final version of the law with the versions considered earlier. At the end of the chapter I make some critical observations about the general structure of his theory and about the acceptability of the categorical imperative (in its various versions) as a fundamental moral principle.

1. *The Formula of the Kingdom of Ends,* C5

Kant's formula of the kingdom of ends is closely related to his formulas *C3* and *C4*. Reflection on *C3* suggests the following observation: "Rational beings all stand under the *law* that each of them should treat himself and all others, *never merely as a means*, but always *at the same time as an end*. By doing so there arises a systematic union of rational beings under common objective laws—that is, [what Kant calls] a kingdom. Since these laws are directed precisely to the relation of such beings to one another as ends and means, this kingdom can be called a kingdom of ends. . . ."[1] In an earlier passage Kant had offered a more detailed account of what he means by a kingdom of ends: "Since laws determine ends as regards their universal validity, we shall be able—if we abstract from the personal differences between rational beings, and also from all the content of their private ends—to conceive a whole of all ends in systematic conjunction (a whole both of rational beings as ends in themselves and also of the personal ends which each may set before himself); that is, we shall be able to conceive a kingdom of ends which is possible in accordance with the above principles."[2] Kant abstracts from the personal differences between rational beings and also from the content of their private ends because he does not want to restrict a kingdom of ends to any particular rational beings with special personal ends. His idea seems to be that, no matter what rational beings might exist and no matter what their personal ends may be, if they and their ends conform to the requirements of universal law, the resulting "systematic conjunction" will amount to a kingdom of ends.

A little later Kant says that a kingdom of ends "is possible"—meaning, I suppose, "can be conceived of"—only on the analogy of a kingdom of nature. As we might expect, a kingdom of nature is a teleological system in which each natural thing acts in harmony with other natural things. In view of his earlier remarks about what is involved in treating a rational being as an end in himself, it would appear that a possible kingdom of ends is a system of rational beings (ends in themselves) each of whom pursues his private ends in ways (a) that do not conflict with others' pursuit of their private ends and (b) that assist, "so far as possible," this pursuit by others. Given the formula C4, which emphasizes that rational beings are necessarily makers of universal law, we can formulate the moral law in a way that underlines the importance of a kingdom of ends. Kant does this by saying:

Act on the maxims of a member who makes universal law for a merely possible kingdom of ends.[3]

This remark is not as explicit as it could be, for a little later Kant says that "every rational being should act as if he were *through his maxims* always a law-making member of a kingdom of ends."[4] In view of this more explicit remark, and in the interest of providing a sufficient as well as a necessary condition for morally acceptable action, I suggest the following as Kant's principle C5:

It is morally permissible to act on m just when having m as a maxim is consistent with being a rational legislator who, through his maxims, makes universal law for a possible kingdom of ends.

By "making law through a maxim *m*" we can understand Kant as meaning "willing that $G(m)$ shall be a universal law."

After introducing his notion of a kingdom of ends, Kant remarks that "morality consists in the relation of all actions to the making of universal laws whereby alone a kingdom of ends is possible." Later on he says, "Now a kingdom of ends would actually come into existence through maxims which the categorical imperative prescribes as a rule for all rational beings, *if these maxims were universally followed*."[5] These remarks prompt the following question: "Are we to understand Kant as saying that a rational maker of universal law is motivated by the aim of realizing a possible kingdom of ends?" If the answer to this question is no, a further question arises in its place: "How, exactly, are we to conceive of the relation between universal law and a possible kingdom of ends?"

From our discussion in earlier chapters, we know that the answer to the first question must be no: Kant is committed to the idea that rational makers of universal law are not motivated by the aim of achieving any "result" by their legislation. The answer to the second question is developed most fully in some remarks Kant makes in his *Critique of Practical Reason*. In these remarks Kant introduces the notion of "an object of pure practical reason," saying that such an object is "an effect possible through freedom."[6] Since a kingdom of ends clearly seems to be an effect of this kind, and since Kant also says that "the sole objects of practical reason . . . are those of the good and evil," it appears that a kingdom of ends is nothing other than what he elsewhere calls "the highest good," that is, the summum bonum.[7] Now, Kant makes it clear that the answer to our first question has to be no: "though the highest good may be the entire *object* of pure practical reason, *i.e.*, of a pure will, it is still not to be taken as the *determining ground* of the pure will: the moral law alone must be seen as the ground for making the highest good and its realization the object of the pure will."[8] This passage leaves no doubt that, although the highest good is "an effect possible through [our] freedom" and, consequently, an object of our pure will, we do not conform to the moral law for the sake of any "effect" that might result from this conformity, whether that effect be the highest good or something else.

On the page immediately following the one on which he makes the statement just quoted, Kant shows us how our second question is to be answered: "But it is self-evident not merely that, if the moral law is included as the supreme condition in the concept of the highest good, the highest good is then the object, but also that the concept of it and the idea of its existence as possible through our practical reason are likewise the determining ground of the pure will."[9] To understand Kant's point in this passage, it is helpful to draw a distinction between a primary and a secondary "determining ground" of the pure will. The primary determining ground of such a will can be represented by the principle:

1. I will act in accordance with the moral law.

But the following is a necessary truth:

2. If I act in accordance with the moral law, I shall be promoting the highest good.

From 1 and 2 a rational being would conclude:

3. I will promote the highest good.[10]

By virtue of this practical argument, we can say, as Kant does, that the highest good is "the object" of the moral law (the effect possible through the free act of making universal law) and that "the concept of . . . [this effect] and the idea of its existence as possible through our practical reason are likewise [that is, secondarily] the determining ground of the pure will."[11] Thus, a rational being necessarily intends to do what he can to realize the highest good, but he does so *only because* he necessarily intends to conform to the universal laws he has freely made.

2. Critical Reflections on C5

If we are to use *C5* as a basic moral principle, we must understand exactly what it means. We have seen that, in Kant's view, rational beings do not make universal laws *for the pur-*

pose of realizing a kingdom of ends. But since universal conformity to these laws would result in such a kingdom, Kant might reasonably contend that acting on a maxim *m* is morally permissible just when it is compatible with laws having this result—that is, when it is compatible with universal laws. When Kant summarizes the argument of his second chapter, he says that if each rational being chooses his maxims "from the point of view of himself—and also of every other rational being—as a maker of law," a world of rational beings, a "*mundus intelligibilis*," would "be possible as a kingdom of ends—possible, that is, through the making of their own laws by all persons as its members." He then continues: "Accordingly, every rational being must so act as if he were through his maxim always a law-making member in the universal kingdom of ends."[12] To act in this way, he adds, is to act on maxims that are consistent with the principle "So act as if your maxims had to serve at the same time as a universal law (for all rational beings)." The "pure" test for a morally acceptable maxim is thus its conformity to universal law, not its ability to promote a kingdom of ends. The reference to such a kingdom in *C5* therefore provides a mere means of identifying the laws to which one should conform; it does not identify a distinct aim or purpose for moral action.

As I have just interpreted it, *C5* seems to have the same basic import as *C1*. This accords with Kant's intentions. Nevertheless, in a later passage Kant introduces another formula concerning a possible kingdom of ends whose content seems very different from that of *C1*. The formula is:

> All maxims as proceeding from our own making of law ought to harmonize with a possible kingdom of ends as a kingdom of nature.[13]

This formula is clearly intended as another typic for the moral law. As I explained in Chapter II, a typic of this kind amounts to a "rule of judgment" for applying the moral law—that is, for determining what the moral law requires us to do, or attempt to accomplish, in the world of experience. The rule just given tells us to conceive of a possible kingdom of ends as a kingdom of nature and to act only on maxims that "harmonize" with this conception. As we might expect, the maxims that can harmonize with this conception are just those maxims that one could will to become universal laws of nature.

The question is, "How might we conceive of a possible kingdom of ends as a kingdom of nature?" The answer seems relatively straightforward. We are to conceive of a world in which each person is treated as an end rather than as a mere means to an end. In view of Kant's remarks on treating persons as ends rather than as mere means to ends, the idea seems to be that we are to conceive of a world in which each person pursues his private ends without thereby interfering with others' pursuit of their private ends, and in which "everyone endeavors also, so far as in him lies, to further the ends of others."[14] A world of this kind involves a "harmony" of human ends; and Kant holds that it is morally permissible to act on a certain maxim when, and only when, doing so is compatible with this harmony.

Though I did not mention the point when I discussed Kant's remarks on treating people as ends, his remarks are idealized in a way that raises a serious problem for his theory. In saying that everyone should endeavor, "so far as in him lies, to further the ends of others," Kant seems to overlook the important fact that some of the ends people have do not deserve to be furthered. A characteristic end of a sadist is to inflict undeserved pain on other people, but Kant would certainly not require us to help such a creature realize this end—in fact, he would insist that we have a positive duty not to do so. When I discussed Kant's account of treating humanity as an end, I avoided this kind of problem by saying that each person ought not to interfere with the permissible or legitimate ends of others and ought, so far as he can, to further their permissible or legitimate ends. But the question is, "Can Kant actually preserve his theory by making this kind of qualification?"

If a morally permissible or legitimate end is simply one that an agent is morally entitled (or permitted) to pursue, then the answer is no. The reason for this is simple. According to Kant, all forms of the categorical imperative are forms of the moral law, which is the fundamental principle from which obligations and permissions are inferred. But if those forms of the law that explicitly require us to treat people as ends rather than as mere means presuppose a distinction between permissible and impermissible ends, they could not possibly serve as fundamental moral principles. To apply them we should have to know how to distinguish permissible from impermissible ends—and this distinction could not then be derived, in a noncircular way, from those principles themselves. Thus, if the law requiring us to treat humanity as an end rather than as a means enjoins us to further some ends at the expense of others, the distinction between these ends must be based on something other than moral permissibility.

Though Kant does not explicitly deal with the difficulty I am raising here, I think his position is relatively clear. In treating a human being as an end in himself, we should further his *rational* ends, those that accord with his nature as a rational being. As sensible beings, we have no direct access to the intelligible world—the world of purely rational beings—and thus no direct means of determining what ends accord with the nature of a rational being. All we have to go on is the moral law. But this law, in any pure form, cannot be applied directly to the sensible world; we have to form an estimate of what it requires by reflecting on a typic for it. When we do this, we reason about a world that serves as an analogue for the world of intelligible beings. Our analogue for a kingdom of ends is a kingdom of nature, and our analogue for the universal laws of rational beings is the universal laws of nature. Since purely rational beings necessarily act in accordance with the universal laws they make for themselves, they necessarily act in accordance with the moral law and their private ends both accord with their rational nature and harmonize with the private ends of other rational beings. Since a kingdom of ends is a union of rational ends (that is, rational beings and their private ends) under universal laws, our analogue for such a kingdom is a union of natural ends (natural beings and their private ends) under natural laws. Any end of a partly rational, natural being that harmonizes with this latter union thus accords with our model for a possible kingdom of ends and deserves to be furthered rather than interfered with. Such an end may be said, "by analogy," to accord with a person's nature *as* a rational being.

These last reflections underline the overriding importance, in Kant's moral theory, of a typic for the moral law. Though Kant makes it perfectly clear in his *Critique of Practical Reason* that we cannot apply the pure moral law to the world of experience, he does not emphasize the point in his *Groundwork*. Yet if the point is not understood and taken account of, his theory is bound to seem incoherent. Since human beings are patently capable of pursuing morally objectionable ends, a distinction must be drawn between those human ends that should not be interfered with and those that should be interfered with. If the categorical imperative is to be the fundamental moral law, this distinction cannot (on pain of circularity) be clarified by reference to moral permissibility, something that is defined by the moral law. The only way to clarify it is to distinguish sharply between rational beings, all of whose ends (however private they may be) are worthy of being realized, and imperfectly rational humanity, whose unlawful or "unnatural" ends are not worthy of being realized. These unlawful or improper ends can be identified as such by a typic for the moral law, according to which natural law represents universal practical law and a kingdom of nature represents a kingdom of ends. If, by treating an imperfectly rational being in a certain way, we promote a kingdom of nature, we can infer, by analogy, that we are acting in accordance with the requirements of the pure moral law, which directly applies to an inaccessible domain of purely rational, intelligible beings.

3. *Comparison of Kant's Formulas*

The considerations raised in the last section make it advisable to compare Kant's various formulations of the moral law. I shall refer to the typic associated with *C5* as *C6*; this gives us six formulas to compare. The formulas are as follows:

  C1: Act only on that maxim through which you can at the same time will that it shall become a universal law.

  C2: Act as though the maxim of your action were by your will to become a universal law of nature.

  C3: Act in such a way that you always treat humanity, whether in your own person or in that of another, never simply as a means but always at the same time as an end.

  C4: So act that your will can regard itself at the same time as making universal law through its maxims.

  C5: Act on the maxim of a member who makes universal law for a merely possible kingdom of ends.

  C6: All maxims as proceeding from our own making of universal law ought to harmonize with a possible kingdom of ends as a kingdom of nature.

Clearly, *C1*, *C4*, and *C5* are intended to be versions of the pure moral law, for each is focused on universal law, which concerns the domain of intelligible beings. By contrast, *C2*, *C3*, and *C6* are really typics, or analogues, of the moral law, which are applicable to the sensible world of nature.

  Though the six formulas given above contain three versions of the pure law and three typics for it, not every pure law has a corresponding typic and vice versa. *C2* is the typic corresponding to the pure law *C1*, and *C6* is the typic corresponding to the pure law *C5*; but while *C3* (by virtue of containing the term "humanity") is a typic and *C4* is pure, *C3* does not correspond to *C4*. Thus, the six formulas Kant gives do not include all the possibilities implicit in his system. To complete his list we might therefore introduce two further laws, a pure counterpart to *C3* and a typic corresponding to *C4*. These laws might be expressed as follows:

  C7: Act in such a way that you always treat rational nature, whether in your own person or in that of another, never simply as a means but always at the same time as an end.

C8: So act that you can regard yourself as making laws for
a teleological system of nature.

Though *C8* is a very odd-sounding law, its content is very
close to that of *C2*, and Kant seems to introduce *C7* himself
when he refers to the principle "So act in relation to every rational being (both to yourself and to others) that he may at the
same time count in your maxim as an end in himself."[15] In
any case the addition of these two principles results in a tidy
system that illustrates the key ideas involved in Kant's various
formulations of the moral law. The tidy system includes four
pure laws, each with a corresponding typic. The key ideas
associated with each pure law and its corresponding typic are
represented in the following table:

Idea	Pure Law	Typic
Conforming to Law	*C1*	*C2*
Respecting ends in themselves	*C7*	*C3*
Making law	*C4*	*C8*
Bringing about a kingdom of ends	*C5*	*C6*

According to the table, Kant's various formulations of the
moral law involve four key ideas. Yet when Kant summarizes
his discussion of the moral law, he says that only three basic
ideas are involved.[16] This discrepancy is not serious, in my
opinion, because Kant is merely running two of the ideas together. He remarks that he has presented "the principle of
morality" in "three ways" (not five or six), these ways being
"at bottom merely so many forms of precisely the same law,
one of them by itself containing a combination of the other
two." Since his subsequent discussion shows that he is concerned mainly with typics and is also including his principle
of autonomy (or universal legislation) as part of a kingdom-
of-ends formulation, there is no doubt, in my view, that he is
simply ignoring some of the distinctions he has previously
drawn.

The three ideas Kant claims to be fundamental to his several
formulations of the moral law are those of universality, rational nature as an end, and a kingdom of ends as a kingdom
of nature. Two of the three formulas he identifies are clearly

typics for the moral law, and the third, which he may regard
as a typic, looks like *C7*, though he does not comment on its
difference from *C3*, which he introduced earlier as one of his
principal versions of the moral law. His point in introducing
these three formulas is to relate the moral law to certain
"categories" that apply to rational willing. His discussion of
these categories is confusing, but it may be useful to say
something about the main points he is trying to make.

One of the categories applicable to the rational will is that
of *unity*. Rational willing, Kant seems to say, is unified by a
certain "form," which is no doubt the "legislative form" he
speaks of in the *Critique of Practical Reason*.[17] The form of such
willing consists, he says, in the universality of the maxim
employed, and a maxim has this universality just when it
could hold as a universal law. Since we, as sensible beings,
ought to will in a rational way, the moral imperative applicable to us may be expressed as "Maxims must be chosen as if
they had to hold as universal laws of nature." Obviously, this
formula is a variant of *C2*. The next category applicable to
rational willing is that of *multiplicity*, which concerns the
"matter" or purposes of rational willing. Such willing is restricted by a concern for all rational beings as ends in themselves. This aspect of rational willing is reflected in the formula: "A rational being . . . must serve for every maxim as a
condition limiting all merely relative and arbitrary ends."
Since this formula contains "rational being" rather than "humanity," it would appear to be a variant of *C7* rather than *C3*,
though Kant might prefer the latter interpretation. The final
category is that of *totality*. This category applies to the objects
of all rational willing—specifically, to the "completeness" of
a rational system of ends. The formula associated with this
category is: "All maxims as proceeding from our own making of universal law ought to harmonize with a possible kingdom of ends as a kingdom of nature."[18]

Since this last formula clearly runs together the formulas of
autonomy and the kingdom of ends (that is, *C4* and *C6*), the
four ideas distinguished in the table are represented in Kant's
discussion. Conforming to law is thus associated with the cat-

egory of unity, respecting rational nature as an end is associated with the category of multiplicity, and the notions of making law and bringing about a kingdom of ends are associated with the category of totality. Though Kant no doubt has his reasons for relating his several versions of the moral law to his three categories of quantity, I shall not speculate about them here.

It should be noted that Kant ends his summary by saying that the main purpose of his three "concepts," or formulas, is to bring the moral law "closer to intuition" and to make its requirements more readily acceptable.[19] As far as actual moral judgment is concerned, it is better, he says, to rely on the "universal formula" of the categorical imperative—namely, "Act on the maxim that can at the same time be made a universal law."[20] Since this last formula is clearly a pure law, and since the others, as means for bringing the requirements of this pure law closer to intuition, are probably intended as typics for it, the possibility must at least be mentioned that, in spite of what Kant seems to imply in his earlier discussion, he really accepts only one pure version of the moral law instead of the family of pure principles I have attributed to him.

Though Kant might have had this simpler system of principles in mind when he composed his summary, there is no doubt that he is actually committed to the principles I have identified. This can be seen as follows. Having emphasized the importance of a typic for the moral law, Kant explicitly introduced both $C1$ and $C2$. But he also introduced two principles concerned with a kingdom of ends, one specifically mentioning a kingdom of nature.[21] Since a kingdom of nature is clearly a sensible analogue for a pure kingdom of ends, the latter being a system of intelligible beings with their private ends, Kant's two principles amount to a pure law, $C5$, and an associated typic, $C6$. His derivation of $C4$ leaves no doubt that this principle is supposed to be pure, and it can therefore be applied only with the help of some typic. Kant did not himself introduce the formula $C8$, but since making law does not seem to differ from legislative willing, $C8$ seems to have the same basic content as $C2$, which he did introduce.

Another formula that he introduced is $C3$, which is a typic even according to his summary; but when he related his formula of the "end in itself" to $C1$,[22] he had to be thinking of a pure counterpart to $C3$, which I have referred to as $C7$. The need for $C7$ is also shown by his derivation of the end-in-itself formula, which was based on the pure notion of a rational being's fundamental motive for action. Thus, however Kant may have viewed his formulas when writing his summary, there is no doubt that his system actually requires the principles I have identified.

To insist that Kant's system requires the principles listed in the table is not to deny that some of these principles have a special status. In fact, if we consider the reasoning by which Kant introduced his pure principles, we must acknowledge that $C1$ and $C7$ are really more fundamental than the others. This point is worth developing, because it will be useful for purposes of evaluating Kant's system.

According to the table, Kant's system contains four pure principles, $C1$, $C7$, $C4$, and $C5$. As I interpret him, Kant introduced his kingdom-of-ends formula, $C5$, in relation to $C1$ and $C7$. Observing that "a kingdom of ends would actually come into existence through maxims which the categorical imperative prescribes as a rule for all rational beings, *if these maxims were universally followed*," Kant seems to have introduced his formula $C5$ as a derivative means of identifying (or characterizing) the universal laws we ought to follow.[23] He emphasized that these laws could not be justified by their tendency to bring about such a kingdom, for they are, as I put it, intrinsically acceptable to a rational being. But this does not mean that they cannot be identified (or characterized) by reference to such a kingdom.

Kant's principle of autonomy, $C4$, is also introduced on the basis of $C1$ and $C7$. Three considerations seem to have been paramount in Kant's thinking here. One concerns the intrinsic acceptability to a rational being of universal laws. Since such laws are not rationally acceptable by virtue of some "effect" that would be brought about by conforming to them, they can be acceptable to a rational being only because they "spring as . . . law[s] from his own will."[24] Another consideration concerns human freedom. As we saw, Kant thought that genuine freedom has a positive component: as a kind of causality, it necessarily requires laws of some kind. But if these laws are not self-imposed, a rational being would be governed by alien causes, and thus not be free at all. The third consideration was based on the notion of human dignity and on man's nature as an end in himself. Kant traced a man's essential dignity to his free will and argued that "a rational being must . . . be regarded as *making universal law*, because otherwise he could not be conceived as *an end in himself*."[25] Since $C7$ establishes the practical necessity of regarding rational beings as ends in themselves, $C4$ is at least partially dependent on $C7$.

In contrast to $C4$ and $C5$, the formulas $C1$ and $C7$ (the pure law corresponding to $C3$) were introduced independently of any other version of the moral law. Kant's derivation of $C1$ was based on the concept of a categorical imperative. As we saw, Kant thought that only the formal principle of conforming to universal law—of doing what, in general, rational beings necessarily do—could support an absolutely categorical imperative. But for obscure and, in any event, untenable reasons, Kant concluded that this formal principle could be expressed as $C1$, which requires us to act only on maxims that we could will to be universal laws. His derivation of the pure principle corresponding to $C3$, that is, $C7$, was based on his conception of the fundamental motive of rational willing, that of respecting rational nature as an end in itself. Since this motive does not, in his opinion, concern some effect to be realized by rational action, it could serve as a rational ground of universal legislation. Arguing that his first law, $C1$, actually restricts morally permissible actions to those that are compatible with treating every rational being as an end in himself, Kant concluded that, in spite of appearances, $C1$ and $C7$ are "at bottom the same . . . principle."[26]

Apart from disclosing the fundamental role of $C1$ and $C7$ in Kant's system, these last remarks clarify the basic relations between Kant's pure versions of the moral law. To round out my discussion of Kant's various formulas, I now want to say something about the typics that he explicitly introduces—namely, $C2$, $C3$, and $C6$.

To begin with, $C3$ and $C6$ are very closely related. To act in such a way that you treat humanity always as an end and never simply as a means is to act in harmony with a possible kingdom of nature. As we have seen, a kingdom of nature is a teleological system of natural ends or things. In such a system each thing pursues its private ends in harmony with other natural things. The highest things, or ends, in our system of nature are human beings; and when each human being acts according to natural law, he does not interfere with other human beings' pursuit of their proper ends but, in fact, furthers those ends to the extent that he reasonably can. In this way a harmony of natural wills is established. It seems clear that the natural law Kant has in mind here cannot be purely descriptive; it must be ideal in some sense. People who commit suicide, engage in "unnatural" sexual acts such as masturbation, and neglect to develop their talents do *not* conform to the natural law he has in mind: they act unnaturally and thus wrongly.

The laws $C3$ and $C6$ are related to $C2$ in a rather complicated way. When I discussed $C2$, I remarked that if it is to be strong enough to render the sadomasochist's actions morally impermissible, the notion of willing relevant to it should be understood as rational willing, this being willing that is consistent with what a rational being necessary wills. But from our present perspective this qualification seems misplaced. The notion of consistent willing appropriate to the pure law $C1$ is rational willing thus understood, but the notion of willing appropriate to $C2$ must (since $C2$ can be applied by a partially rational being) be understood in a different way. As I see it, $C3$ and $C6$ show us how this willing is to be understood: it is willing that is not self-contradictory and also consistent with (*a*) other things the agent wills in acting on the relevant maxim and (*b*) the teleological laws of nature. If these laws of nature specify certain natural purposes and affirm that these purposes are to be realized by certain kinds of behavior, then any willing consistent with these laws cannot promote contrary behavior. The sadomasochist, Kant would no doubt say, is inconsistent with natural law (or natural purposes) in willing to gain pleasure by harming others and being harmed himself; the purpose or function of pleasure is to further activities of a healthier kind. The development of this idea will have to be postponed to later chapters, where we shall consider Kant's views on ethics. But it seems clear what direction his thinking will take.

A rational being necessarily wills the happiness of other rational beings. Since such beings necessarily conform to the requirements of the moral law—that is, they necessarily act according to the universal laws they make for themselves—their happiness is always deserved. But Kant makes it clear that a rational being does not necessarily will the unqualified happiness of every human being. As he says on the first page of the *Groundwork*, "A rational and impartial spectator can never feel approval in contemplating the uninterrupted prosperity of a being graced by no touch of a pure and good will."[27] Kant seems to think that a rational being wills that an imperfectly rational being is happy in proportion to his moral merit: happiness is a good thing only when it is deserved.[28] This fact explains why a person using C2 cannot rule out the sadomasochist's maxim by appealing to a notion of rational willing that requires one to be consistent with a rational being's will that others are happy. The others in question here would seem, strictly speaking, to be other *rational* beings; a rational being's attitude toward the happiness of particular beings in the sensible world will depend on his view of the moral character and circumstances of those beings—and this is something that cannot be known a priori.

It should be admitted that there is a sense in which rational beings do will the happiness of even imperfectly rational beings: they ought to be virtuous and, in consequence of their virtue, happy. The happiness of imperfectly rational beings is thus a kind of ideal: they ought to be virtuous and they deserve to be happy in proportion to their virtue. But as matters actually stand in the world of sense, many imperfectly rational beings deserve the unhappiness of severe punishment; and although only "the supreme lawgiver" has the moral title to inflict punishment,[29] a perfectly rational being would not positively will the unqualified happiness of a person who deserves to be punished.

4. Critical Remarks on Kant's Moral Theory

From the perspective of the last two sections, the fundamental weakness of Kant's moral theory lies in its appeal to a teleological system of nature in which things have certain natural functions or purposes. As I remarked, the natural laws that represent universal laws for us are not (or cannot be) purely descriptive, for immoral men act contrary to them. Kant says: "By a natural purpose I mean such a connection of cause with an effect that, without attributing intelligence to the cause, we must yet conceive it by analogy with an intelligent cause and so as if it produced the effect purposefully."[30] But this does not prevent him from acknowledging that patently observable behavior may be unnatural and contrary to some natural purpose: "Lust is called *unnatural* if man is aroused to it, not by its real object, but by his imagination of this object, and so in a way contrary to the purpose of the desire, since he himself creates its object."[31] Since everything that happens is natural in a purely descriptive sense of the word "natural,"[32] Kant's sense is clearly normative in some way. This generates problems for his moral theory because disputes about the natural purpose of sex, self-love, and numerous other things could not then be settled by an empirical investigation of nature. People with different moral commitments will want to resovle such disputes in different ways (for example, some will insist while others will deny that contraception is unnatural), but no morally neutral way of resolving them would seem to be available. If this is so, an appeal to Kant's typics for the moral law will be useless in many (if not most) serious moral disputes.

Contemporary philosophers interested in rehabilitating Kant's moral theory would no doubt wish to eliminate all reference to natural purposes and teleological laws of nature, but doing so will unfortunately generate as many problems as it avoids. Two key difficulties stand out here. One concerns the distinction between morally allowable and morally objectionable ends or purposes. If we are to treat human beings as ends in themselves, we shall have to be able to distinguish the private ends that should not be interfered with (and even promoted) from those that do not deserve to be realized. But if this distinction cannot be based on natural purposes or on the requirements of the moral law (the latter would involve a vicious circularity), it is difficult to see how it could be made without the addition of further moral principles. Such an addition would, of course, destroy the unity of Kant's moral theory, for the categorical imperative would not then be the fundamental moral law. Another difficulty concerns the example of the sadomasochist. If his favorite maxim is not to be ruled out as incompatible with some natural purpose or teleological law of nature, some other means of ruling it out must be found. If this can be done only by reference to further moral principles, Kant's theory is undermined; if it is to be done by reference to certain principles of rationality, we have to know what these principles are and be able to defend them. This last alternative would preserve the spirit of Kant's approach to morals, but it is not easy to see how it might be developed.

One implication of the sadomasochist case is that, if we disregard Kant's dubious appeal to a doctrine of natural purposes or a teleological conception of nature, we shall have to say that the categorical imperative is in danger of being an excessively weak moral principle: without supplementation of some kind, it is not strong enough to show that action on a patently objectionable maxim is, in fact, morally impermissible. I now want to consider an objection from the opposite direction—namely, that the categorical imperative is, in a way, too strong, for it implies that certain intuitively acceptable forms of behavior are morally impermissible.

The objection is as follows.[33] Consider the maxim m:

I will buy a clockwork train but never sell one.

Given the way things now stand in the world, we are clearly entitled to act on this maxim. But consider the universalized form of m:

$G(m)$: Everyone will buy a clockwork train but never sell one.

Since a person can buy something only if someone sells it to him, it is obvious that $G(m)$ is inconsistent with m. In view of $C1$ or $C2$, action on m must then be morally forbidden, for no one having m could consistently will that $G(m)$ should be a law. Since, intuitively speaking, action on m is perfectly all right, Kant's categorical imperative has the unacceptable consequence that a morally innocent maxim must be regarded as morally impermissible.

Though this objection seems reasonable, I think Kant has a tenable reply to it: the statement m above is not a proper maxim. As I interpret Kant,[34] a proper maxim is a hypothetical principle, which relates an action to a "subjective condition" and thus provides a possible reason for action. There is, I must admit, one important exception to this view of a maxim. The exception is a maxim that corresponds to a categorical imperative. A rational being who wills to conform to universal law does not do so for any purpose, and the maxim on which he acts can be formulated as "I will conform to universal law as such." Kant tells us that, strictly speaking, there is just one truly categorical imperative, and so, he would add, just one truly categorical subjective principle or volition, or maxim. This is not to say that a categorical volition is impossible—only that a categorical volition is not a "principle of volition," that is, a maxim. With the exception of universal lawgiving, a rational act is always done for some purpose, and a principle of volition formulates a purpose for a possible action. On the other hand, when an agent acts on a maxim, he decides (or wills) to do a certain thing because he believes (thinks, hopes) that he will thereby satisfy some purpose. But although the decision (or volition) "So, I will do

A" may thus be categorical, this decision is not a principle of volition: it does not involve a "general determination" of the will.

If an ordinary maxim must be hypothetical, at least tacitly, the objection stated above cannot reasonably be made out. Let P formulate an appropriate purpose associated with buying but never selling a clockwork train. The law corresponding to the maxim is then:

> For every person s, if s has P, s will buy but never sell a clockwork train.

But this law is not self-contradictory, not inconsistent with the qualified maxim m, and not inconsistent with natural law, at least if the purpose P is, as it should be, a naturally contingent one, which every person need not possess. Thus, the objection fails.

A tenacious critic presented with this line of criticism will naturally seek a related example involving a maxim that raises problems for Kant's theory even though its form is hypothetical. The following maxim has this character:

> m: If I decide to be a parent, I shall marry and impregnate some woman who also decides to be a parent.

Though somewhat contrived, m seems to be a possible maxim on which a man might legitimately act. But consider the generalized form of m:

> $G(m)$: If anyone decides to be a parent, he (or she) shall marry some woman who also decides to be a parent.

$G(m)$ is both self-consistent and consistent with m, but it raises a problem for Kant's principle $C2$. To see the problem, we need only consider "how things would stand" if $G(m)$ were a law of nature. If no one decided to be a parent, then the human race would either die out or be significantly limited, which is contrary to nature's purposes. If, on the other hand, someone did decide to be a parent, then some woman would decide to be a parent. But then, by $G(m)$, some woman

would marry and impregnate another woman, which is physically impossible or contrary to natural law. In either case
natural law is violated. Thus, $G(m)$ cannot be willed to be a
universal law of nature; it has consequences inconsistent with
natural law. Consequently, by Kant's principle $C2$, it is morally impermissible to act on the maxim m.

It seems to me that this example, unlike the one concerning
the clockwork trains, unquestionably succeeds in exposing a
fundamental difficulty with the generalization test implicit in
the categorical imperative. As we shall see when we discuss
the *Metaphysics of Morals*, Kant works hard to show that the
system of duties recognized (in his opinion) by "the common
moral consciousness" can be derived from the categorical imperative, but he makes no effort to show that only such duties
can be derived from it. Since no one, I think, would seriously
contend that it is morally impermissible for a male human
being to act on the maxim we have just considered, it seems
fair to say that the categorical imperative, at least in the
applied form of $C2$, is, in a way, too strong to be a satisfactory moral principle. The mere fact that the generalization of
a maxim could not be a law of nature is insufficient to show
that one makes a moral error, or does something immoral, in
acting on it.

Someone might object that even though Kant's generalization test has the consequence that it is morally impermissible
for a man to act on the maxim m, it does not have the consequence that it is morally impermissible for him to act on a related maxim whose content is very close to that of m, namely:

$m\star$: If I decide to be a parent, I shall marry and impregnate
    some person of the opposite sex who also decides to be
    a parent.

Since a man who realizes his purpose of becoming a parent by
marrying and impregnating a woman thereby marries and
impregnates a person of the opposite sex, the fact that Kant's
generalization test disallows action on the maxim m is morally
trivial and does not undermine that test: the test really allows

as permissible the actions we should want to allow—namely, those done on the related maxim $m^\star$.

This objection is confused and misses the point of my criticism. That point is very simple: By any plausible standard, action on m is morally innocent and thus permissible; Kant's test implies that such action is impermissible; therefore, Kant's test is defective. The fact that it is perfectly all right, according to his test, to act on a maxim closely related to m is logically irrelevant to my objection. To counter my objection one must argue either that, contrary to what one would naturally think, it really is morally impermissible to act on m or that Kant's test does not actually have the consequence that such action is morally impermissible. Yet neither of these points was supported in the objection above, and I, for one, find it hard to believe that anyone not emotionally committed to Kant's philosophy should find either in the least degree tempting.

Though the acceptability of my criticism is not increased by saying this, I might add that the cautious reader of Kant should *expect* to find numerous counterexamples to the generalization test. According to that test, it is immoral to act on a maxim that could not, for *any* reason, become a universal law of nature. This implies that if a maxim, generalized or taken by itself, is defective for purely logical reasons, actions based on it are immoral. But this should strike us right off as far too strong. If a particular maxim were patently contradictory, one would no doubt be very stupid to act on it, but one would not necessarily be immoral in doing so, particularly if one did not thereby violate anyone's moral rights—or so it would seem.

It is helpful to consider an analogy here. In ordinary life people frequently employ a variant generalization argument in support of their belief that some action is immoral. The argument is usually formulated in an elliptical way: "What if everyone did that?" The presumption is that if it would be morally disastrous (or very bad) if everyone did that, it is wrong for a particular person to do it. Without elaboration the argument is poor: It would be morally disastrous if everyone refused to grow food, but it certainly does not follow that it is morally objectionable for Joe Smith to refuse to grow it. With suitable elaboration the argument can be compelling, however. If, for example, there is a kind of action that (a) everyone would like very much to perform and (b) could not be performed by everybody, or nearly everybody, without a morally disastrous consequence, then unless there is some special reason why Joe Smith should be allowed to perform it when others cannot, it is not right for Smith to perform it.

A person who is not aware of the limitations of unqualified generalization arguments might think that the mere impossibility, morally speaking, of everyone doing a certain thing shows that it is wrong for a given person to do it. But the kind of elaboration that puts such arguments in a better light makes it clear, I think, that the moral objection to the person's action lies in a tacit appeal to *fairness*: roughly speaking, it is not right (fair) for one person to do what everyone (or nearly everyone) wants to do but cannot do. One ought to feel a strong suspicion that something similar should be true of Kant's generalization test. The mere fact that a certain maxim could not become a law of nature should not render immoral all actions based upon it. A confused or ignorant admirer of Thomas A. Edison might adopt the maxim "I will construct a perpetual motion machine if the condition C obtains," but if it should happen that the condition C is a tautological one that must obtain, so that, given the impossibility of a perpetual motion machine, his maxim could not possibly become a law, it would be absurd to conclude that the would-be inventor who acts on the maxim does something immoral. As we shall see in Chapter V, Kant thinks that the impossibility of a maxim's becoming a law indicates that allowable human freedom is curtailed in some way. Yet although a limitation of human freedom may in most cases constitute a moral wrong, not every limitation of human freedom would seem to do so.

Before concluding this section I want to say something

about Kant's notion of "the" ordinary moral consciousness. In the first chapter of the *Groundwork* he argued that if we accept the dictates of this consciousness, we shall have to admit, at least on reflection, that the only thing in or out of the world that is good without qualification is a good will, that a good will is precisely one that acts for the sake of duty, and that acting for the sake of duty amounts to acting out of respect for practical law, which is the same as (or equivalent to) acting in obedience to the categorical imperative. Although this derivation of the categorical imperative is (as we have seen) unsuccessful, an alternative strategy was possible for Kant: he could have argued that his categorical imperative qualifies as the moral law because the class of duties derivable from it coincides exactly with the class of duties recognized by the ordinary moral consciousness. Viewed this way, the categorical imperative could count as a moral axiom whose acceptability is determined by its consequences.[35] Unfortunately, the arguments I have developed in this chapter show that, to the extent that the requirements of the ordinary moral consciousness are clearly identifiable, the categorical imperative does not have the right consequences: among other things, it yields "duties" that the ordinary moral consciousness does not recognize.

Though the point is perhaps obvious, it is worth observing that any attempt to establish a comprehensive moral axiom by reference to "the" ordinary moral consciousness is bound to be dubious at the present time. The difficulty is that we are now faced with a variety of conflicting moral consciousnesses, or (as Marxists say) "ideologies," no one of which can claim to be standard or ordinary. This is illustrated to some extent by current attitudes to the examples Kant discusses. Though most people today would no doubt agree with Kant that it is wrong to make false promises and right to help others in distress, the prohibition against suicide is accepted only by some (mostly Roman Catholics) and very few would agree that we have a moral obligation to develop our talents. But far more significant examples of basic moral disagreement are easy to find: just think of current arguments about the allowable forms of sexual behavior; the morality of abortion, contraception, sterilization, or euthanasia; and the acceptability of private property, economic equality, or compensatory discrimination. In view of the undoubted sincerity of most parties in these arguments, it seems preposterous to suppose that there is any one moral consciousness whose dictates are now generally (let alone universally) accepted. To say this is not to deny that there is widespread agreement on some moral requirements. But this kind of agreement seems far too limited to yield a comprehensive moral axiom that everyone, or even most people, could accept.

It might be objected that, contrary to what I have been claiming, Kant himself located a comprehensive moral axiom that most people tacitly accept in spite of their differences on particular moral issues. This principle is $C3$, which requires us to treat rational beings always as ends and never as mere means to ends. Anyone who makes moral distinctions attaches an intrinsic value to human life and thus tacitly accepts Kant's formula of the end in itself whether he realizes it or not. Surely this principle, which Kant takes to be equivalent to his universal law formulas, has the deductive power of a moral axiom and could be used to resolve at least a good share of the moral disputes facing us today.

The trouble with this objection is that it does not pay sufficiently close attention to the actual content of Kant's principle $C3$. As we have seen, Kant says that treating humanity as an end involves two things: not interfering with others' pursuit of their private ends and endeavoring, so far as we can, to further those ends. But Kant was speaking loosely when he said this; he did not mean to imply that every private end should not be interfered with, let alone furthered. He meant that we should not interfere with a person's *rational* ends—these being, for imperfect human beings, ends that accord with nature's purposes. Yet as I pointed out in criticizing Kant's view, there is no morally neutral way of identifying nature's purposes, and there is certainly no agreement, at the present time, that nature has any purposes at all. Consequently, Kant's law $C3$, which is really a typic for the pure law $C7$, is not something people could agree upon today. Many people, particularly those with some smattering of Kant's philosophy, might approve of Kant's formula, but if they do not also agree with his teleological view of nature, they will not be able to apply the formula in the way Kant intended.

In the absence of reasoned agreement about nature's purposes, one might, of course, attempt to apply the pure law corresponding to $C3$ (namely, $C7$) by developing an alternative account of the distinction between ends that deserve to be furthered and ends that deserve to be frustrated. But as the vitality of current disputes about sexual behavior, economic equality, and so forth seem to indicate, people with differing moral views will almost certainly want to develop the distinction in different ways, so that any one account is not likely to be generally accepted. Some people will no doubt insist that some private ends are "rational" while others will not; yet if a theory of rationality is to be used in applying Kant's principle, it will necessarily involve some moral bias that some people will reject. Is it irrational for women to seek abortions? Is a desire for economic equality more rational than a desire for personal wealth and prestige? I can think of no generally acceptable way of answering such questions. It seems to me that the distinction between ends that deserve to be furthered and ends that deserve to be frustrated is clearly a moral one, which must be drawn *before* Kant's pure principle can be applied.

Very recently, it has been argued that Kant's formula $C3$ could serve as an adequate first principle of morals if it were interpreted as requiring "respect" for every human being.[36] But this view does not seem very plausible either: the notion of respecting a person strikes me as far too limited to yield a comprehensive system of moral duties. As we shall see, Kant himself thought that duties of respect do not even exhaust our duties of virtue, let alone our duties of justice. Kant's notion of respect might, of course, be less comprehensive than the one in question. But since any system of morals will inevitably require that some human ends be rejected and others furthered, a single moral axiom based on respect for rational nature will have to involve some kind of distinction between worthy and unworthy ends. Yet how can the bare notion of respecting rational nature yield this kind of distinction? I don't think it can. I may be very shortsighted about this matter, but we shall have a much better idea of the difficulties it involves when we consider the complicated system of moral duties that Kant develops in his *Metaphysics of Morals*. I shall deal with this system in the chapters to follow.

Chapter V: The Basic Principles of Justice

IN the *Metaphysics of Morals* Kant works out the basic principles of two systems of moral duties: duties of justice (or juridical duties) and duties of virtue (or ethical duties). His discussion of juridical duties occurs in part one of the *Metaphysics of Morals*; the German title of this part is "*Metaphysische Anfangsgründe der Rechtslehre*," which may be translated as "The Metaphysical Elements of Law" or, more satisfactorily, as "The Metaphysical Elements of Justice." My concern in this chapter is mainly with Kant's basic claims about our duties of justice. I shall not attempt to comment on the entire scope of the "*Rechtslehre*," for it contains a good deal of political philosophy.

1. Duties of Justice and of Virtue

In his introduction to the *Metaphysics of Morals* Kant tells us that the laws of freedom—the universal laws freely adopted by rational beings—include juridical as well as ethical laws. Though fundamentally descriptive of the behavior of perfectly rational beings, these laws indirectly specify obligations for us as imperfectly rational beings, for we ought to behave as perfectly rational beings necessarily do behave. Since Kant defines a duty as "an action to which we are obligated,"[1] we thus have both juridical and ethical duties. These two kinds of duties make up the system of moral duties that Kant discusses, in a general way, in the *Groundwork*.

At least initially, Kant distinguishes juridical from ethical duties in two principal ways: by the kind of legislation establishing them, and by the kind of restraint they impose upon us.[2] Generally speaking, juridical legislation establishes what is permitted or required in an "external" sense. If one's voluntary behavior accords with juridical law, it is right (or just) no matter what one's aim or purpose might be. Fundamentally, juridical legislation is concerned with "the external and . . . practical relationship of one person to another in which their actions can in fact exert an influence on each other (directly or indirectly)."[3] The effect of such legislation is to bring the free actions of different people into a certain kind of agreement or "harmony": roughly, the free actions of one person should not conflict with the free actions of others. The kind of restraint appropriate here is coercion or legal compulsion. As far as justice is concerned, what we ought to do coincides with what we can be compelled to do by an appropriate legal authority.

By contrast, ethical legislation is called "inner legislation."[4] As Kant argued in the *Groundwork*, an action has moral value only when it is done for the sake of duty; and ethical legislation is associated with this idea. To the extent that it is successful, ethical legislation brings our will (or the maxims on which we act) into the right relation to the moral law, and it does this by prescribing ends that we ought to pursue. The compulsion or restraint associated with ethical legislation is provided by the thought of duty. Ethically speaking, what we ought to do coincides with what we are constrained to do by our awareness of (or respect for) the moral law.

Since universal laws in Kant's sense are "laws of freedom," both ethical and juridical laws are concerned with freedom. Kant calls juridical laws "laws of outer freedom," for they concern the relation of one person's free actions to the free actions of others. In line with this, juridical duties (duties of justice) apply to actions that we can be compelled by others to perform or omit consistently with everyone's moral title to express his or her freedom. Ethical laws, on the other hand, are "laws of inner freedom"; they concern our freedom to pursue rational ends in opposition to various nonrational urges or inclinations. Ethical duties concern the ends that we are constrained to pursue (or reject) by our respect for the moral law. Since one such end is conformity to universal law as such, it turns out that we have an ethical duty to seek the fulfillment of our juridical duties. For this reason, Kant says that our juridical duties may be termed "indirectly ethical."[5]

Kant's distinction between ethical and juridical duties does not correspond to a distinction that we commonly draw today between ethical and nonethical duties. For him, the duty of keeping promises is not an ethical duty, at least directly; it is a juridical duty, or duty of justice.[6] Since we should nowadays regard promise keeping as an ethical requirement, Kant's conception of juridical duties falls, at least partly, within the subject of ethics as we now understand it. In the sections to follow I shall have a lot more to say about Kant's distinction, but a key point to keep in mind is that he views a juridical duty (or duty of justice) as closely associated with a moral right of some kind. Thus, if you act unjustly toward a person, you infringe on some right that he possesses; and if you treat him justly, you treat him in a way that he has a right to be treated. As Kant sees it, ethical duties are not generally associated with some moral right. We have, Kant thinks, an ethical duty to be beneficent—to help others who need our help—but no one has a moral right to our beneficence. When we do our ethical duty, we show our moral merit, and our action is worthy of respect and esteem. When we do our juridical duty, we do what others can rightfully demand that we do, but our action need not be done for a moral motive and it may thus lack the kind of moral value that Kant discusses in the first chapter of the *Groundwork*.

2. The Notion of an Externally Right Action

Having introduced, in a general way, Kant's distinction between juridical and ethical duties, I now want to attend to the fine points of his conception of a just, or juridically right, action. As we might expect, Kant attempts to extract his theory of just action from the categorical imperative by attending to those universal laws that count as juridical. He calls these laws "natural laws," meaning "prescriptive natural laws," and contrasts them with "positive laws," which are the enacted laws of some actual state or society.[7] Laws of this latter kind are just, he says, only to the extent that they conform to prescriptive natural laws. For this reason, prescriptive natural laws, at least when established by "outer legislation," may be viewed as basic laws of justice.

As I have pointed out, juridical laws are supposed to be

laws of outer freedom; they concern the relation of external
actions to one another, and their effect is to promote each person's allowable external freedom. External freedom consists,
essentially, in the absence of compulsion or duress by other
agents, and it is permissible, Kant says, only when it can
"coexist with the freedom of everyone according to universal
law."[8] In view of his basic conception of allowable external
freedom Kant formulates the Universal Law of Justice as follows:

> Act externally in such a way that the free use of your will
> is compatible with the freedom of everyone according to a
> universal law.

Corresponding to this universal law he lays down the principle:

> Every action is just [or right] that in itself or in its maxim is
> such that the freedom of the will of each person can coexist
> with the freedom of everyone in accordance with a univer-
> sal law.[9]

The predicate "just" here has the sense of "juridically right"
or, as we might say, "juridically all right" or "juridically
permissible."

Although some readers may find Kant's principle of justice
clear and unproblematic, I find it ambiguous and very difficult to interpret. The ambiguity concerns the scope of the
modifier "according to a universal law." On the face of it, we
could construe the sentence "*A*'s freedom is consistent with
the freedom of everyone according to a universal law" in at
least two ways:

1. *A*'s freedom is consistent, according to a universal law,
   with the freedom of everyone.
2. *A*'s freedom is consistent with the freedom, according
   to a universal law, of everyone.

Apart from this ambiguity, which is by no means insignifi-
cant, there is a problem about the significance of "a universal
law" (*einem allgemeinen Gesetz*). In his introduction to part

two of the *Metaphysics of Morals* Kant says that the doctrine of law (or justice) "deals only with the *formal* condition of outer freedom (the consistency of outer freedom with itself if its maxim were made universal law)."[10] This remark suggests that, to be juridically permissible, *A*'s freedom need only be consistent with everyone's freedom according to a *possible* universal law, not some actual universal law.

To develop a satisfactory interpretation of Kant's principle of justice, we might begin by considering why Kant should think it necessary to mention universal law when characterizing a juridically permissible (or just) action. Could he not have said, more simply, that an action is juridically right if, and only if, it does not interfere, directly or indirectly, with anyone's freedom? One reason why Kant would insist on a negative answer is this. It is always a matter of principle, and not of mere contingent fact, that a certain sort of action is right or just. In doing *a*, I might inadvertently, accidentally, or mistakenly interfere with another's freedom, but my act would not be wrong merely on that account. If I act unjustly, my action must be incompatible with someone's right (or freedom) in a necessary or essential way. When he discusses juridical duty, Kant says that the motive or purpose of an action is not crucial for its juridical status, but he did not mean to imply that the "form" (as opposed to the "material" or specific content) of the agent's maxim is juridically unimportant. On the contrary, an externally free action is always voluntary, or based on a maxim, and its moral status, whether specifically ethical or juridical, is based entirely on the "formal" character of its maxim. Thus, if an action is right or just, it is so because its maxim is related in some necessary (or lawful) way to the freedom of others.

Another reason for introducing the notion of universal law into his account of a just (or right) action is this. If each person pursued his private ends without any heed to the will of others, the result would be a world of "lawless freedom" (as Kant calls it) in which the freedom of one person would often destroy the freedom of others. Since destroying another's freedom amounts, in most instances, to an act of injustice, a just world must be one in which "lawful freedom" is the rule. In a world of this kind, individual choice would be restricted by laws that promote a "harmony" of wills (or willed actions). To be just or right, an action must be consistent with such laws, which may be called "laws of external freedom."

Though these last remarks do not fully clarify Kant's conception of just action, they do allow some reformulation of the somewhat garbled statement of Kant's principle of justice that I cited in the second paragraph of this section. That statement was garbled because the clause following the "such that" does not succeed in qualifying its subject. As I have pointed out, Kant is clearly assuming that only willed actions (that is, those based on a maxim) can be considered just or unjust; and the idea behind the principle would seem to involve the claim that

> An action on a maxim m is just (right) if and only if the agent's freedom in acting on m is compatible with everyone's lawful freedom.

To be compatible (in the relevant way) with everyone's lawful freedom an action on m must conform to universal laws that would, if universally obeyed, create a world of lawfully free agents.

The principle just formulated obviously requires us to think of a lawfully free action as something different from one that merely does not interfere with some agent's pursuit of an end. If a state of lawless freedom is to be avoided, the wills of some people must be restricted—that is, they must be prevented from pursuing certain antisocial ends. As Kant says: "If a certain use of freedom is itself a hindrance to freedom according to universal laws (that is, is unjust), then the use of coercion to counteract it, inasmuch as it is the prevention of a hindrance to freedom, is consistent with freedom according to universal laws. . . ."[11] This remark leaves no doubt that a state of lawful freedom is not only consistent with but, in practice, actually requires the repression of some free acts. But how, exactly, are these objectionable free acts to be identified? They may interfere with the freedom of others, but their repression would always seem to interfere with the freedom of someone.

Kant's evident solution to this problem was worked out in the last chapter: the free acts we may interfere with and need not respect are those that do not accord with universal law or with our analogue for universal law, the teleological laws of nature. To verify this interpretation, we should consider the relation of Kant's principle of justice to the categorical imperative.

As a first step, we might recall $C3$, the formula of the end in itself. According to our discussion in Chapter III, Kant's conception of treating people as ends in themselves involved a negative as well as a positive requirement. The negative requirement is that we should not interfere with a person's pursuit of his rational ends; the positive requirement is that we should endeavor to further those ends in certain ways. Kant's discussion in both parts of the *Metaphysics of Morals* makes it clear that these contrasting requirements correspond to the distinction between juridical and ethical duties. Fundamentally, our juridical duties boil down to the requirement of not acting in ways that necessarily interfere with someone's pursuit of a rational end. The obligation, roughly put, of doing what we can to further the rational ends of others is the foundation of our ethical duties, or our duties of virtue.

When I discussed Kant's formula $C3$, I pointed out that a person's rational ends are those that accord with universal law, and that universal law describes the behavior of perfectly rational beings, who belong only to the intelligible world. Since we, as imperfectly rational beings, have no direct cognitive access to the intelligible world, we have no direct way of knowing what a person's rational ends are; we have to reason by analogy. Our analogue for universal law is teleological natural law, and our analogue for a rational end is a natural purpose. The concept of a natural purpose thus provides the key to Kant's view of lawful freedom. If a particular action accords with nature's purposes and is also consistent, in an appropriate way, with the freedom (according to natural law) of every human being, then we are entitled to call it "just" or "juridically all right": it satisfies our typic for the pure law of justice. The pure law differs from our typic in referring to universal law and rational beings where our typic refers to natural law and human beings.

Kant's remarks on the "law of nature" formula of the categorical imperative—that is, C2—cast further light on his principle of justice. In discussing C2 Kant observed that the categorical imperative can be applied in two ways to derive two distinct kinds of moral duties, perfect and imperfect ones. In his introduction to "The Doctrine of Virtue" he claims that all imperfect duties are duties of virtue, that is, ethical duties.[12] He acknowledges later on that certain perfect duties are also ethical, but with just a few exceptions these are duties of a person to himself and do not involve other persons in any essential way. Thus, he holds that perfect duties that concern interpersonal actions are, on the whole, juridical. Since he provides a specific test for identifying perfect duties, we can reconstruct the reasoning by which he would identify those that are juridical.

The formula C2 patently applied to voluntary actions. The test was that an action on a maxim m is morally permissible just when the agent could consistently think of himself as having m as his maxim and as willing that a generalized form of m should become a universal law of nature. Now, Kant thought that this test yields two subtests. As he put it: "Some actions are of such a nature that their maxim cannot even be *thought* as a universal law of nature without contradiction. . . . In others this internal impossibility is not found, though it is still not possible to *will* that their maxim should be raised to the universality of a law of nature, because such a will would contradict itself."[13] Kant proceeds to remark that the first kind of action conflicts with the "stricter or narrower" kind of duty, which is perfect duty; the latter conflicts with the "broader" kind of duty, which is imperfect. In view of this we might say that if a maxim concerning an external action directly involving more than one person "cannot be thought as a universal law of nature without contradiction," then action on that maxim is contrary to juridical duty—that is, it is juridically wrong to perform it.

How does this suggestion relate to the view of juridical right that I developed from Kant's remarks on *C3*? Kant's answer, I believe, would be this. If an appropriately generalized version of a maxim concerning more than one person is contradictory or inconsistent with natural law, then it is impossible for everyone to act in accordance with it. This means that, if a certain person expresses his freedom by acting on such a maxim, at least one other person *cannot* act on it: his freedom to do so is ruled out. This key point can be expressed more abstractly by saying that any maxim involving more than one person whose generalized version is contradictory or inconsistent with natural law is necessarily such that a person's freedom in acting on it is *not* compatible with the freedom, according to natural law, of everyone else. Since natural law is our analogue for universal law, we can thus conclude that a maxim involving more than one person whose generalized version could not become a universal law is necessarily such that one person's freedom in acting on it is not compatible with the rational freedom (or freedom according to universal law) of everyone.

Though the answer just given accords nicely with Kant's general theory, it is not entirely satisfactory. The difficulty is that, even if we apply Kant's test only to maxims concerning more than one person, we shall not find that whenever his test fails for such a maxim, one person's action on it will interfere with the freedom of someone else. Consider the maxim I introduced in the last chapter:

m: If I decide to be a parent, I shall marry and impregnate some woman who also decides to be a parent.

Since, by virtue of natural law, one woman cannot impregnate another woman, the generalization of this maxim could not be a universal law. But if a man acts on it, he will not thereby limit anyone's freedom according to natural law. It may be true that *some* nongeneralizable maxims are such that, if anyone acts on them, someone else's freedom is thereby limited. But this does not hold as a general matter. Consequently, the test for juridical duty implicit in *C2* breaks down: it does not give the right results for every maxim to which it is appropriately applied.

Having considered Kant's strategy for deriving juridical duties from the categorical imperative, we should discuss his approach to juridically permissible (that is, right or just) actions. Does he hold that if the generalization of a maxim *could* be regarded as a law of nature, it is *not* juridically wrong to act on that maxim? There can be little doubt about this matter: Kant must hold this view because he insists that the principles of justice can be derived from the categorical imperative. If *C2*, at least when applied to interpersonal maxims, did not allow us to prove that certain actions are right or just (that is, juridically permissible) it would not fulfill its central purpose in Kant's moral theory.

On the assumption, then, that Kant holds the view in question, we might ask how the possibility of a maxim's becoming a law of nature relates to the subject of human freedom. Is it reasonable to suppose that, if the generalization of Jones's maxim *m* can be "thought" as a law of nature, then Jones's freedom in acting on *m* is compatible with everyone's rational freedom? A couple of preliminary points can be made right away. If Jones's maxim can be universalized in this way, Jones's action on it is compatible with nature's purposes, the teleological laws of nature, and, therefore, with the universal laws that natural laws represent for us. Thus, his free action is not objectionably unnatural and, consequently, not nonrational like an act of pederasty, which Kant condemns and says should be punished by castration "after the manner of either a white or a black eunuch in the sultan's seraglio."[14] Since the maxim of his action is consistent with natural law, the performance of his action does not entail that anyone else acts in an objectionably unnatural (and therefore nonrational) way. So far so good. But we also have to know that no one's rational freedom is limited by Jones's action, and this does not seem to follow from the assumption that the generalization of his maxim could be "thought of" as a law of nature. Though one may be unable to "will" that anyone who feels offended by another person should punch the other on the nose, there is no evident reason why this principle could not be "thought" as such a law. Yet it does not seem juridically right (or permissible) for a person to act on the maxim of punching another in the nose if he feels offended by him. Consequently, the generalization test implicit in *C2* does not adequately support Kant's principle of justice or juridical permissibility.

Though Kant's strategy in deriving his Universal Law of Justice from the second version of his categorical imperative does not appear to succeed, the preceding discussion makes the content of the law fairly clear. The idea is that action on a maxim concerning more than one person is juridically permissible (right or just) when and only when (*a*) it accords with nature's purposes or with natural law (and therefore, by analogy, with universal law) and (*b*) it is consistent, according to natural and therefore universal law, with the rational freedom of everyone else. Kant formulates this complicated condition by saying merely that the agent's free action must be "compatible with the freedom of everyone in accordance with universal law," but a careful analysis of his view requires that the modifier "in accordance with universal law" must be applicable not only to the freedom of the relevant actions but to their compatibility with one another.

3. *Justice and Moral Rights*

According to Kant, "anything that is unjust is a hindrance to freedom according to universal laws." But anything that "contradicts the hindrance of an effect promotes that effect and is consistent with it." Certain uses of coercion hinder unjust actions. Therefore, certain uses of coercion promote freedom and are, in consequence, just. Kant says: "It follows by the law of contradiction that justice [a right] is united with the authorization to use coercion against anyone who violates justice [or a right]."[15] I shall have a lot to say about this argument later on in the chapter; the point I want to attend to now is that Kant's conclusion extends the notion of justice to cover moral rights as well as right (or just) actions.

According to Kant, an action is morally right (or just) if it is compatible with everyone's lawful freedom. But this condition does not seem sufficient to show that anyone has *a right* to do (let alone to have) something. Kant tells us that a moral right is a "moral capacity to bind others" and that "right" ("*Recht*") and "authorization to use coercion" mean the same thing.[16] His meaning here can be clarified by an example. To say that "a creditor has a right to demand from his debtor the payment of a debt . . . means only that the use of coercion to make . . . the debtor do this is entirely compatible with everyone's freedom, including that of the debtor, in accordance with universal laws."[17] In view of this last remark we might say that "S has a right to do or possess X" means something like "S's doing or possessing X can justly be realized or protected by the use of coercion." To say that something can *justly* be realized by an act of coercion is to say, of course, that such an act would be compatible with everyone's freedom according to universal law.

The meaning I have suggested for "S has a moral right to do or possess X" is extremely vague. Unfortunately, Kant is not very precise in speaking about rights. In spite of this imprecision his basic approach to moral rights—his leading idea—is easy enough to identify. To develop his idea we should observe that Kant acknowledges moral rights of at least three kinds: rights to do things, rights to possess things (where possessing includes having things done by others), and rights to be in some state or condition. I would not claim that rights of these three kinds are irreducible or exhaustive, but Kant's basic idea about rights must apply to all of them. Presumably, he would approach them somewhat as follows. A person has a moral right to do something A just when coercion could rightfully (or justly) be used to prevent others from interfering with his attempt to do A. He has the moral right to possess something, on the other hand, just when coercion could rightfully be used either to prevent others from taking it from him or to put him in possession of it (at least if he wills to possess it). Finally, a person has the right to be in a certain state just when coercion could rightfully be used to prevent others from interfering with his being in that state or, possibly, to cause others (if they are appropriately obligated) to bring it about that he is in that state. In all three cases the appropriate use of coercion must be compatible with everyone's freedom according to universal law. The explanations I have given here are not, of course, watertight, but they do illustrate Kant's general approach to moral rights.

We can form a better idea of Kant's approach to rights if we consider his claim that moral rights are based on juridical duties. Kant says: "Inasmuch as duties and rights are related to each other, why is moral . . . philosophy usually . . . labeled the theory of duties and not also rights? The reason for this is that we know our own freedom (from which all moral laws and hence all rights as well as duties are derived) only through the moral imperative, which is a proposition commanding duties; the capacity to obligate others to a duty, that is, the concept of a right, can subsequently be derived from this imperative."[18] To relate this passage to what I have said about moral rights, we must connect Kant's notion of a juridical duty or obligation with his notion of just coercion.

In an important passage where Kant introduces the concept of strict justice he tells us that "justice [or a right] cannot be conceived of as composed of two separate parts, namely, the obligation implied by a law and the authorization that someone has . . . to use coercion to make the other fulfill [his obligation]. Instead, the concept of justice [or a right] can be held to consist immediately of the possibility of the conjunction of universal reciprocal coercion with the freedom of everyone. . . . [Strict] justice, inasmuch as it contains no ethical elements, requires no determining grounds of the will besides those that are purely external."[19] Kant's view here is the following. Although, as we know from the *Groundwork*, what we ought to do is just what rational beings necessarily do, a juridical obligation can be identified (so far as the sensible world is concerned) with the possibility of rightful or just coercion. What is important for justice is that people act in ways that are compatible with everyone's lawful freedom—not that they act for this or that motive. Consequently, justice need not be viewed as involving two "separate parts," juridical obligation *and* the authorization to use coercion. Instead, we can in effect identify juridical obligation with an appropriate authorization to use coercion.

Kant's view, in the passage above, of the relation between justice and the authorization to use coercion can be further explained as follows. Everyone has a right to exercise his lawful freedom and would act unjustly if he interfered with the lawful freedom of anyone else. Given that coercion is just when it is compatible with everyone's freedom according to universal law, we may infer that coercion can rightfully be used against anyone attempting to interfere with another's lawful freedom. Since every person is a possible violator of another's lawful freedom, it is thus juridically possible for every person to be subject to appropriate coercive restraint. By the same token, each person has the right to have his lawful freedom protected by the lawful coercion of a potential violator of his freedom. Since each person is both a possible violator of another's freedom and a possible subject of violation by another, a perfectly just world would involve, as Kant says, "the *possibility* of a general reciprocal use of coercion" that, to be just, is "consistent with the freedom of everyone in accordance with universal law."

With this understanding of Kant's view of justice, we can return to his concept of a moral right. Originally, I explained Kant's conception of moral rights in relation to the possibility of lawful coercion, but in view of his account of the relation between coercion and obligation, his conception of moral rights could equally be explained in relation to juridical obligation. Thus, since according to the Universal Law of Justice it is juridically wrong, or unjust, for anyone to interfere with the lawful freedom (or freedom according to universal law) of anyone else, each person may be said to have the moral right to exercise his lawful freedom. Again, if Jones, by virtue of making a promise to Smith, incurs an obligation to perform a certain service to Harris, then Smith has a moral right to Jones's service, which implies that Jones may justly be coerced to perform that service if Smith (not Harris) so wills. As these two examples show, different moral rights are apt to involve the notion of juridical obligation or lawful coercion in slightly different ways. For this reason, it is difficult to provide a schematic definition applicable to moral rights of every kind.

The key reason, I suppose, why Kant defines rights in relation to coercion rather than obligation is that not all moral obligations involve or generate moral rights. As Kant views morals, it is principally juridical obligations that imply moral rights; with one important exception, ethical obligations (or duties of virtue) imply no rights at all. Since a crucial difference, for Kant, between duties of justice and duties of virtue is that the former "constrain the will" by the coercion they authorize, Kant avoids confusion by defining strict moral rights in relation to lawful coercion. He did not have to proceed this way, but his point in doing so seems reasonable enough.

In the last paragraph and in an earlier quotation I referred to *strict* moral rights and to strict justice. Insofar as "justice" is concerned with rights, it has, for Kant, both a narrow and a wide sense, designating *jus strictum* or *jus latum*. Thus far I have been concerned entirely with strict justice, which is, as Kant says, "united with the authority to use coercion." But Kant admits that we can also think of justice or rights in a wider sense, "where the authority to use coercion cannot be stipulated by any law." In his view "there are two true or supposed rights of this kind—equity and the right of necessity." The first, he says, "admits a right without any coercion; the second, coercion without any right."[20]

According to Kant, "the motto (*dictum*) of equity is: 'The strictest justice is the greatest injustice.' " He makes no attempt to define equity, but he gives two examples to illustrate it. One of them is this: "A domestic servant [is paid] . . . through the end of the year in a currency that has in the intervening period become depreciated. . . . [The result is] that he can no longer buy what he could have bought with the same money at the time of concluding the contract. . . ." Such a person cannot, Kant thinks, "appeal to a right to be compensated for the loss. . . . He can only appeal to equity . . . , because nothing was stipulated about this in the contract, and a judge cannot pronounce in accordance with unstipulated conditions." Kant says that there can be no remedy for such cases in actual legal proceedings. The claim to justice involved here "belongs solely to the court of conscience."[21]

As an example of "the imagined right of necessity," Kant describes the case of a man "who has been shipwrecked and finds himself struggling with another man—both in equal danger of losing their lives—and who, in order to save his own life, pushes the other man off the plank on which he had saved himself." Kant says that a penal law against such behavior would be pointless and, thus, unjustifiable: "It could never have the effect intended, for the threat of an evil that is still uncertain (being condemned to death by a judge) cannot outweigh the fear of an evil that is certain (being drowned)."[22] But even though a law against such cases would, Kant thinks, be pointless, those cases are still unjust in a broad sense.

Kant calls the right to equity and the supposed right of necessity "equivocal rights" because, in thinking about them, one is apt to confuse "the objective with the subjective grounds of the exercise of justice (before reasons and before a court)."[23] In cases of equity one will have good grounds for considering something just that would not be regarded as just by a court, and in cases of necessity a good person will recognize as unjust something that "will be treated with indulgence by a court." Kant's discussion of these equivocal rights is very short, and is, in fact, inserted in an appendix to his "Introduction to the Elements of Justice." It is a pity that he did not discuss these rights (or supposed rights) at greater length, for both involve a notion of "justice as fairness" that is not adequately taken account of by his Universal Principle of Justice.

It seems obvious that a good many cases of what we should regard as just behavior cannot be adequately handled by his general principle. Consider the following case, for example.

Jones and Smith are neighbors, but their ways of life conflict. Jones is fond of loud music and enjoys playing it on his stereo system, which has such a powerful amplifier that it makes his walls shake. What others might call "peace and quiet" is, to him, painfully dull; it makes him want to scream. Smith, on the other hand, is a passionate chess player who cannot bear loud noise. Clearly, Jones's freedom to play loud music is limited by Smith's freedom to play effective chess, and vice versa. In view of Kant's principle, it would seem that neither person's freedom could be justly exercised in the circumstances. Yet if one of the people, Jones say, restricted his favorite activity to just one hour per day in view of the other's interest, then it would seem that he acts fairly and, therefore, justly even though he does limit the other's freedom for one hour per day.

On the face of it, Kant would probably agree that, subject to certain qualifications, "Agreements ought to be kept" expresses a universal law. If so, he might say that if Jones and Smith had worked out some agreement about how often they would each engage in their favorite activities, their behavior at various times could be shown to be right or wrong, just or unjust, by reference to their agreement. I think there can be no doubt that, if a proper agreement of this kind were made, we should want to appeal to it in settling disputes about whether Jones or Smith are treating the other fairly. Nevertheless, in the absence of such an agreement I think we should still feel justified in making at least rough and ready estimates of their fairness to one another, and it is hard to see how these estimates could be supported by Kant's Universal Principle of Justice.

It is worth observing here that Kant might well admit that Jones and Smith have *ethical* obligations to limit their favorite activities in consideration of the other's needs. As we shall see, Kant thinks we have an ethical obligation to promote the happiness of others—at least to the extent that their happiness is deserved. Since their favorite activities are crucial for their happiness, Jones and Smith would no doubt be neglecting their ethical duty to one another if they did not restrict their activities in consideration of the other's interests. This ethical duty is, of course, a moral duty, but it is not a duty of justice. It seems to me that a broad notion of justice nevertheless applies to this case (a general notion of fairness) but this notion does not appear to be one that Kant develops in his ethical writings.

4. *Rights and Moral Value*

As we have seen, Kant describes moral rights as "moral capacities (*moralische Vermögen*) to bind others." His main division of moral rights is into innate and acquired rights. Since innate rights belong to everyone "by nature, independently of any juridical act," they could equally be called "natural rights," though Kant does not describe them this way. Acquired rights always depend on some "juridical act."

According to Kant, there is only one innate right: the right to lawful freedom—that is, to independence from the constraint of another's will insofar as this independence is compatible with the freedom of everyone in accordance with universal law. This innate right to freedom "contains within itself," Kant says, a number of subsidiary rights. These are:

> Innate equality, that is, independence from being bound by others to do more than one can reciprocally bind them to do; hence also the attribute of a human being's being his own master (*sui juris*) and of being an irreproachable man (*justi*), inasmuch as, prior to any juridical act, he has done no injustice to anyone; finally, also the authorization [or liberty] to do anything to others that does not by itself detract from what is theirs and that would not detract if only they themselves were not willing to submit themselves to it; an example of this would be merely sharing one's thoughts with others or telling or promising them something, no matter whether what is said is true and honest or false and dishonest . . . , for it is entirely up to them whether they want to believe him.[24]

In another context Kant includes under "innate equality" the right of equality before the law and the right to "rise," in a community, "to any status or class (appropriate to a subject) to which talent, industry, and luck may take him."[25] Concerning the right to be one's own master, he elsewhere seems to include within it the right to own "some sort of property —among which may be counted any skill, craft, fine art, or science that supports him"; for "whenever he needs to acquire things from others in order to live," he may do so by "*disposing* of what is *his own*."[26] Finally, as a general comment on freedom "as a principle for the constitution of a community," he says, "No man may compel me to be happy after his fashion, according to his conception of the well being of someone else."[27] For him, a paternalistic government is "the worst conceivable *despotism.*"[28]

Most of the rights Kant insists upon here are perfectly reasonable in view of his general position, but one of them raises special problems of interpretation. This is the right that includes "sharing one's thoughts with others or telling or promising them something, no matter whether what is said is true and honest or false and dishonest." This alleged right is problematic, because in his famous article "On A Supposed Right to Tell Lies from Benevolent Motives" Kant insists that, if a person must speak at all, "veracity is [for him] an unconditional duty."[29] He also says that "the duty of veracity . . . is the supreme condition of justice in utterances"[30] and that "truthfulness is a duty that must be regarded as the basis of all duties founded on contract, the laws of which would be rendered uncertain and useless if even the least exception to them were admitted."[31] I am not at all sure how to square these remarks with the quotation above. Perhaps he would say that the duty of veracity is applicable mainly to contexts in which our listeners have a right to take our words seriously—not to contexts in which we are joking or merely trying out ideas on someone. Such an interpretation may be suggested by his remark: "To be *truthful* (honest) in all declarations is therefore a sacred unconditional command of reason, and not to be limited by any expediency."[32] Perhaps we are entitled to a little dishonesty if we are not in the serious position of making a declaration.

Kant calls innate rights "inner property" (*das innere Mein und Dein*) and acquired rights "external property" (*das äussere Mein und Dein*).[33] External property, or rights, can be acquired in many ways, principally by various kinds of contracts. Although Kant did not explicitly include the right to make contracts in his list of the special cases of the right to freedom, he makes it clear elsewhere (for example, in his discussion of the right to be one's own master, to which I have called attention) that the right to freedom includes this right. It is possible that, because contracts come close to being multilateral promises, Kant did not think it necessary to provide a justification for the right to make contracts.

It is worth observing at this point that if making a certain contract is compatible with everyone's freedom according to universal law, then anyone who accepts Kant's Universal Law of Justice would have to acknowledge that a person is morally entitled to make such a contract and thus has a moral right to do so. In view of the close connection between contracts and promises, it is reasonable to suppose that anyone accepting the categorical imperative as a valid moral principle would acknowledge that at least some contracts generate moral duties. Thus, if Jones and Smith agree (promise) to perform certain morally permissible actions for one another if certain conditions are met, then if those conditions are met, Smith and Jones are thereby obligated (at least *prima facie*) to perform the relevant services. The obligations generated here can be derived from the categorical imperative in just the way that the obligation to keep any other promise can be derived from that imperative. Kant's account of how this derivation can be accomplished was developed in the *Groundwork*, and there is no need to discuss it here.

If all moral rights are ultimately based on the innate right to freedom, then human freedom would seem to possess a supreme moral value—at least to the extent that it accords with universal law. This consequence is not surprising, for as we saw in Chapter III when we discussed the account of moral value that Kant developed in the *Groundwork*, Kant traces the "dignity" (or intrinsic value) of human nature back to its capacity for moral autonomy, which is nothing other than rational freedom. To the extent that the theory of justice is a branch of moral philosophy, it is thus natural for Kant to view it as fundamentally concerned to further our human dignity, or rational freedom. Since the value of this freedom is unqualified and intrinsic, the justification for valid rules of justice cannot be based on their tendency to promote universal human happiness. Consequently, although Kant's commitment to the importance of human freedom is in many ways similar to the commitment expressed by J. S. Mill in *On Liberty*, it differs sharply from the latter in not tracing this importance to social utility.

Kant's view of innate rights is apt to be criticized nowadays for being excessively narrow. According to the Universal Declaration of Human Rights adopted by the General Assembly of the United Nations, each person has important rights that cannot, at least in any obvious way, be justified by a more fundamental right to freedom. In particular:

> *Article 25*: (1) Everyone has the right to a standard of living adequate for the health and well being of himself and his family, including food, clothing, housing and medical care and necessary social services. . . .
>
> *Article 26*: Everyone has the right to education. Education shall be free, at least in the elementary and fundamental stages.[34]

Given his general theory, Kant cannot recognize these alleged rights as natural or innate. He could, as we shall see, allow that, in a particular society, each citizen might have an acquired right to the benefits described in the articles above, but this right could not be natural or innate. Who, for instance, would have the corresponding obligation? In a state of nature each person would have an *ethical* obligation to be beneficent —to help others in need—but this obligation does not correspond to a right to be helped. As Kant sees it, one peculiarity of a purely ethical obligation is that it does not, generally speaking, imply some corresponding right.

I shall comment on Kant's approach to social welfare in the

next section; I want to end this one by some further remarks
on his view of our innate right to freedom. As I have described this right, the only limitation it places on our freedom
is that it cannot conflict with anyone's freedom "according to
universal law." It should be clearly understood that this limitation differs from the one emphasized by such writers as J. S.
Mill. According to Mill, the only purpose for which a person's freedom can be rightfully limited is "to prevent harm to
others."[35] Kant would allow this limitation only when the
"harm to others" consists in limiting their liberty in a way incompatible with universal law. It is possible that Kant would
disallow every exercise of freedom that Mill would disallow,
but he would always offer a different rationale for doing so. If
a Dostoevskian husband exercises his freedom by senselessly
beating his wife, he will be acting wrongly, Kant would say,
because in so beating her he is limiting her allowable freedom.
This allowable freedom does not consist in being *free from* a
beating; it consists, I should think, in having her available
choices arbitrarily restricted during the time (at least) of her
beatings. If she willed to be beaten at the time because she
demanded punishment for some offense, her freedom *might*
not be wrongfully limited at the time. What matters is not the
pain she suffers, but how the pain interferes with her free
exercise of choice. I myself think that Kant's view here makes
it awkward to deal with certain examples of patent injustice,
but I do not doubt that he can nevertheless disallow every
patently unjust exercise of freedom that Mill would disallow.
On the other hand, it is easier on Kant's view to explain why
it is not unjust but merely cruel to beat a dog or horse: the
latter may feel pain just as we do, but since they lack (at least
in Kant's opinion) the capacity for free choice, they lack
moral rights and thus cannot suffer the injustice of having
their rights infringed or violated.

5. *Private and Public Law*

Kant divides prescriptive law into private law and public law.
The key difference between these kinds of law is that public
law "requires public promulgation in order to produce a

juridical condition," or to be binding on us.[36] Public law can also be called "civil law," for it is based on the "general legislative Will" of a civil society.[37] Private law is valid, or universally binding, even in a state of nature, and it cannot be abrogated by statutory or public law. Thus, private law constitutes the foundation of all prescriptive law.

Private law or justice is what I have been discussing thus far in this chapter; as I have explained, Kant thinks that this law "can be known a priori by every human being."[38] The Universal Principle of Justice thus belongs to private law; and though I have not mentioned it, private law provides the basis for determining what things are legitimate "objects of external legislation." As Kant explains in great detail, these legitimate objects of external legislation include external property, services by others, institutions, and many different kinds of contracts. Although private law has a very large scope, it possesses important limitations: roughly speaking, it cannot provide the juridical machinery for settling disputes over rights (this requires a public judiciary), and it cannot deal adequately with what we might call social obligations, which are based on the general will of a community.

The importance and distinctive character of public law emerges most clearly in connection with the notion of property. According to Kant, "a thing is externally mine [my property] if it is such that any prevention of my use of it would constitute an injury to me even if it is not in my possession. . . ."[39] Since Kant conceives of an injury as a violation of one's freedom, he concluded that, if an object is mine (my property), everyone else has an obligation not to interfere with my use of it. But, Kant argues: "By an individual act of my own will I cannot obligate any other person to abstain from the use of a thing in respect of which he would otherwise be under no obligation; . . . such an obligation can arise only from the collective will of all. . . ."[40] The collective will of a community is embodied, Kant says, in a "constitution"; and when a community of people have such a collective will, they "constitute a civil society."[41] Consequently, only in a civil society "can a thing be externally yours or mine."[42]

Kant does not deny that there is a sense in which something—a piece of land, say—could be possessed in a precivil state of nature. In fact, he explicitly allows that a limited form of possession is possible in such a state and that the possessor may *rightfully* resist others who seek to deprive him of what he thus possesses. But this "provisional *de jure* possession" (as Kant calls it) is right only when it is held "in expectation and preparation for a civil society" and when it accords with a possible public law governing property.[43] For something to be owned or possessed in the fullest sense—for it to be "peremptorily possessed"—it must be held in accordance with the provisions of a public law that specifies the conditions under which something may properly belong to one person rather than another and that provides a means of settling disputes about possessions. Since men feel a natural inclination not to respect the rights of others, a state of nature is inevitably a state of lawless freedom. Consequently, anyone who is "so situated as to be unavoidably side by side with others" has an obligation to "abandon the state of nature and enter, with all others, a juridical state of affairs," that is, a civil society.[44]

It may seem obvious that, if private property is morally permissible, there must be laws and principles that specify the rights and obligations pertaining to it and that determine the means by which it may legitimately be acquired, transferred to others, and the like. On the other hand, it may not seem obvious that private property really is morally permissible and, if it is morally permissible, that the relevant laws of property must be based on the "united will" of the relevant community. But Kant offers specific arguments for both these points.

As far as the possibility of private property is concerned, Kant's argument is essentially that the mere existence of private property is not incompatible with anyone's freedom according to universal law. It is true, as I mentioned earlier, that Kant conceives of property in a broad way, so that it may include an action promised or contracted by another; but he makes it abundantly clear that he regards the private ownership of land as morally acceptable. In view of the numerous arguments that have been offered against the moral acceptability of private property, it is not possible to provide a thorough defense of Kant's position in the few pages I can devote to it here. It is possible, however, to show that Kant's position is extremely reasonable and far more difficult to refute than opponents of private property might believe.

The first point to observe is that to claim, as Kant does, that the private ownership of land is morally permissible or right is not thereby to commit oneself to any particular account of how such ownership may be acquired or transferred to others, or even of how extensive it might be. These matters can be determined only by the relevant laws concerning such ownership. It may well be that the existing laws governing the ownership of property in this or that society have the effect of greatly curtailing the lawful freedom of many human beings. Yet even if all existing laws governing the private ownership of land had this character, it would not follow that the private ownership of land is per se objectionable. This would follow only if all conceivable (or possible) laws governing such ownership had unjust consequences. But this last possibility seems extremely dubious: it is hard to imagine it nailed down by a sober argument, least of all one that accords any value to individual freedom or autonomy.

However this may be, Kant's conception of private ownership is somewhat peculiar, in a way that deserves to be pointed out.[45] He seems to hold that a person can have peremptory possession of a piece of land only in the sense that he is entitled to *use* it in certain ways and to be protected in his use of it by the civil law. Strictly, or in a deeper sense, the land is "possessed in common" with all the members of society. Thus, Kant says: "Right in a thing is a right to the private use of a thing, of which I am in possession—originally or derivatively—*in common with all others*. . . ."[46] The reason he gives for this is that the obligation others have to abstain from using something to which one has peremptory possession can arise only "from the collective will of all united in a relation of common possession."[47] In giving this reason he is clearly assuming that people can legislate collectively about something only if they "possess" it collectively. The sense of "common possession" he has in mind might be that in which United States citizens could be said to enact property legislation only for land that they possess—that is, land belonging to the United States. The key point of interest in his claim is that the private possession of property amounts to a private or special *right* to use a common possession.

The next thing I want to consider is why Kant thinks that the laws of property must be public, expressing the collective will of a community. The answer rests squarely on Kant's view of moral autonomy. As he puts it: "A citizen [or person generally] . . . has the lawful freedom to obey no law other than one to which he has given his consent."[48] Since the will from which "all rights ensue . . . must . . . be incapable of wronging anyone," there is just one will for which this is possible: "The will of the people as a whole (when all decide about all, and each, accordingly, decides about himself)— because the one man to whom each person can do no legal wrong is himself. If it is otherwise, any decision made for all by a will other than the will of all might be an injustice. . . ."[49] Public law, which secures the rights of each person "by an effective power that is not his own," is thus based on the "united and consenting Will of all."[50]

6. *The Original Social Contract*

Kant says that public law, as the expression of the general will, "can only be singular" and may be called "the original contract." By saying this he does not mean to imply that the collective act of making this contract should be regarded as an actual historical occurrence. On the contrary, he thinks that the notion of such a contractual act should be accepted as

> a *mere idea* of reason, albeit one with indubitable practical reality, obligating every lawmaker to frame his laws so that they *might* have come from the united will of an entire people, and to regard every subject who would be a citizen as if he had joined in voting for such a will. For this is the

touchstone of the legitimacy of all public law. If a law is so framed that all the people *could not possibly* give it their consent . . . the law is unjust; but if it is *at all possible* that a people might agree on it, then the people's duty is to look upon the law as just. . . .[51]

In Kant's view the general will of the people is "represented" by a lawmaker or head of state—a "moral person," who may be constituted by any number of actual people.[52] Ideally, the aim of the lawmaker is to secure, by his legislation, a stable, enduring social order that guarantees the right of each citizen to "pursue his happiness in the manner that seems best to him," provided, of course, that he does not thereby infringe on anyone's freedom according to universal law.

Although Kant insists that the end to be promoted by public law is not the happiness of the citizens but a "juridical condition" that secures and protects their rights (or lawful freedom), he claims that this end can be realized only in a stable, enduring social order. To ensure that the state or civil order is stable, "strong enough to resist foreign enemies," and able to "maintain itself as a community," the lawmaker may pass laws that do contribute to the happiness and prosperity of the people. Kant says, for example: "The general Will of the people has united itself into a social order to maintain itself continually, and for this purpose it has subjected itself to the internal authority of the state in order to supply those members of the society who are not able to support themselves."[53] What we should call "welfare legislation" is therefore justifiable, according to Kant, when and only when it is necessary for the continued existence of a civil society. Its ultimate aim is not, as he puts it, "to make the people happy, against their will as it were"; it is to "make them exist as a community."[54]

It is important to realize that, to be fully justified, welfare legislation must always accord with the general will—however necessary it may be to a particular social order. The obvious reason for this is that, according to Kant, the *raison d'être* of any legitimate social order is to guarantee each citizen's basic freedom. If welfare legislation, which inevitably places burdens on prosperous citizens, did not accord with *everyone's* will, its enactment would limit some citizens' freedom to pursue their happiness in a way that is compatible with everyone's freedom according to universal law. Yet if such legislation does accord with everyone's will—if every citizen *could* consent to it—its enactment will not necessarily conflict with any citizen's freedom to act, lawfully, as he wills.

To understand Kant's view of justifiable public legislation we must, of course, understand his meaning when he says that a public law is unjust when and only when "all the people *could not possibly* give it their consent." What sense of "possibility" is involved here? In one passage Kant implies that the answer is "logical, or formal, possibility": "Just as long as it is not self-contradictory to assume that all the people consent to . . . a law, however distasteful they may find it, the law is in accord with justice."[55] But this passage does not represent Kant's best thinking on the matter. His first example of a law to which the people could not possibly give their consent is one "granting the hereditary *privilege* of *master status* to a certain class of *subjects*.[56] Obviously, there is nothing self-contradictory about this law. In fact, it would not really be surprising if all the members of a feudal society actually assented to a law of this kind. In a later passage Kant clarifies matters by speaking of a monarch's "true will." He asks whether a community "*may* enact a law to the effect that certain tenets of faith and outward religious forms, once adopted, should remain forever," and then answers in the negative, saying that such a law "would be null and void in itself, because it runs counter to the destiny and to the ends of mankind."[57]

In view of these last remarks I think we must interpret Kant as having in mind the kind of rational legislating that he discussed in the *Groundwork*. Ideally, public law, though "concerned only with the juridical form of men living together," is a species of universal law, which is freely adopted by rational beings.[58] Consequently, in thinking about the idea of an original contract, we should conceive of the community of citizens as rational beings (which, indeed, they are "in them-

selves") who have certain rational ends and who have sufficient knowledge of themselves and their circumstances to
make a reasonable estimate about "how things would stand"
(as Kant says in the *Groundwork*) if they adopted a certain law.
The question we should ask ourselves, if we want to know
whether a particular law is consistent with the general will of
the relevant community, is whether all the members of that
community, considered as rational beings with certain factual
information and certain "essential ends," could *consistently* as-
sent to that law, or will that it should govern their associa-
tion. The notion of consistency appropriate here is *relative
consistency*, the consistency of a decision with, or relative to,
certain aims and information.

Although Kant tries to prove, in his "Doctrine of Virtue,"
that rational beings necessarily have certain specifically ethical
aims (namely, their own moral perfection and the happiness
of others), it is doubtful that he would allow public legislation
to be evaluated for moral acceptability by reference to ethical
aims or ends. After all, he is a firm opponent of paternalistic
legislation and says again and again that the purpose of public
law is *not* to make people happy. In view of these disclaimers,
I should say that the "ends of humanity" by reference to
which the "true will" of a citizen on the acceptability of a possible public law can be determined probably comprise a fairly
short list. Prime candidates for the list include:

1. the agent's freedom to pursue his own happiness in
ways compatible with the freedom of everyone according to universal laws;
2. the agent's will to enter "a condition of society in which
what is to be recognized as belonging to . . . [each per-
son] must be established lawfully and secured to him by
an effective power that is not his own . . .";[59]
3. the agent's will that the civil society into which he is en-
tering "maintain itself continually";
4. the agent's will that public positive laws be enacted and
enforced that insure the continued existence of his civil
society and permit its development into a more perfect,

enlightened society that can unite with other societies in
the interests of achieving perpetual peace.[60]

If each potential citizen possess these and related ends, the
united and general will of all would agree on the kind of public law that will characterize what Kant considered a just civil
society.

To underline that rather narrow range of considerations
relevant to judging the moral acceptability of a public law, it
is worth emphasizing that a just social order could permit
"the greatest inequality in the quantity and degree of . . . [its
citizens'] possessions, whether these be physical or mental
superiority, external gifts of fortune, or simply rights (of
which there can be many) with respect to others."[61] On the
other hand, the moral equality of subjects in a community requires that "each member of the community must be permitted to rise in it to any status or class (appropriate to a subject)
to which his talent, industry, and luck may take him."[62]
Kant's conception of a just social order is thus firmly in the
tradition of political liberalism. He does allow some room for
welfare legislation, but he insists, as we have seen, that it is
justifiable only as a means of maintaining a social order that
protects its citizens' lawful freedom "to pursue their happiness in their own way."

7. Kant's Theory of Punishment

Kant's conception of just punishment is explicitly retributivist. He says flatly: "Judicial punishment can never be used
merely as a means to promote some other good for the criminal himself or for civil society, but instead it must in all cases
be imposed on him only on the ground that he has committed
a crime; for a human being can never be manipulated merely
as a means to the purposes of someone else. . . ."[63] The kind
and degree of punishment appropriate to a given crime cannot
be determined by utilitarian considerations either; this is determined by "the principle of equality (illustrated by the
pointer on the scales of justice), that is, the principle of not
treating one side more favorably than the other. . . . Only the

Law of retribution (*jus talionis*) can determine exactly the kind and degree of punishment. . . ."[64] Kant also speaks of the principle of equality as "the principle of returning like for like" and says that just punishment must always be "proportional" to the crime.[65]

One of Kant's claims here is both clear and reasonable—the claim, namely, that a person can be justly punished only on the ground that he has committed a punishable offense. But Kant's principle of equality is neither clear nor plausible. He says that just punishment should be "proportional" to the offense; yet this proportion can be understood in more than one way. Some retributivists would say that the severity of the punishment should be proportional to the seriousness of the offense; others would say that the effect of the punishment should be proportional to the harmful effect of the offense. Although the first view seems the most satisfactory, Kant appears to hold the second one, for he says that "the spirit" of the principle is satisfied when "the effects" of the punishment are similar to the effects of the offending act. By way of illustration he remarks that a person who inflicts a verbal injury upon another might rightfully be punished by being required "not only to make a public apology to the offended person, but also to kiss his hand, even though he be socially inferior."[66] He also remarks that if "a man of a higher class" violently attacks a social inferior, he could rightfully be condemned "not only to apologize, but to undergo solitary and painful confinement," because in addition to feeling significant discomfort, his pride will be "painfully affected" in a way that will "compensate for the offense as like for like."[67] In view of these remarks it seems reasonable to interpret Kant's principle of equality as requiring that the harm inflicted by just punishment should be proportional to the harm caused by the relevant offense.

Interpreted this way, Kant's principle of equality or retribution seem appropriate, at best, for fairly simple offenses in which one person deliberately harms another in some publicly identifiable way. Three kinds of offenses for which his principle is patently objectionable immediately come to mind. First, willful acts of robbery, rape, or murder may be bungled or even foiled by the authorities; yet attempts to commit these offenses are rightly regarded as crimes and punished according to their presumed seriousness as crimes—not according to the actual harm they cause someone, which could be negligible. Second, and by way of contrast, certain offenses may cause a great deal of very serious harm and yet be deserving of fairly mild punishment. An example would be a reckless act that accidentally resulted in a death. Because of the recklessness, the act may count as an offense, but it would not merit the punishment accorded to an act of willful murder, though the results in both cases might be equally harmful. Finally, many punishable offenses are considered more or less serious even though there is no effective way of estimating the harm they cause in particular cases. Examples of such offenses include discharging limited amounts of toxic wastes in a large river, cheating on one's income tax, covering up offenses committed by subordinates, embezzling funds from a bank, or deserting one's army unit in the heat of battle. Many cases of this kind clearly deserve punishment if anything does; yet the actual harm they cause may be virtually impossible to determine.

As far as I can tell, there is no simple principle by which punishment is rightly assigned to offenses of the kinds just described. On the face of it, a number of different principles seem appropriate.[68] One such principle is clearly utilitarian: we want to discourage acts of armed robbery and willful murder, and we find it useful for this purpose to punish those who merely attempt to commit such crimes. Yet in doing this we also consider the amount of harm that results from the act, and we are moved by a sense of fairness and a feeling of respect for the offender's dignity as a person. Consequently, we do not punish attempts as severely as we punish successes, and we avoid "cruel and unusual punishment." In cases of willful murder some people insist on applying something like Kant's principle of equality, thus requiring a death for a death; but others contend that even in these special cases Kant's principle must be qualified to be consistent with the value they (or we) attach to human life. Since I believe that there is no simple way of formulating and systematizing the various principles on which a morally acceptable theory of punishment could be based, I shall not attempt to do so here. I shall merely say that, in my judgment, Kant's principle of equality or retribution is far too simple to deal satisfactorily with the wide variety of offenses that should be covered by a reasonable system of penal law.

Whether I am right or wrong about the acceptability of Kant's principle, an important question remains to be discussed: How does Kant attempt to justify that principle? The answer, unfortunately, is that Kant did not offer an explicit defense for his principle. He insisted that it provides the only acceptable basis for just punishment, but he did not attempt to derive it from his basic principles. To unearth his reasons for insisting upon the principle, we have to rely on various incidental remarks he makes and also consider how the principle fits in with his general theory of justice.

Since punishment is, for Kant, a form of justifiable coercion, an important clue to his conception of just punishment might be found in his remarks on the authorized use of coercion. The crucial passage is this: "Everything that is unjust is a hindrance to freedom according to universal laws. Coercion, however, is a hindrance or opposition to freedom. Consequently, if a certain use of freedom is itself a hindrance to freedom according to universal laws (that is, is unjust), then the use of coercion to counteract it, *inasmuch as it is the prevention of a hindrance to freedom*, is consistent with freedom according to universal laws; in other words, this use of coercion is just."[69] But this kind of reasoning cannot support Kant's principle of equality in any direct way. The kind of coercion it directly justifies is not punishment for acts already committed but lawful interference with unjust acts—a kind of coercion that prevents unjust acts from occurring. Thus, if Jones is engaged in giving Smith an undeserved beating, Kant's reasoning would justify someone (perhaps an official) in interfering with or hindering Jones's action; it would not, at least obviously, justify punishing Jones after his act is completed.

I have said that the reasoning given above does not directly justify the imposition of punishment for acts already committed, but it may indirectly justify such punishment. Kant makes it abundantly clear that, in his view, a state of lawful freedom can exist only in a civil society with public laws and both judicial and executive authorities.[70] Such a society maintains a state of lawful freedom by enforcing its laws—by holding trials and imposing just punishment. Now, the prospect of being punished for a legal offense undoubtedly has a *coercive* effect on the wills of the citizens: it hinders them from performing unjust acts that they might (or would) otherwise perform. Viewed this way, retributive punishment is just coercion in an indirect form. Punitive acts do not hinder or interfere with the offensive acts for which they are penalties; they hinder, interfere with, or, more exactly, *deter* potential offenses, which might (or would) have been committed *if* those punitive acts had not been known to occur.

There is no doubt that the line of thought just sketched does represent part of Kant's thinking about the justification of punishment or of penal legislation. After all, the penal law is, for him, just part of public law, which is needed to establish and maintain a state of lawful freedom in a community of people. Also, in one passage he makes it clear that "the effect intended" by the death penalty is to deter (at least among other things) acts of homicide.[71] But however true to Kant's position these last observations may be, they are not sufficient to justify his principle of equality. What we want to know is why Kant thinks that just punishment, which admittedly serves the instrumental function of promoting a state of lawful freedom or universal justice, must also conform to his principle of equality. And this matter is not clarified by the line of thought we have been discussing.

On the assumption that Kant thinks some system of punishment is necessary for the crucial goal of lawful freedom, we might ask why he should suppose that a system conforming to his principle of equality is the only sort that is truly justifiable. A possible answer to this question is suggested by Kant's remark that "all other standards [except the principle of equality] fluctuate back and forth and, because extraneous considerations are mixed with them, they cannot be compatible with the principle of pure and strict legal justice."[72] His claim here might be that the other standards such as that provided by "the winding paths of a theory of happiness" will not really promote the goal of lawful freedom. As he maintains elsewhere, if government (and so, we may add, law) were founded on the "principle of benevolence toward the people," it would be paternalistic and have the effect of canceling "every freedom" of the citizens, leaving them "no rights at all."[73] Obviously, any principle having this consequence could not be consistent with "pure and strict" justice.

It seems to me that this reasoning does represent part of Kant's basis for his principle of equality. He unquestionably holds that a state of lawful freedom requires a system of penal law (at least at this stage of civilization) and that only a system based on his principle is compatible with pure and strict justice. But the soundness of this reasoning is certainly open to question. Not only does Kant fail to consider every possible rival to his principle of equality, but he deals very casually with the rival that he does explicitly consider—namely, some version of the utilitarian principle. Of course, Kant may have felt that "the principle of benevolence" provides the only serious alternative to his principle, and he may have felt that since, in his view, a just world is one of lawful freedom in which people are entitled to pursue ends that (contrary to their estimate) bring them unhappiness rather than happiness, no principle of benevolence could possibly provide a satisfactory foundation for legal justice. But to be compelling, to a modern reader at least, these attitudes require careful defense.

Regardless of the merits of this last line of argument, Kant clearly has some other, possibly more fundamental basis for his principle of equality. In a well-known passage he says this: "Even if a civil society were to dissolve itself by common agreement of all its members . . . , the last murderer remaining in prison must first be executed, so that everyone will duly receive what his actions are worth and so that the blood-guilt thereof will not be fixed on the people because they failed to insist on carrying out the punishment. . . ."[74] If the principle of retribution must be satisfied even when a society is in the process of dissolution, it cannot be justified only as a means of preserving the state of lawful freedom secured by that society: some further justification must be possible. Since Kant speaks of "bloodguilt" in the passage above and says elsewhere that certain crimes can be "expiated" only by death, this further justification might be connected, in his mind, with the notions of guilt and expiation. He introduces a related notion when he remarks, in his "Doctrine of Virtue," that "the function of [punishment] is to *avenge* the crime upon its perpetrator (not merely to make good the injury)."[75]

Since Kant did not provide an explicit justification for his principle of equality, we thus have to ask: "What kind of justification, apart from the inadequate one we have considered, can Kant possibly give for his principle?" An interesting answer to this question has been suggested by Jeffrie Murphy. According to him,

> Kant offers a theory of punishment . . . based on his general view that political obligation is to be analyzed in terms of *reciprocity*. If the law is to remain just it is important to guarantee that those who disobey it will not gain an unfair advantage over those who obey it voluntarily. Criminal punishment attempts to guarantee this, and, in its retribution, its attempts to restore the proper balance between benefit and obedience. . . . [Since a citizen] derives benefit from [the laws of his society] . . . , he owes obedience as a *debt* to his fellow-citizens for their sacrifices in maintaining them. If he chooses not to sacrifice by exercising self-restraint and obedience, this is tantamount to his choosing to sacrifice in another way—namely, by paying the prescribed penalty. . . . This analysis of punishment regards it as a *debt* owed to the law-abiding members of one's community; and, once paid, it allows re-entry into the community of good citizens on an equal basis.[76]

This analysis has the merit of providing a rationale for the principle of equality that fits in nicely with an otherwise puzzling remark Kant makes about reciprocity and with his scattered words about vengeance and atonement. The remark about reciprocity is that in a state of lawless freedom men cannot wrong each other by fighting back and forth: "whatever goes for one of them goes reciprocally for the other as though they had made an agreement to that effect."[77] The relation of the analysis to Kant's words on vengeance and atonement are obvious. If you are required to atone or pay for a debt created by an offense you commit, those to whom the debt is owed and who demand its payment must have some interest in the payment you make. Thus, if, as in the case of murder, you are to atone for your offense by giving up your life, your fellow citizens, who demand this form of repayment, must have some interest in seeing you die. But what can this interest be if it is not the desire (or will) for vengeance? Nowadays, moralists do not condone acts of vengeance, but Kant uses the word with approval, and it may express his attitude better than "desire (or will) to secure a fair balance of benefits and burdens," which a philosopher such as Murphy would probably prefer.

Even though Murphy's analysis accords with some of Kant's scattered remarks, it is essentially conjectural and does not, I believe, accord well with Kant's principal claims about justice. As Kant emphasizes, "the concept of external law as such derives completely from the concept of *freedom* in the external relations of men to one another."[78] The basic principle of his theory of justice is his Universal Law of Justice, and this law is specifically concerned with the requirements of lawful freedom, not with the need for balancing social benefits and burdens in a fair way. Murphy does not found his analysis on Kant's Universal Law of Justice but on Kant's notion of the original contract; yet in speaking of that contract Kant does not introduce the notion of fairness at all. Referring to what he calls Kant's "basic model of rational decision," Murphy says that a government is based on consent, for Kant, "if it could have been chosen by a group of rational beings as a fair way of resolving their conflicts."[79] But this seems to describe John Rawls's view of an original contract far better than it describes Kant's.[80] There is no textual evidence that Kant thought of intelligible makers of external universal law as being moved by a principle of fairness. As we saw in the last section, the considerations that do move them seem, rather, to be focused squarely on human freedom.

These remarks do not, of course, prove that Murphy's analysis is mistaken; they simply render it doubtful. But another analysis, equally conjectural, is at hand, and it is not affected by these considerations. Like Murphy's analysis, this one is based on Kant's remarks about reciprocity. When Kant first introduced the notion of justice as "the possibility of a general reciprocal use of coercion," he argued that his principle of justice as reciprocity is derivable from the Universal Principle of Justice by virtue of the law of contradiction. As we have seen, his key claim was that "if a certain use of freedom is itself a hindrance to freedom according to universal laws . . . , then the use of coercion to counteract it, inasmuch as it is the prevention of a hindrance to freedom, is consistent with freedom according to universal laws. . . ."[81] Although this argument is not (as I have argued) adequate to justify Kant's principle of equality, a tempting argument for the principle can be obtained if we disregard the clause beginning with "inasmuch as" in the passage above. The idea behind the new argument would be that an unjust hindrance to freedom can justly be "counteracted" by a corresponding hindrance to the freedom of the offender, for in a world of freedom according to universal law no one should have more freedom than anyone else. A person who acts unjustly hinders someone else's freedom and, as a result, has a greater freedom than the person he hinders. To redress this imbalance, the offender's freedom should be hindered in a way "proportional" to his hindrance of the other's freedom. If, at the cost of some awkwardness but no outright absurdity, we think of retributive punishment as simply a hindrance of an offender's freedom—either partial, as by a term in jail, or complete, as by the death penalty—we shall have a derivation of Kant's principle of equality (or retribution) from his Universal Principle of Justice.

Would Kant have accepted this argument? Did he have it, or something like it, tacitly in mind when he propounded his principle of equality (or retribution)? It is hard to say. Since he did not, at least in any obvious way, offer an explicit defense for his principle, any account of his reasons for holding the principle must be based largely on conjecture. Unlike Murphy's analysis, the argument above is focused specifically on lawful freedom, and it keeps Kant's principle closely tied to his fundamental principle, the so-called Universal Law of Justice. Apart from this, it suggests a way of relating Kant's words on vengeance to his claims about justice. The idea is that rational vengeance consists of limiting an offender's freedom in a way comparable to the limitation he imposed on someone else's freedom. If "freedom according to universal law" requires equal freedom for all, the aim of this "rational" vengeance would be "pure and strict legal justice" in Kant's technical sense, that is, a state of what I have been calling "lawful freedom." Though the matter is highly uncertain and conjectural, it seems to me that this approach to Kant's principle has a lot to commend it.

Chapter VI: The Basic Principles of Ethics

THE subject of this chapter is the "doctrine of virtue" that Kant develops in the second half of his *Metaphysics of Morals*. This doctrine is concerned with specifically ethical duties, or duties of virtue. Since all moral duties are, for Kant, either duties of justice or duties of virtue, this chapter will complete my discussion of Kant's moral theory.

1. *The Basis of Ethical Obligation*

The role of ethical duty in Kant's moral theory is easy to appreciate if we recall his claim, in the *Groundwork*, that actions have moral value only when they are done for the sake of duty. His idea was that, although a scoundrel may act justly in repaying a debt merely out of fear of his creditor, his act is not thereby worthy of our respect and esteem; a craven act is not to anyone's moral credit, and it lacks moral value even though, in satisfying the provisions of an external law, it must be considered right or just. To have moral value and to merit our moral approbation, an action must be done for a moral motive—specifically, "for the sake of duty." The aim of doing one's duty would, of course, be empty and useless if it did not involve less abstract, more specific aims. Kant's "Doctrine of Virtue" is concerned with identifying these more specific aims and with proving that we have a moral obligation to pursue them. According to his terminology, any aim or "end" that we have an obligation to pursue is an ethical end. Such ends "are also duties," and the system of them exhausts the subject of "pure" ethics.

A person is morally virtuous to the extent that he acts for the sake of duty. For this reason, ethics is properly called "the doctrine of virtue." Kant's notion of virtue is not entirely traditional, however. Aristotle conceived of a virtuous person as one who habitually acts virtuously, but Kant thinks that a virtuous person acts virtuously only because he has a virtuous attitude, this being a state of moral fortitude that enables him to resist urges and inclinations opposed to the demands of duty. According to Kant, "men, natural beings," are "unholy enough that pleasure can induce them to transgress the moral law, even though they recognize its authority." When they do obey the law, typically they do so *"reluctantly* . . . and so under *constraint*."[1] For the special case of ethical obligation, this constraint is provided by the sense of duty, which amounts to reverence for the moral law. A person in whom the sense of duty is strong thus has moral fortitude and may be called "morally virtuous."

Although morally virtuous people are morally constrained to do their duty, they nevertheless do it freely, for moral constraint is a form of self-constraint. As Kant sees it, intentional action is always directed to some end; and when a person acts contrary to his natural urges or inclinations, he acts for the sake of ends that he has set for himself. The specific laws of ethics (or virtue) prescribe ends that are necessary means to the primary end of doing one's duty or obeying the moral imperative. Since these prescribed ends are freely adopted by a rational being, the laws of ethics may be called "laws of inner freedom." As this terminology suggests, we are "internally" free when we master our animal impulses and pursue the rational ends that virtue (or ethics) requires.

As we saw in Chapter II, a person who acts for the sake of duty is motivated, Kant thinks, by a basic intention or "principle of the will" that can be expressed as

P1: I will conform my actions to universal law as such.

He also seems to think[2] that this basic intention can be expressed by

P2: I will act on a maxim m only when I can at the same time will that m should become a universal law.

The intention expressed by these formulas might be called "the moral intention," because it discloses one's commitment to conform to the requirements of the moral law. The categorical imperative *C1* tells us to act only on maxims that we could consistently will to become universal laws, and *P2* expresses the intention to do just this. Since Kant thinks that *C1* actually amounts to the imperative

P3: Conform your actions to universal law,

we can say that *P1* also expresses an intention to conform to the moral law.

As we have seen, Kant contends that a person who does what the moral law requires does not necessarily act virtuously. What he does is right or lawful, but to be virtuous—to have moral value—his action must be done for the sake of the moral law. Since ethics is the doctrine of virtue, Kant expresses the Universal Ethical Command as "Do your duty from the motive of duty."[3] Yet if *P1* and *P2* express the basic moral intention, we might add that a person acts virtuously when his action is ultimately motivated by this intention.

Now, Kant claims that the duties generated by the Universal Ethical Command are duties to pursue certain rational ends. The rationale for his claim can be built on the following argument:

1. You ought to act on the moral intention *P1*.
2. Your acting on *P1* requires your acting on the derivative intention *I*.
3. Therefore, you ought to act on the derivative intention *I*.

Since to act on an intention is necessarily to act for some end, the conclusion of the argument here allows us to add that you (or, more generally, we) ought to act for some end. But an end we must act for (or pursue) if we are to realize the moral intention is an ethical requirement: in Kant's terminology, it is an end that is also a duty.

The question is, "What ends does ethics require us to pursue?" In one place Kant says that the "highest, unconditioned end" that we are morally required to pursue is virtue itself.[4] But he also says that we "widen our concept of duty beyond the notion of *what is due*" (that is, beyond merely juridical duty) by making "the right of humanity, or also the rights of men, our end."[5] Given Kant's view of the relation between virtue and ethical duty, we can easily see why he might say that our highest end is to pursue virtue itself. The second remark is based on a more complicated consideration, however. According to the doctrine of the *Groundwork*, the categorical imperative can also be expressed in the form of *C3*—namely, "Act in such a way that you always treat humanity, whether in your own person or in the person of any other, never simply as a means but at the same time as an end." Since ethics requires us to act on an intention corresponding to the moral law, it requires us to act on an intention corresponding to *C3*. We might express this intention as:

   IC3: I will always treat humanity, whether in myself or in the person of any other, always as an end and never simply as a means.

If we assume that treating humanity according to the requirements of *C3* amounts to treating human beings in the way they have a moral right to be treated, it would not seem unreasonable to say that anyone acting on the intention *IC3* has "the rights of men" as his end.

   Apart from speaking of the rights of men, or of humanity, as our fundamental ethical end, Kant says, more simply, that "we should make ourselves and others our end" and that "man is obligated to regard himself, as well as every other man, as his end."[6] In view of this, we might say that our fundamental end in acting on *IC3* is to treat humanity as an end in itself. Since this end is what is declared obligatory by ethics, the ethical requirement is not just to *treat* humanity as an end in itself but to *act on the intention* of doing so. As Kant insists, ethics is a doctrine of ends, not of "external actions," which fall under the scope of outer, juridical duty. Kant does say that "[our] ethical obligation extends over juridical obligation," but he adds that this does not justify us in calling juridical obligations "duties of virtue."[7] His idea is that since juridical laws are universal laws, the moral intention *P1* requires us to have the subordinate intention of doing what is required by juridical laws. Although we have a juridical duty to do what those laws require, our ethical duty is not just to obey them (which we could do for a nonmoral motive) but to make it our end or purpose to obey them.

Kant argues that the primary subordinate ends that ethics requires us to pursue (or to have) are *our own perfection* and *the happiness of others*. He says that we cannot interchange "perfection" and "happiness" here, for *"one's own happiness* and the *perfection of others* cannot be made into obligatory ends of the same person."[8] He argues that we could not have a duty to pursue our own happiness because we *naturally* seek our happiness, and duty is a form of "necessitation to an end that we adopt reluctantly." Consequently, it would be "contradictory to say that we are *under obligation* to promote our own happiness to the best of our ability."[9] As for the perfection of others, Kant says that it would be equally contradictory to suppose that we had a duty to pursue this end. His reason for this is based squarely on his conception of perfection. As he conceives of it, another's perfection "as a person" consists "precisely in *his own* power to adopt his end in accordance with his own conception of duty."[10] Since it is self-contradictory to demand that I do what only another person can do, *another person's perfection* could not possibly be an obligatory end *for me*.

The bulk of Kant's "Doctrine of Virtue" is devoted to the analysis of the ends of one's own happiness and the happiness of others, and to argumentation supporting the claim that we have a duty to have (or pursue) them. In the sections to follow I shall consider Kant's principal claims about these ends and then discuss certain more general matters of fundamental importance to his conception of ethics or virtue.

2. One's Own Perfection as an Obligatory End

According to Kant, the concept of perfection appropriate here belongs to teleology and concerns the adequacy of a thing's qualities to some *telos* or end. The perfection of ourselves that ethics requires us to pursue is both natural and moral. As far as natural perfection is concerned, our fundamental duty is to cultivate our natural powers for promoting the ends that "reason puts forward." The natural powers pertinent here are those of the mind, the soul, and the body. Powers of the mind are concerned with the use of reason in a priori subjects such as logic and mathematics; in perfecting them we perfect the power for abstract thought needed for solving problems that may arise for us. Powers of the soul, as Kant calls them, are those powers of mind that are guided by experience. These powers include memory, imagination and the like, "on which we can build learning," as well as taste. Powers of the body, finally, are those that must be cultivated to maintain one's "animal vigor," which is necessary for the pursuit of all sorts of rational ends.

Although the cultivation of these natural powers is clearly helpful for a satisfying life, it is by no means obvious that we have an actual duty to cultivate them. But Kant argues as follows:

> That natural perfection is a duty and so an end in itself, and that the cultivation of our powers even without regard to the advantage it brings has an unconditioned (moral) imperative . . . at its basis, can be shown this way. The power to set an end—any end whatever—is characteristic of humanity (as distinguished from animality). Hence, there is also bound up with the end of humanity in our own person the rational will, and so the duty, to make ourselves worthy of humanity by culture in general, by procuring or promoting the *power* to realize all possible ends, so far as this power is to be found in man himself.[11]

Obviously, Kant's reasoning here is highly abbreviated. Although it recalls his treatment of his Third Example in the *Groundwork*, it introduces a new idea. This is that, as sensible beings, we are partly rational animals who, to be virtuous, must do what we can to make our animal nature serve our rational ends. We must be "worthy of our humanity." Since the power of setting ends is partly constitutive of our rational nature, we have the duty of developing the physical powers (the "talents" as Kant put it in the *Groundwork*) necessary for realizing the ends that we might set for ourselves as rational beings.

I shall have more to say about Kant's reasons for acknowledging this last duty later; I now want to consider the other aspect of our perfection that Kant says ethics requires us to pursue—namely, our moral perfection. The basic requirement for pursuing this is having "the maxim of striving with all [our] might to make the thought of duty for its own sake the sufficient motive for every dutiful action."[12] It is very easy to misunderstand this last requirement. The point is not that we should make the thought of duty the sufficient motive for everything we do; this would be moral fanaticism, which Kant rightly deplores: "That man may be called fantastically virtuous who admits *nothing* morally *indifferent* . . . and strews all his steps with duties, as with mantraps; it is not indifferent, to him, whether I eat meat or fish, drink beer or wine, supposing that both agree with me . . . [This attitude turns] the sovereignty of virtue into a tyranny."[13] The requirement, rather, is that we should strive with all our might to do what duty requires *because* duty requires it. *If* duty requires that we do a certain thing, then we should do it—and do it for the reason that duty requires it, whether we have a natural inclination to do it or not.

As far as I can tell, Kant does not offer a specific argument for his claim that we have an ethical duty to seek our own moral perfection. Yet if this kind of perfection consists essentially in striving to do our duty just because it is our duty, Kant may have thought that his claim requires no special defense. The Universal Ethical Command is, he says, "Do your duty from the motive of duty," and if we conscientiously obey this law we shall, it would seem, be pursuing our moral perfection. As we shall see, Kant seems to subsume certain specific duties, which cannot be defended in this simple way, under the generic duty of pursuing one's moral perfection. But his remarks about these special duties, such as that of never telling a lie, strongly suggest that he thinks they follow readily from the categorical imperative.

Since the categorical imperative is the basic principle of

Kant's moral theory, we should consider how it can be used to justify the ethical injunction to pursue our own perfection. There should be more than one way of developing such a justification, for Kant offers several formulations of the categorical imperative. The reasoning in each case should, of course, be similar in a fundamental respect: since ethics requires us to act on the maxim of conforming to the moral law, we have to show that this requirement has the consequence that we should seek our own perfection. The difference in each case is that, in considering what is required by action on this maxim, we have in mind a different interpretation of the moral law or categorical imperative.

In the *Groundwork* Kant shows us how he thinks the formulas C2 and C3 can be used to prove that we have a duty to cultivate our natural talents. Since cultivating our natural talents amounts to pursuing our natural perfection, Kant shows us, in effect, how he thinks the required justification can be constructed. His reasoning based on C3, which is really a typic for the pure moral law, is essentially this. Our analogue for universal law is teleological natural law. According to this latter law, every human being has numerous capacities that form "part of nature's purpose" for him. If we are to fulfill the requirements of C3 and treat the humanity in our person as an end in itself, we must develop these capacities, for ends are the sort of thing that a rational being wills to be realizes as fully as possible. Neglecting to develop the capacities that form part of nature's purpose for our humanity "can admittedly be compatible with the *maintenance* of [our] humanity as an end in itself, but not with the *promotion* of this end."[14] Since treating the humanity in us as an end in itself requires "promoting" our humanity, or realizing it to the greatest extent possible, the ethical requirement to act on C3 entails the requirement to seek (or pursue) our own natural perfection.

Like C3, C2 is a typic for the moral law rather than the real thing. The requirement to act on it amounts to the requirement to act only on lower-order maxims that we could consistently will to become universal laws of nature. On the basis of this requirement Kant argues that no maxim of "neglecting [one's] natural gifts" is morally acceptable. He allows that "a system of nature could always subsist" under natural laws corresponding to such maxims, but one could not consistently *will* that a system of this kind should actually exist. The reason is that, "as a rational being," we "necessarily will that all [our] powers should be developed, since they serve [us], and are given to [us], for all sorts of possible ends."¹⁵ Yet if, for this reason, we are forbidden to act on every maxim "of neglecting our natural gifts," we are ethically obligated to seek their cultivation or, what amounts to the same thing, to pursue our natural perfection.

Though neither of these arguments is very compelling, the first is better than the second. If treating humanity in our own person as an end in itself requires us to develop the capacities in which human perfection consists, then anyone who accepts C3 as a valid moral principle will have to agree that we have an obligation to develop whatever capacities are associated with human perfection. To this extent, at least, Kant's argument is a success. Unfortunately, the ideas on which Kant builds the argument—that of nature's purposes and teleological laws of nature—are highly problematic. If human perfection must be characterized by reference to nature's purposes and the teleological laws that specify those purposes, then Kant's conception of human perfection is just as problematic as these other ideas. Since we explored the basic problems with these ideas in Chapter IV, there is no need to discuss them here.

The second argument has two key flaws. One occurs in the last step: even if we have established that it is ethically forbidden to act on every maxim of neglecting our natural gifts, it does not *follow* that it is ethically obligatory to pursue one's own perfection. To pursue one's own perfection is to have a "maxim of ends," as Kant calls it; and the requirement to have some positive maxim is not entailed by the requirement *not* to act on any maxim of a certain class. Kant may be able to support at least a qualified version of the claim that any live, kicking, and even moderately rational person who has no maxim of neglecting a natural gift necessarily pursues (at least to some extent) his own natural perfection. But until such a claim is supported by a plausible line of reasoning, we are entitled to be highly critical of Kant's second argument.

The second flaw came to light in our discussion of the *Groundwork*.[16] The essential point is this: Even if we allow that any rational being necessarily seeks to develop whatever powers he deems necessary for attaining an end he actually has, we need not concede that he thereby seeks to develop all the powers he deems necessary for attaining ends that he might *possibly* have. It is, of course, true, as Kant observes, that we cannot say what ends might, at some time, be ours, but this is not a good reason for thinking that we are *obligated* to pursue the development of *all* our natural powers. In fact, if seeking to develop a natural power requires some effort on our part, it would appear that we could not reasonably hope to develop all our powers. The time available for self-perfection is always limited, and even Renaissance men and women must neglect some of their natural powers or talents.

Oddly enough, Kant is fully aware of this last point, for he says: "As to which of these natural perfections should take *precedence* among our ends and in what *proportion* to one another we should make them our ends in keeping with our duty to ourselves, it remains for us to choose, according to our rational deliberation about what sort of life we should like to lead and whether we have the powers necessary for that way of life (*e.g.* whether it should be manual labor, commerce, or scholarship)."[17] I am not sure how this passage can be brought into line with Kant's claim that we have a duty to procure or promote "the *power* to realize all possible ends, so far as this power is to be found in us." Perhaps his view is that, although we have as an end the cultivation of all our talents, we cannot possibly give equal attention to all these talents at any one time. For this reason, some of our ends must take precedence over others, at least at particular times. At any moment, the ends that we should actively pursue are those somehow appropriate to our circumstances, our other duties, and our rational plans of life.

Kant emphasizes that our duty to pursue our own perfection is an "imperfect duty of wide obligation," and further light can be shed on his conception of that pursuit by a careful analysis of what he calls "wide obligation." I shall attempt such an analysis in section 4 of this chapter. In the remainder of this section I want to say something about a number of specific duties that Kant associates with our general duty to seek our own perfection.

Kant says that our ethical duties to ourselves fall under two divisions. The first is "objective." According to it, every ethical duty to ourself is either "material" or "formal." Material duties of this kind are immediately concerned with our self-perfection: Kant says that they pertain to our "moral wealth," which consists in having the power to realize all our ends, "so far as this can be achieved." Formal ethical duties to ourselves are all negative or limiting: they forbid us to act contrary to our natural end, and so concern or "moral preservation" or "moral health." Although Kant says in his introduction that all ethical duties are imperfect, of wide obligation, these formal duties are all perfect, forbidding us to do fairly specific things. The main prohibitions that Kant lists are "self-murder" (including self-mutilation), "carnal self-defilement," and "self-stupefaction by the immoderate use of food and drink." Kant says that the principle of negative duties to oneself lies in the dictum "Live according to nature" or "Preserve yourself in the perfection of your nature"; the principle of positive duties to oneself lies in the saying "Make yourself more perfect than mere nature made you."[18]

The other division is "subjective" and based on two ways of viewing ourselves: as a moral animal or a merely moral being. Considered as a moral animal, we are subject to vices associated with certain of our animal instincts. Nature's purpose for these various instincts is (a) to preserve our physical existence, (b) to preserve our species, and (c) to preserve our ability to enjoy the animal pleasures of life. Our ethical duties to ourself as a moral animal consist of prohibitions against indulging in these vices, which are self-murder, carnal self-defilement (or "the unnatural use of [one's] sexual desire"), and "such *immoderate consumption of food and drink* as weakens [our] capacity for using [our] powers purposefully."[19] Our ethical duties to ourselves as merely moral beings "consist,"

Kant says, "in what is *formal* in the harmony of [our] maxims of the will with the *dignity* of humanity in [our] person."[20] The principal vices to be avoided here are lying, avarice, and false humility (or "servility"). As in the case of our formal duties to ourselves, which coincide with our subjective duties to ourselves as moral animals, the duties to avoid lying, avarice, and false humility are all "perfect, of narrow obligation." I shall have more to say about such duties in section 4 of this chapter.

The brief account I have just given of Kant's two divisions of our duties to ourselves makes it clear that, contrary to his initial claim, some of our ethical duties do not *consist* in the pursuit of ends. Those that do not consist in this kind of pursuit are all negative or limiting: they forbid us to do things incompatible with our nature as moral animals or mere moral beings. The justification for calling them ethical is that, in fulfilling them, we "preserve ourselves in the perfection of our nature"—and this is something we must do if we pursue our own perfection. As perfect duties they cannot, of course, be justified by the line of reasoning used to justify obligatory *ends*. But, as the account I have given indicates, Kant thinks they are easily and directly justified by reference to the categorical imperative. Kant's arguments against self-murder, carnal self-defilement, and the immoderate use of food and drink parallel his argument against suicide in the *Groundwork*: since such vices are contrary to nature's purposes, the maxim of committing them *could not be* a universal law of nature. His arguments for the duties of refraining from lying, avarice, and false humility are not developed very clearly, but presumably he thinks they can be inferred from *C3* or *C2*. These vices are not, he says, compatible with the "dignity of humanity in our person"; and lying springs from a purpose (or maxim) that is "directly opposed to the natural purposiveness of the power of communicating one's thoughts."[21]

3. *The Happiness of Others as an Obligatory End*

The ethical duty of promoting the happiness of others consists, Kant says, in making others' ends one's own, "in so far as these ends are only not immoral."[22] If we think of immoral ends as those contrary to nature's purposes, this account is not circular, but it is certainly inexact. Kant is clearly not implying that if marrying Sarah is Tom's end, I have the ethical duty of pursuing this end myself. His point, rather, is that I should make it my end to help others realize their ends. In particular, I should be "beneficent": I should seek "to promote, according to [my] means, the happiness of others who are in need, and this without the hope of gaining anything by it."[23] Beneficence thus understood is "practical benevolence"; and it is (or appears to be) the principal ingredient in the ethical duty of promoting the happiness of others.

In line with the argument he gave in the *Groundwork*[24] Kant claims that "the proof that beneficence is a duty follows from the fact that our self-love cannot be divorced from our need of being loved by others (*i.e.* of receiving help from them when we are in need), so that we make ourselves an end for others. Now our maxim cannot be obligatory [for others] unless it qualifies as a universal law and so contains the will to make other men our ends too. The happiness of others, is, therefore, an end which is also a duty."[25] Since Kant offers this argument with confidence and little elaboration, he must believe that it contains a sound line of reasoning. Our task is to clarify the reasoning and then evaluate it.

Perhaps the first thing to say about Kant's argument is that it appears to derive a duty from a psychological fact concerning "our" need of being loved by others. Yet if the derivation is to have any plausibility at all, the "we" in question must be rational beings, or human beings to the extent that they are rational. Since Kant defines obligation in relation to what rational beings necessarily do, his argument here would seem to involve (or require) an inference from some necessary fact about the psychology of rational beings to the conclusion that beneficence is a duty, that is, that rational beings are necessarily beneficent.

The next point to make about the argument is that, if the *we* in question is all rational beings, there must be some maxim relating to self-love that all rational beings necessarily have. What is this maxim? The penultimate sentence suggests that this maxim is such that, if it expresses our will, we shall be committed to making other men our end. Yet what maxim could have this property? Two possibilities come to mind:

1. Other men shall make me their end.
2. If I need help, other men shall help me.

If these maxims express our will as *rational* beings, they express universal laws. But a universal law cannot merely concern my relation to others; it must equally concern others' relation to me. As Kant points out elsewhere, "since all *other* men with the exception of myself would not be *all* men, . . . the maxim would not then have the universality of a law."[26] The universal law expressed by 1 and 2 must therefore have the sense, respectively, of 3 and 4:

3. All men shall make other men their end.
4. If anyone needs help, all others shall help him.

Since 1 and 2 express our will as rational beings, so do 3 and 4. But 3 and 4 "contain the will to make other men our ends." Thus, 1 and 2 express our will to make other men our ends. Since this will has the status of universal law, we have an obligation, as imperfectly rational beings, to make other men our ends and to help them if they need help.

Understood this way, Kant's argument seems weak in two places. The first weakness concerns the maxims 1 and 2: it is not entirely clear why we should suppose that these maxims express the will of a rational being. I think, however, that Kant would clarify this point as follows. As an autonomous agent, a rational being necessarily wills his own happiness or well-being. But a necessary condition of realizing this end in a world like ours is that other people make him their end, or help him when he needs help. Since a rational being necessarily wills what he knows to be necessary for the realization of his ends, he thus wills that others make him their end, or at least help him when he needs help. Consequently, a rational being (or a human being to the extent that he is rational) necessarily accepts the maxims 1 and 2.

In the *Groundwork* Kant asserts that "*one* end that can be presupposed in all rational beings (so far as they are dependent beings to whom imperatives can apply) . . . [is that] of happiness"; they have this end, he says, "by a natural necessity."[27] Although the point is not absolutely certain, he would presumably also accept the principle that a rational being necessarily wills what he knows to be necessary for realizing his ends. If this is right, he would no doubt accept the reasoning in my last paragraph. It seems to me that his assertion about happiness and the principle about willing are highly plausible, but that a rational being need not therefore accept maxims as strong as 1 and 2. The difficulty is simply that the future happiness of any one person is not actually dependent on the benevolent attitude toward him of *everyone* else. It is conceivable that my future happiness will depend on the beneficent action of an obscure beggar now living in Ceylon, but there is no good reason to suppose that I will actually require his help. If I am rational and motivated solely by self-interest, I might reasonably will that anyone who can contribute to my happiness shall will to do so, but this volition would not require *everyone* to make me their end.

The other weakness of Kant's argument is, I believe, fatal. Even if all rational beings do accept the maxims 1 and 2, it remains to be shown that they thereby will to make other people their ends, or will to help them when they need help. Kant claims, of course, that a universally valid maxim—one accepted by all rational beings—expresses a universal law, but this claim needs an argument that Kant has not supplied. On the face of it, there is no reason why a rational being who wills that other people make him their end could not consistently will to ignore other people in need of his help. From a logical point of view, the following complex volition does not seem objectionable:

> Other people shall make me their end but I will not make anyone else my end.

This complex volition seems consistent because, in willing not to make others one's end, one does not thereby will that they take the same attitude to oneself. It is one thing to believe, as Kant obviously does, that every maxim acceptable to a rational being expresses (or corresponds to) a strictly universal practical law, but quite another thing to prove that this belief is true.

An obvious line of objection might be raised against me at this point. Even though the complex volition described above is logically consistent, it does not follow that a rational being who wills his own happiness could reasonably accept it. As Socrates argued in the *Republic*, anyone who expects others to help him when he needs help had better show others that he is prepared to do the same for them: a perfectly selfish person is bound to earn the enmity of others. Thus, if a rational being considered "how things would stand" if he adopted the selfish volition (or maxim) described above, he would see that his aim of being happy, which requires that he be helped when he needs help, could not then be realized. The selfish volition is therefore rationally objectionable even though it is logically consistent.

Though plausible at first sight, the objection does not really succeed. It may be true that people will hesitate to help a person whom they regard as utterly selfish and unfeeling toward them, but a person who accepts the selfish maxim given above does not have to flaunt his indifference to the welfare of others. In fact, he can adopt the maxim of gaining others' regard by making them think he regards them as his ends. To realize his aim of being happy, he must be careful not to *appear* indifferent to the needs of others, but this will not require him actually to make their happiness his end. Occasional acts of beneficence are entirely compatible with thoroughgoing selfishness.

At a later stage of his "Doctrine of Virtue" Kant offers a more elaborate argument for the duty of beneficence, which lacks the drawbacks of the one just considered. The argument is this: "Every man who finds himself in need wishes to be helped by other men. But if he lets his maxim of not willing to help others in turn when they are in need become public, *i.e.* makes this a universal permissive law, then everyone would likewise deny him assistance when he needs it, or at least would be entitled to. Hence the maxim of self-interest contradicts itself when it is made law—that is, it is contrary to duty. Consequently, the maxim of common interest—of beneficence toward the needy—is a universal duty of men. . . ."[28] The key line of reasoning here can be set down as follows:

1. If it is morally permissible for me to act on the maxim of not helping others who need my help, then I can consistently will that this maxim should become a universal law of nature.
2. But if this maxim were a universal law of nature, others would not help me if I needed help.
3. As a rational being, I cannot will that others do not help me if I need help.
4. Therefore, I cannot consistently will that the maxim in question should become a universal law.
5. Consequently, it is *not* morally permissible for me to act on the maxim of not helping others who need my help.
6. Thus, I have a duty of beneficence toward the needy.

Although the move from 5 to 6 is objectionable, 5 does appear to follow from the preceding premises. If we accept the principles of volitional consistency set forth in Chapter II, section 2, we must grant that 4 follows from 1, 2, and 3. Assertion 5 then follows from 4 and 1. Thus, the first part of the argument seems valid. But is it sound? Are the premises acceptable? Premise 1 is an immediate consequence of Kant's formula $C2$, which, for the sake of argument, we may allow to be acceptable. Premise 3 is adequately supported by the reasoning I gave in connection with Kant's first argument for the duty of beneficence. Premise 2 thus appears to be crucial. If this premise is acceptable, we may regard at least the first part of Kant's argument as sound.

Premise 2 is related to the point of weakness in Kant's first argument, but it does not require us to suppose that any rational being who wills to be helped by others necessarily wills to help others. It merely specifies a consequence of a certain maxim's becoming a universal law. To evaluate this premise we must, of course, answer a question that arises in connection with Kant's first argument—namely, "What universal law of nature does my maxim of not helping others who need my help become?" Kant pretty clearly supposes that the answer is "No one helps others who need his help"—and this answer would render the premise true. But if, as I have supposed in earlier chapters, the universal law of nature that a maxim is to be viewed as becoming is a generalization of that maxim, it is arguable that the law should be "No one with the characteristics I have helps others who need his help." This answer would not confirm the premise, because only I have the characteristics I have, and so only I must be supposed not to help others who need my help. However this may be, the notion of a maxim's becoming a universal law is Kant's, and he clearly thinks that the law in question is "No one helps others who need his help." If we allow that a universal law in Kant's sense is a practical principle, his view is highly plausible, for it would appear that a maxim could "become" a universal law of nature only by becoming the maxim of all beings in nature capable of reason. Clearly, if everyone had the maxim of not helping others who need their help, no one would help me if I needed help.

In view of these considerations I think it is fair to say that the first part of Kant's argument is sound: given that *C2* is acceptable, Kant's assertion 5 is a logical consequence of acceptable premises. Unfortunately, the conclusion he is after here—namely 6—does not follow from 5. The latter tells us that we are morally forbidden to act on a certain maxim, but this does not imply that we ought to pursue any particular end. Kant makes it clear, as we have seen, that we are always obligated or forbidden to act on some maxim or other, so a duty of beneficence is a duty to act on some maxim of ends. But as I pointed out in the last section, a duty to act on some particular maxim cannot be inferred (at least directly) from a duty *not* to act on some other maxim. Thus, if we are forbidden to act on the maxim of not helping others who need our help, it does not *follow* that we are obligated to act on the maxim of helping others who need our help. As far as logic is concerned, the maxim we are obligated to act on could perfectly well be "I will do whatever maximizes human happiness."

Although 6 does not follow from 5, Kant does offer a reason for accepting 6. He says that beneficence toward the needy is a universal duty of men for this reason: "Men are to be considered fellow-men—that is, rational beings with needs, united by nature in one dwelling place for the purpose of helping one another."[29] If we assume that "nature's purpose" for uniting men in one dwelling place is to have them help one another, then we may infer, by virtue of his typic for the moral law, that men have a duty to help one another. Of course, if we find this kind of appeal to nature's purposes dubious or downright unacceptable (as I do), this reason for accepting 6 will carry little weight with us.

As in the case of our ethical duties to ourselves, Kant embeds our fundamental ethical duty to others in a whole system of ethical duties. His main division of this latter system is into duties of love and duties of respect. His word "love" in this connection means "practical love" or "active benevolence . . . that has to do with the maxims of actions."[30] A distinctive feature of a duty of love is that, in fulfilling it, we also obligate others; at the least, we generate a duty of gratitude in them. Kant says that duties of love are all imperfect, of wide obligation; and he subdivides them into duties of beneficence, gratitude, and sympathy. Duties of respect, on the other hand, do not create, by their fulfillment, any further obligations. Any human being has a *right* to our respect. (This is the only *ethical* right that Kant recognizes.) All duties of respect are negative; they are all based on the principle of not exalting ourself above others. The crucial vices to avoid here are those of pride, calumny, and mockery. Our ethical duties to avoid these vices are of narrow obligation; they appear to be perfect duties.

4. Perfect and Imperfect Duties

As we saw in section 1 of this chapter, Kant claims that ethics goes beyond law (or justice) in prescribing obligatory ends.

As a doctrine of ends, Kant says, ethics "can prescribe only the maxims of actions, not actions themselves. . . . [Consequently] it leaves a play-room (*latitudio*) for free choice in following the law, *i.e.* the law cannot specify precisely what and how much one's actions should do toward the obligatory end."[31]

Thus, while ethics requires us to pursue certain ends, it does not tell us exactly what we must do in particular circumstances as a means to those ends. Nevertheless, Kant warns us that "a wide duty [*i.e.* to pursue certain ends] is not to be taken as a permission to make exceptions to the maxim of actions, but only as a permission to limit one maxim of duty by another (*e.g.* love of one's neighbor in general by love of one's parents)—a permission that actually widens the field for the practice of virtue. As the duty is wider, so man's obligation to action is more imperfect; but the closer to narrow duty (Law) he brings the maxim of observing this duty (in his attitude of will), so much the more perfect is his virtuous action."[32] By speaking of a duty as imperfect, Kant means only that we have a significant degree of freedom in deciding how to comply with it: it does not itself specify *how* we are to act. A perfect duty, on the other hand, does specify a particular action. If, for example, I enter into a just contract that requires me to do a certain thing at a particular time (for example, repay a loan) then I have a perfect duty: a definite task is required of me.

It is tempting to suppose that the distinction between perfect and imperfect duties is not really as sharp as Kant's remarks might suggest. When I have a perfect duty to repay a loan, I certainly have some "play room" for deciding how to comply. I may decide to send a check in the mail, to appear in person and hand over the cash, or to have my lawyer deliver a bank note. Consequently, though I do have a duty to do a certain thing, this "certain thing" is not a specific action that can be performed only in a specific way. In the *Groundwork* Kant defined a perfect duty as one "which allows no exceptions in the interest of inclination,"[33] but this definition does not render his distinction any sharper. Clearly, my duty to pursue obligatory ends does not allow exceptions "in the interest of inclination" either: I always have these obligations. Since perfect duties can be fulfilled in more than one way, it seems reasonable to say that the difference between them and imperfect duties is really one of degree, and that the terms "narrow" and "wide" convey this difference better than "perfect" and "imperfect." A wide duty allows the agent considerable scope in deciding how to comply; a narrow duty limits this scope to a considerable extent. Intuitively speaking, there are only so many ways of paying a debt, but no end to the ways of being beneficent.[34]

I think these observations succeed in showing that a perfect duty is really wider than Kant's remarks suggest, but they do not show that the difference between perfect and imperfect duties is merely one of degree. As we have seen, Kant claims that ethical duties require us to pursue certain ends. But the duty of pursuing an end does not itself specify some action that we must perform. Consequently, such a duty is imperfect: it does not specify "what and how much one's actions should do toward the . . . end." A juridical duty is not imperfect in this way. It may leave some play room for a choice of how to comply, but it does specify a definite action in at least general terms. When I consider the duty of paying a certain debt, I know in general terms what I must do, or what action I must perform; I have only to decide *how* to do it. But when I consider my duty of pursuing or, better, having a certain end, I do not know what I must *do*, even in general terms, until I consider what means are appropriate to that end—and even then I may be in doubt about what I am required to do.

The doubt that may persist here is worth some discussion, because a definite ethical requirement to adopt a certain means to an obligatory end is hard to establish on Kant's theory. Consider the following reasoning, which might occur to me on seeing a blind man attempt to cross a busy street:

1. I ought to pursue the end of helping others who need my help.
2. If I help that blind man cross the street, I shall be pursuing, or helping to realize, this obligatory end.

3. Helping that blind man cross the street is morally permissible; it is not explicitly forbidden by any moral law.
4. Therefore, I ought to help that blind man cross the street.

This reasoning cannot be acceptable to Kant. The premises locate an obligatory end and tell us that one particular action, which is permissible in principle,[35] is an available means to that end. But this is not enough to establish the conclusion. The difficulty is that incompatible actions can be available means to the same end: for example, a very small child may also be trying to cross the street but be in such a position that I could not possibly help both him and the blind man. Since Kant explicitly denies that we can have conflicting duties,[36] he must also deny that we have a moral duty to do something *merely* because it is an available means to an obligatory end.

Even though Kant must reject the reasoning given above, he does not deny that we may be ethically obligated to perform specific actions. In the very passage in which he denies that there can be conflicting obligations, he says that there can be conflicting "*grounds* of obligation." He adds that "when two such grounds conflict with each other, practical philosophy says, not that the stronger obligation takes precedence . . . , but that the stronger *ground of obligation* prevails."[37] Given this passage, we might say that when some particular action contributes to an obligatory end and is morally permissible, there is a ground of obligation for performing it. To this we might add, though no passages in Kant explicitly support the idea, that if we have a ground of obligation for performing an action A but no such ground for doing something incompatible with A, then we have a *derivative* or *specific ethical duty* to do A.

There is another way of deriving specific ethical duties. It seems to be a necessary truth that if one has an obligation to do X and doing X entails doing Y, then one has an obligation to do Y. As we have seen, Kant clearly subscribes to this principle, at least tacitly, for he relies upon it in arguing that our ethical obligation to act out of respect for the categorical imperative entails the more specific obligation to seek our own perfection and the happiness of others. Given this principle, we might reason as follows when we observe a blind person trying to cross a busy street:

1. I ought to pursue the end of helping others who need my help.
2. If, in the circumstances, I do not help that blind man, I shall not be pursuing (but positively neglecting) the obligatory end of helping others who need my help.
3. Therefore, I ought to help that blind man cross the street.

On the assumption that premise 2 affirms that, in the circumstances, pursuing the obligatory end entails, or necessarily requires, helping the blind man, the argument is valid. Although it is not obvious how we could be said to know that a premise like 2 is, in fact, true, we can nevertheless say that, if it is true, we have a specific ethical duty to perform a particular "positive" action.

My remarks in the last two paragraphs make a place in Kant's system for specific, nonnegative, perfect ethical duties, but they do not, of course, fully characterize those duties. To do this, they would have to show us how to deal with "conflicting grounds of obligation." Kant says that when two grounds of obligation conflict, "the stronger ground of obligation prevails," but he never explains how one ground of obligation *can* be stronger than another.[38] In the course of discussing one of the "casuistical questions" that he poses but does not answer in his "Doctrine of Virtue," he calls our attention to one possible conflict among our grounds of obligation. Observing that since nature's purpose in the intercourse of the sexes is procreation, he concludes that "one may not, at least, act contrary to that end." But he then asks whether it may yet be permissible in some cases to "use the sexual power *without regard to that end*." Citing the example of a man having intercourse with a pregnant or sterile wife, he asks whether in this case there is "a permissive law of morally-practical reason, which in the clash of its determining grounds makes permissible something that is not in itself permitted (indulgently, as it were), in order to prevent a still greater transgression?"[39] He does not attempt to answer this question, but he suggests, at least, that in some circumstances we may be entitled on ethical grounds to opt for the lesser of two evils. Presumably he would allow that it may sometimes be our ethical duty to make this kind of choice.

Kant's failure to provide clear directions for resolving conflicts between various grounds of obligation is perhaps explained by a remark he makes toward the end of his "Ethical Doctrine of Elements," which is the principal section of his "Doctrine of Virtue." The remark is that "the duties of men to one another with regard to their *circumstances*" do not call for a special chapter in a system of pure ethics; they can be specified only by the application of pure principles to experience. To deal with the full range of moral problems that arise for us, we thus need, he says, a transition from pure to applied ethics—one that, by "applying the pure principles of duty to cases of experience, would *schematize* these principles, as it were, and present them as ready for morally-practical use." Without such a transition, we shall not have, he adds, a "complete exposition" of our system of ethics.[40] Unfortunately, he does not include such a transition in his "Doctrine of Virtue."

Although the metaphysics of morals, in Kant's technical sense, is properly restricted to a priori principles, he himself admits that the system of juridical and ethical duties he presents in his *Metaphysics of Morals* is not entirely pure. As he says in his introduction, he "will often have to take as [his] subject the particular *nature* of man, which is known only by experience, to show in it the implications of the universal moral principles."[41] The "impurity" of the system he actually presents is obvious: his prohibitions concerning "carnal self-defilement" and "the immoderate use of food and drink" are plainly based on his conception of man's nature as an animal being. This impurity was also present in the *Groundwork*, for his doctrine of the typic for the moral law was used to show us how the pure versions of the moral law can be applied to our experience. Thus the transition he deems necessary for the complete exposition of his system is at least partly contained in his works on the metaphysics of morals.

If we consider some of the questions that Kant thinks can be resolved only by developing a transition between pure and applied ethics, we shall see that the transition he is thinking of must be far more extensive than what he supplies in his *Metaphysics of Morals*. Kant asks: "How should one behave . . . to men who are morally pure or depraved? to the cultivated or the crude? to the learned or the ignorant . . . ? How should men be treated by virtue of their differences in rank, age, sex, health, prosperity or poverty and so forth?"⁴² To answer these questions we must do more, it seems, than merely consider human nature or nature's purposes for creatures like us. But it is not clear what other considerations he thinks we can appeal to. The exposition of his system is simply not complete.

5. *On the General Structure of Kant's Moral Theory*

In the preceding sections of this chapter I have been mainly concerned with various details of Kant's moral theory. I now want to make some remarks about the general structure of his theory—specifically, about the role or function in it of the categorical imperative.

Although Kant makes it abundantly clear, both in the *Groundwork* and in the *Metaphysics of Morals*, that he is specifically concerned with the metaphysics of his subject, most readers nevertheless assume that his categorical imperative is intended to provide a means of identifying our moral duties in specific circumstances. We have seen that this assumption is incorrect. As the "first principle" of morals, the categorical imperative is properly used to derive a complex system of juridical and ethical duties, which must in some way be applied to cases that arise in experience. This conception of the categorical imperative has great theoretical importance, for it shows us that even if Kant's arguments are invariably successful, his system of pure (or relatively pure) morality resolves just one of two key problems that moral philosophers continue to struggle with.

One of these problems, the one that Kant purports to solve with his categorical imperative, concerns the basis, or foundation, of the system of duties recognized by what Kant calls "the ordinary moral consciousness." As Kant emphasizes, ordinary people commonly recognize and agree upon a wide class of moral duties, such as promise keeping, truth telling, self-perfection, and beneficence to others. But what rational basis do we have for these duties? Why should we accept them as binding on us? Kant's answer is that these duties are founded on (and so inferable from) the moral law, which is (as he says in the *Groundwork*) the only imperative that is truly unqualified or categorical. In his view, when we fully understand this law and realize why it is binding on us as imperfectly rational beings, we have a rational basis for working out the subordinate laws of justice and virtue, and thus for systematizing and justifying the duties of justice and virtue, that we commonly recognize. With the aid of his principle, we can give a rational account of these various duties, showing how they are related to one another, how they are related to various kinds of moral "legislation," and why we are rationally committed to recognizing them.

The other problem, the one that Kant does not even attempt to resolve in the works we have studied, concerns what W. D. Ross called our "absolute" duties. Even if we have fully resolved the problem of systematization and justification mentioned above, we still face a difficult problem about what we are morally required to do in specific circumstances. This problem arises from the fact that the duties we commonly recognize—our *"prima facie* duties" in Ross's terminology— occasionally enjoin physically incompatible actions. Though Kant seems to speak of "conflicting grounds of obligation" only in connection with duties of virtue, the problem is really a general one that arises equally for duties of justice. It is not just that a duty like self-perfection may sometimes conflict with, say, the duty of benevolence, but that a single duty (for example, that of keeping promises) may impose incompatible requirements in a particular case. I may have promised to help Jones repair his roof on the first sunny day but also, being fully confident that it will rain tomorrow, have promised to take my children to the movies that day. Everything considered, what must I do if it is sunny tomorrow—help Jones with his roof and break my promise to the children, or take them to the movies and break my promise to Jones? Or should I do neither? The difficulty here is that it is totally unclear what principles I should appeal to in solving the problem. It would be highly agreeable to think that the categorical imperative could help with this kind of case, but as Kant himself admits, a pure (or relatively pure) principle cannot itself resolve an issue in applied ethics. Apart from this, it seems obvious that numerous maxims concerned with conflicting promises could be willed to become universal laws: for example, "In cases of conflicting promises, the first takes precedence over the others" or "In cases of conflicting promises, do whatever will maximize the happiness of the deserving parties involved."

I mentioned earlier that, in Kant's view, "a conflict of duties and obligations is inconceivable." He supports this view by saying that "the concepts of duty and obligation as such express the objective practical *necessity* of certain actions, and two conflicting rules cannot both be necessary at the same time: if it is our duty to act according to one of these rules, then to act according to the opposite one is not our duty and is even contrary to duty. . . ." He admits, however, that there can be "two *grounds* of obligation . . . both present in one agent and in the rule he lays down for himself. In this case one or another of these grounds is not sufficient to oblige him . . . and is therefore not a duty."[43] These remarks are extremely puzzling in the light of Kant's major claims about morality. If, as he says elsewhere, I have an obligation (a duty of justice) to keep my promises, then it would seem that I have a duty both to help Jones and to take my children to the movies, for I have promised to do both these things. But these duties or requirements conflict in the sense that it is physically impossible for me to fulfill both. To be consistent it would appear that Kant must either deny that we have an unqualified duty to keep our promises or else allow that our duties (as opposed to our "grounds of obligation") may indeed conflict.

I really have no idea how Kant would attempt to resolve this kind of problem. The matter is serious, because there is no doubt that the duties Kant explicitly recognizes often do conflict in particular cases. It might be argued that the actual duties of virtue and justice implied by the categorical imperative involve qualifications that Kant did not bother to formulate, but this strategy does not seem very promising: to my knowledge, at least, no philosopher has ever formulated a plausible system of ethical and juridical duties that could not possibly conflict in particular cases.[44] For my part, the most promising strategy for Kant to adopt is to regard his system of moral duties as *prima facie* duties in Ross's sense. His basic theoretical contribution to moral philosophy (assuming that it is sound) would then be his derivation of the total system of such duties from the categorical imperative. This would leave him with the stubborn problem of providing an acceptable rationale for identifying a person's "absolute duties" in particular circumstances, but this problem has not, at least to my knowledge, been solved by anyone else.

The next matter I wish to discuss concerns Kant's view of the relation between the kind of moral obligation immediately established by the categorical imperative and the more specific forms of obligation associated with justice and virtue. In the *Groundwork* Kant makes it clear that the categorical imperative yields what might be called a general principle of morality. The principle associated with $C1$ is this:

> It is morally permissible for s to act on m just when s could consistently will that m should become a universal law.

As we have seen, this principle can be viewed as providing two distinguishable tests for a person's maxim:

1. Could the maxim possibly *become* a universal law?
2. Given that the maxim could become a universal law, could the agent consistently *will* that it should become such a law?

Since Kant contends that the first test may establish "stricter or narrower" duties and the second "broader (meritorious)" duties, and since he holds that the former duties are juridical and the latter are ethical, it seems reasonable to conclude that he would accept the following as derivative principles:

D1: It is juridically permissible for s to act on m just when m could become a universal law.

D2: It is ethically permissible for s to act on m just when, given that m could actually become a universal law, s could consistently will that m should become such a law.

If these principles are accepted, the unity of Kant's system of morals is exhibited by the following principles, which follow from D1 and D2:

D3: It is morally permissible for s to act on m just when it is both juridically permissible and ethically permissible for s to act on m.

D4: It is morally obligatory for s not to act on m just when it is either juridically obligatory or ethically obligatory for s not to act on m.

It seems to me that these last two principles provide an accurate view of the relation between moral obligation (and permission) as Kant describes it in the *Groundwork* and the ethical and juridical obligations (and permissions) that Kant develops in the *Metaphysics of Morals*. The general idea is that we are morally permitted to do something (that is, act on some maxim) just when there is no moral prohibition, either juridical or ethical, against doing it; and we are morally forbidden to do something just when there is a moral prohibition, either juridical or ethical, against doing it. The principle D4 does not, it is true, explicitly cover positive moral obligations that require us to act on some maxim; but as I pointed out when criticizing one of Kant's attempted derivations of a positive duty, there is no plausible way of deriving such duties from C1. We may use C1 to show that we have an obligation *not* to act on a certain maxim, but we may not thereby infer, at least on logical grounds, that we have an obligation to act on some other maxim. If a defender of Kant should disagree with me on this point, he can regard *D4* as the principle from which positive moral duties are derivable.

What about the principles *D1* and *D2*? Are they also acceptable? I think they would be acceptable if Kant held to the view of juridical and ethical duty that he expressed in his introduction to the *Metaphysics of Morals*—namely, that juridical duties are all perfect, of narrow obligation, while ethical duties are all imperfect, of wide obligation. If Kant held to this view, the principle *D2* would be particularly valuable, for it provides a very simple means of deriving ethical duties from the categorical imperative.

When I introduced Kant's approach to ethics, I outlined a fairly complicated strategy for deriving ethical obligations. Beginning with his claim that a virtuous action is distinguished by being performed for the moral motive (that is, to comply with the requirements of the moral law) I identified the primary ethical duties by considering what specific ends a person must pursue if he is to implement this motive in his actions (see section 1 of this chapter). This complicated strategy for identifying our ethical duties would not be necessary if *D2* were a fully satisfactory principle.

As it happens, neither *D1* nor *D2* can be regarded as satisfactory when the details of the *Metaphysics of Morals* are taken into account. Although Kant begins by claiming that ethical duties are imperfect, of wide obligation, he ends up arguing that we have perfect ethical duties both to ourselves and to others. These perfect duties are all negative, but they are perfect nevertheless—and the maxims of actions disallowed by them could not *become* universal laws. (Recall Kant's argument against suicide.) Similarly, although Kant begins by claiming that juridical duties are invariably perfect and derivable by the first test implicit in *D1*, he eventually argues, when he develops his conception of the original contract, that certain juridical laws can be considered just (and therefore duty-generating) only when they could be accepted, or "willed," by all the people subject to it. Kant's remarks on this

matter make it clear that his second test, the one implicit in
D2, is needed to establish at least some duties of justice. Thus,
although Kant starts out with a view of ethical and juridical
obligations for which *D1* and *D2* appear to be satisfactory
principles, he ends up with a more complicated view for
which they fail.

It might be suggested that even though *D1* and *D2* are not
compatible with Kant's final view of ethical and juridical obligations, the tests they contain may still be put to good use if
they are applied to the right sort of maxim. Generally speaking, two kinds of maxims have a special significance for
ethics. One kind might be called (for want of a better word)
"egocentric," for they do not contain any reference to another
person. An example of such a maxim is "If my life becomes
utterly gloomy and unpleasant, I will end it." Since duties of
justice always concern our relation to others, any duty established by applying the first test to an egocentric maxim
should count as ethical. For this reason, all perfect duties to
oneself may reasonably count as ethical even though they are
established by the first test. The other kind of maxim having a
marked ethical import includes what Kant calls "maxims of
ends." Unlike the maxims associated with duties of justice,
these maxims do not prescribe "external" actions as means to
ends; rather, they prescribe the adoption of ends either for
their own sake (such as the end of doing one's duty) or for the
sake of some high-order end. If, by applying one of Kant's
tests to a maxim of this kind, a duty is identified, it is reasonable to count that duty as ethical.

These considerations no doubt improve our understanding
of Kant's conception of ethical and juridical duties, but they
are not really sufficient to establish a sharp distinction between those kinds of duties. For one thing, it is not obvious
that the maxims associated with our perfect duties to ourselves must be fully egocentric in the sense described. The
duty to avoid "carnal self-defilement" is a perfect ethical
duty; yet it would certainly seem that acts prohibited by this
duty might well involve another person. Again, if some juridical laws *must* satisfy the condition of being in principle ac-

ceptable to, or willable by, all the members of some community, then it is at least doubtful that only ethical duties are associated with maxims of ends. It seems to me that even if we set aside all duties involving particular circumstances (that is, all absolute duties in Ross's sense) we shall not be able to discover any purely formal way of distinguishing all the ethical and juridical duties that Kant eventually recognizes. The strategies he begins with are too simple, or too idealized, to accommodate the variety of his final system.

Notes

Chapter I

[1] *Groundwork*, 393; trans. H. J. Paton, *Groundwork of the Metaphysic of Morals* (New York, 1964), p. 61.

[2] *Critique of Practical Reason*, 62; trans. L. W. Beck, *Critique of Practical Reason* (New York, 1956), p. 63.

[3] For a discussion of the most common utilitarian formulas for distribution, see Ronald J. Glossop, "Is Hume a 'Classical Utilitarian'?" *Hume Studies*, 2, no. 1 (1976): 1-16.

[4] *Groundwork*, 396; trans. L. W. Beck, *Foundations of the Metaphysics of Morals* (New York, 1959), p. 12.

[5] Alasdair MacIntyre, *A Short History of Ethics* (New York, 1966), p. 192.

[6] I discuss this matter in chap. VI, sec. 2.

[7] *Groundwork*, 398; Beck, p. 14.

[8] Ibid.

[9] See *Groundwork*, 396, where Kant says that the purpose of doing one's duty "restricts in many ways—indeed can reduce to less than nothing—the achievement of the . . . conditional duty, happiness" (Beck, p. 12). See also *Religion Within the Limits of Reason Alone*, trans. T. M. Greene and H. H. Hudson (New York, 1969), note to p. 3, where Kant says that the duty of furthering the happiness of others is only "conditional" because every act must "be weighed according to the moral law before it can be directed to the happiness of others."

[10] *Groundwork*, 400; Beck, p. 16.

[11] I have defended this conception of a reason for action in my book, *Reason and Action* (Dordrecht, Holland, 1977), pp. 61-65.

[12] *Critique of Practical Reason*, 19; Beck, p. 17.

[13] See my *Reason and Action*, pp. 63f., 156f., 165.

[14] As one might expect, there are exceptions to this flat-footed claim. For a thorough discussion of the contrast between "shall" and "will," see Wilson Follet, *Modern American Usage* (New York, 1966), appendix 1.

[15] *Critique of Practical Reason*, 19; Beck, p. 17.

[16] *Metaphysics of Morals*, 382; trans. Mary J. Gregor, *"The Doctrine of Virtue": Part II of the "Metaphysics of Morals"* (New York, 1964), p. 40.

[17] One might think that the maxim Kant mentions in discussing the example of suicide in *Groundwork*, 422, refutes my claim about the logical form of a maxim. The maxim he mentions is "From self-love I make it my principle to shorten my life if its continuance threatens more evil than it promises pleasure" (Paton, p. 89). Yet the principle mentioned within this supposed maxim fills the bill for what he elsewhere calls a maxim, and it is clearly a conditional practical principle whose tacit universality attaches to time or cir-

cumstances. Note that to make his treatment of the example plausible, Kant incorporates into the maxim the purpose or intention that, if I am right, should be viewed as generating the maxim. Also note that the maxim described in his second example (*Groundwork*, 422) is a universal conditional that does not contain any reference to the purpose that might be taken to generate it.

[18] *Critique of Practical Reason*, 28; Beck, p. 28.

[19] *Groundwork*, 427; Beck, p. 45.

[20] Ibid., 400; Beck, p. 16.

[21] I discuss the concept of volition in *Reason and Action*, pp. 65–73.

[22] *Groundwork*, 400; Beck, p. 16.

[23] See fn. 12 above.

[24] *Groundwork*, 401; Beck, p. 27.

[25] Although a maxim is a volitional statement, the general statement corresponding to it is not: if true, the general statement expresses a descriptive law. For future reference, note that when I speak of the "generalization" of a maxim, I mean, strictly speaking, the general statement corresponding to the maxim.

[26] *Critique of Practical Reason*, 27; Beck, p. 27.

[27] *Groundwork*, 401; Beck, p. 17.

[28] See *Critique of Practical Reason*, chap. 3.

[29] *Groundwork*, 402; Paton, p. 70.

[30] Ibid.

[31] Ibid., 421; Paton, p. 88.

[32] Ibid., 424; Paton, p. 91.

[33] *Metaphysics of Morals*, 221; Gregor, p. 20.

[34] See W. D. Ross, *The Right and the Good* (Oxford, 1930), chap. 2. Here I ignore the problems generated by Ross's distinction between *prima facie* and absolute duties. I comment on these problems in chap. VI, sec. 4.

[35] See the last part of chap. III, sec. 3.

Chapter II

[1] *Groundwork*, 413; trans. L. W. Beck, *Foundations of the Metaphysics of Morals* (New York, 1959), p. 30.

[2] Ibid., 413; Beck, p. 31.

[3] Ibid., 415; Beck, p. 32.

[4] Ibid., 416; Beck, p. 34.

[5] Ibid., 418; Beck, p. 35.

[6] Ibid., 418; Beck, pp. 35f.

[7] Ibid., 418; Beck, p. 36.

[8] Ibid., 419; Beck, p. 37.

[9] Ibid.

[10] Ibid.

[11] Ibid., 420; Beck, p. 37.

[12] Ibid., 420f.; Beck, p. 38.

¹³ *Critique of Practical Reason*, 21; trans. L. W. Beck, *Critique of Practical Reason* (New York, 1956), p. 191.

¹⁴ *Groundwork*, 421; Beck, p. 39.

¹⁵ *Metaphysics of Morals*, 221; trans. Mary J. Gregor, *"The Doctrine of Virtue": Part II of the "Metaphysics of Morals"* (New York, 1964), p. 20. See also *Groundwork*, 440; Beck, p. 58.

¹⁶ In this book I am using the S-operator a little carelessly, for my purposes do not require a great deal of precision. According to the more exact account I give in *Reason and Action* (Dordrecht, Holland, 1977), pp. 144-158, the S-operator yields a statement expressing an intention only when it is prefixed to an indicative sentence in the future tense.

¹⁷ *Groundwork*, 417; Beck, p. 34.

¹⁸ For a detailed discussion of this and other forms of volitional consistency, see my *Reason and Action*, pp. 144-158. I might add that, though I find the S-operator useful for various purposes, I actually believe that it (or some equivalent) is not positively needed to clarify the principles of volitional consistency and that these principles are, in fact, no different from the familiar principles of assertoric consistency. For details, see the pages I have referred to in *Reason and Action*.

¹⁹ See *Reason and Action*, chap. 4.

²⁰ *Metaphysics of Morals*, pt. 2, 385; Gregor, p. 44.

²¹ *Critique of Practical Reason*, 67-71; Beck, pp. 70-74.

²² *Groundwork*, 422; trans. H. J. Paton, *Groundwork of the Metaphysic of Morals* (New York, n.d.), p. 90.

²³ *Groundwork*, 422; Paton, p. 89.

²⁴ *Critique of Judgment*, 423; trans. J. C. Meredith, *Kant's Critique of Judgment* (Oxford, 1952), pt. 2, p. 66.

²⁵ *Groundwork*, 423; Beck, pp. 40f.

²⁶ See chap. VI, sec. 2.

²⁷ *Groundwork*, 423; Beck, p. 41.

²⁸ Ibid., 422; Beck, p. 39.

²⁹ *Critique of Practical Reason*, 69; Beck, p. 72.

³⁰ Ibid., 70; Beck, p. 73.

³¹ A problem worth thinking about arises here: If we need a typic for the moral law because we have no direct access to the domain of perfectly rational beings, how can Kant's typic, which requires us to view nature as a rational system, possibly be comprehensible to us? It would appear that we can view nature as a rational, teleological system only if we know what rationality is. I am not exactly sure how Kant would resolve this problem. Perhaps he would say that we need a typic for the moral law, not because we don't directly know what rationality is, but because we don't directly know "how things would stand" in the intelligible world of rational beings if a certain maxim were a law of that world.

³² A classic statement of these problems can be found in Nelson Goodman, *Fact, Fiction, and Forecast*, 2nd ed. (New York, 1965), pp. 3-30. Another rele-

vant discussion is Nicholas Rescher, "Belief Contravening Suppositions," *Philosophical Review* 70 (1961): 176-196.

[33] *Critique of Practical Reason*, 69; Beck, p. 72.

[34] For a discussion of the metaphysical question of whether it is advisable to include events among the furniture of the world, see my *Reason and Action*, pp. 26-49.

[35] The practice of speaking of actions as having various properties only "under certain descriptions" seems to have been introduced into recent philosophy by G.E.M. Anscombe in *Intention* (Oxford, 1959), p. 65.

[36] *Metaphysics of Morals*, 224; Gregor, p. 24.

[37] Ibid., 467f.; Gregor, pp. 139f.

[38] See W. D. Ross, *The Right and the Good* (Oxford, 1930), chap. 2.

[39] See sec. 3 of this chapter.

Chapter III

[1] *Groundwork*, 427; trans. H. J. Paton, *Groundwork of the Metaphysic of Morals* (New York, n.d.), p. 95.

[2] Ibid., 402; Beck, p. 70.

[3] Ibid., 429; Beck, p. 96.

[4] *Critique of Judgment*, 371; trans. J. C. Meredith, *Critique of Judgment*, pt. 2, p. 18.

[5] Ibid., 371; Meredith, p. 19.

[6] Ibid., 435; Meredith, p. 99.

[7] I speak of man as a "perverse" creature, but a stronger adjective would seem appropriate to anyone who appreciates the point of Swift's description of the race of Yahoos or of the conversation Voltaire relates in chapter 21 of *Candide*.

[8] Recall Xenophanes' remark that "if oxen and horses and lions had hands, and could draw with their hands and do what man can do, horses would draw the gods in the shape of horses, oxen in the shape of oxen, each giving the gods bodies similar to their own." I quote from J. M. Robinson's translation in *An Introduction to Early Greek Philosophy* (New York, 1968), p. 52.

[9] *Groundwork*, 429f.; trans. L. W. Beck, *Foundations of the Metaphysics of Morals* (New York, 1959), p. 47.

[10] Ibid.

[11] *Groundwork*, 437; Paton, p. 105.

[12] Ibid.

[13] Ibid.

[14] Ibid., 430; Paton, p. 97.

[15] Ibid., 430; Paton, p. 98.

[16] As it happens, a permissible or legitimate end cannot really be defined this way. I discuss the matter fully in chap. IV, sec. 2.

[17] See chap. VI, sec. 4 below.

[18] *Groundwork*, 430; Paton, p. 98.

[19] *Groundwork*, 431ff.; Beck, pp. 49ff.

[20] See chap. I, sec. 5.
[21] *Groundwork*, 431; Paton, pp. 98f.
[22] Ibid., 432f.; Paton, p. 100.
[23] Ibid.
[24] Ibid.
[25] Ibid., 440; Paton, p. 108.
[26] *Paton*, p. 34.
[27] *Groundwork*, 439; Paton, p. 107.
[28] See chap. II, sec. 4.
[29] See chap. I, sec. 5.
[30] See the middle of sec. 4, chap. I.
[31] See the first part of sec. 5, chap. I.
[32] See chap. I, sec. 3.
[33] *Critique of Practical Reason*, 39; trans. L. W. Beck, *Critique of Practical Reason* (New York, 1956), p. 41.
[34] *Groundwork*, 434; Paton, p. 102.
[35] *Critique of Judgment*, 434; Meredith, pt. 2, p. 99.
[36] *Groundwork*, 439; Beck, p. 57.
[37] *Critique of Practical Reason*, 98; Beck, p. 101.
[38] *Groundwork*, 446; Paton, p. 114.
[39] Ibid., 440; Paton, p. 108.
[40] *Groundwork*, 439; Beck, p. 57.
[41] *Groundwork*, 439f.; Paton, pp. 106f.
[42] Ibid., 393; Paton, p. 61.
[43] Ibid., 446; Paton, p. 117.
[44] Ibid.
[45] Ibid.
[46] *Religion Within the Limits of Reason Alone*, trans. T. M. Greene and H. H. Hudson (New York, 1960), p. 18n.
[47] *Groundwork*, 450f.; Paton, p. 118.
[48] Ibid.
[49] Ibid., 453; Paton, p. 121.
[50] *Critique of Pure Reason*, B232-256; trans. N. K. Smith, *Immanuel Kant's Critique of Pure Reason* (New York, 1961), pp. 218-233.
[51] *Groundwork*, 453; Beck, p. 82.
[52] Ibid., 448; Beck, p. 115.
[53] Though I do not discuss the matter in the text, it is important to note that in the *Critique of Practical Reason* Kant offers a very different justification of our belief in human freedom. In this later work Kant declares that the moral law is a "fact of pure reason" needing "no justifying grounds," and that our consciousness of this fact justifies our belief that our wills are free, because if we ought to do something, we must be able to do it. See *Critique of Practical Reason*, 31f. and 47-50; in Beck, pp. 30f. and 48-51.
[54] I discuss the method of hypotheses in my book, *Rationalism, Empiricism, and Pragmatism* (New York, 1970), pp. 153-178.

[55] See *Critique of Practical Reason*, 50-57; Beck, pp. 52-58. My interpretation here is partly based on Kant's discussion of pure and schematized concepts in his *Critique of Practical Reason*, B176-187.

[56] The ideas sketched in this paragraph are discussed at length in my book, *Reason and Action* (Dordrecht, Holland, 1977), chap. 2.

[57] *Groundwork*, 446; Paton, p. 114.

[58] Ibid.

[59] See *Religion Within the Limits of Reason Alone*, p. 18n.

[60] *Groundwork*, 459f.; Paton, pp. 127f.

[61] For example, see Wilfrid Sellars, "Fatalism and Determinism," in *Freedom and Determinism*, ed. Keith Lehrer (New York, 1966), pp. 141-174. Some of my early views on the subject can be found in my essay, "Abilities, Modalities, and Free Will," *Philosophy and Phenomenological Research* 23 (1963): 397-413.

[62] *Groundwork*, 429; Paton, p. 96.

[63] Ibid., 460; Paton, p. 128.

Chapter IV

[1] *Groundwork*, 433; trans. H. J. Paton, *Groundwork of the Metaphysic of Morals* (New York, n.d.), p. 101.

[2] Ibid., 433; Paton, pp. 100f.

[3] Ibid., p. 439; Paton, p. 106.

[4] Ibid., p. 438; Paton, p. 106.

[5] Ibid.

[6] *Critique of Practical Reason*, 58; trans. L. W. Beck, *Critique of Practical Reason* (New York, 1956), p. 59.

[7] It is a little odd that Kant should speak of "the highest good" here, for he elsewhere describes the highest good as involving happiness in proportion to virtue, and this is not something that *we* can realize through our freedom.

[8] *Critique of Practical Reason*, 109; Beck, p. 113.

[9] Ibid., 110; Beck, p. 114.

[10] The inference here is valid according to the principles of volitional consistency discussed in chap. I.

[11] *Critique of Practical Reason*, 110; Beck, p. 114.

[12] *Groundwork*, 438; Paton, p. 106.

[13] Ibid., 436; Paton, p. 104.

[14] Ibid., 430; Paton, p. 98.

[15] Ibid., 437; Paton, p. 105.

[16] Ibid., 436f.; Paton, pp. 103f.

[17] *Critique of Practical Reason*, 29; Beck, p. 28.

[18] *Groundwork*, 436; Paton, p. 104.

[19] Ibid.

[20] Ibid.

[21] Ibid.

[22] Ibid., 437f.; Paton, p. 105.

[23] See sec. 1 of this chapter.

[24] *Groundwork*, 433; Paton, p. 100.

[25] Ibid., 434; Paton, p. 102.

[26] Ibid., 437; Paton, p. 105.

[27] Ibid., 393; Paton, p. 61.

[28] Ibid. See also chap. I, fn. 9, and chap. V, sec. 7.

[29] *Metaphysics of Morals*, 460; trans. Mary J. Gregor, *"The Doctrine of Virtue": Part II of the "Metaphysics of Morals"* (New York, 1964), p. 130.

[30] Ibid., 423; Gregor, p. 87.

[31] Ibid.

[32] See J. S. Mill's famous discussion of this point in his essay "Nature," included in *The Philosophy of John Stuart Mill*, ed. Marshall Cohen (New York, 1961), pp. 445–488.

[33] The objection is developed by Onora Nell in *Acting on Principle: An Essay on Kantian Ethics* (New York, 1975), p. 76.

[34] See chap. I, sec. 3.

[35] Compare John Rawls's conception of moral philosophy as "the attempt to describe our moral capacity," in Rawls, *A Theory of Justice* (Cambridge, Mass., 1971), pp. 46–53.

[36] See Alan Donagan, *The Theory of Morality* (Chicago, 1977), pp. 66–111. Donagan is concerned with what might be called the traditional moral consciousness, and he tries to show how, in detail, its requirements can be derived from a formula corresponding to *C3*. Donagan's strategy in constructing his derivations turns on establishing what he calls "specificatory premises," which assert that anyone who acts in a particular way forbidden by the traditional moral consciousness is not respecting someone as an end in himself. Though I am very doubtful about the success of Donagan's efforts, I recommend his book to anyone interested in Kant's moral theory.

Chapter V

[1] *Metaphysics of Morals*, 222 (hereafter cited as *MM*); trans. Mary J. Gregor, *"The Doctrine of Virtue": Part II of the "Metaphysics of Morals"* (New York, 1964), p. 21.

[2] Ibid., 219; Gregor, p. 18.

[3] *MM*, 230; trans. John Ladd, *"The Metaphysical Elements of Justice": Part I of the "Metaphysics of Morals"* (New York, 1965), p. 34.

[4] *MM*, 219; Gregor, p. 18.

[5] Ibid., 220; Gregor, p. 19.

[6] Ibid., 219; Gregor, p. 18.

[7] Ibid., 229; Ladd, p. 33.

[8] Ibid., 231; Ladd, p. 35.

[9] Ibid.

[10] Ibid., 380; Gregor, p. 38.

[11] Ibid., 231; Ladd, p. 38.

[12] *MM*, 389; Gregor, p. 49.

[13] *Groundwork*, 424; trans. L. W. Beck, *Foundations of the Metaphysics of Morals* (New York, 1959), pp. 47f.

[14] *MM*, 365; Ladd, p. 132.

[15] Ibid., 231; Ladd, p. 36.

[16] Ibid., 232; Ladd, p. 37.

[17] Ibid.

[18] Ibid., 239; Ladd, p. 45. See fn. 53 to chap. III above.

[19] Ibid., 232; Ladd, p. 36.

[20] Ibid., 234; Ladd, p. 39.

[21] Ibid., 234f.; Ladd, pp. 40f.

[22] Ibid., 235f.; Ladd, p. 41.

[23] Ibid., 236; Ladd, p. 42.

[24] Ibid., 238; Ladd, p. 44.

[25] Kant, *On the Old Saw: That May be Right in Theory But It Won't Work in Practice*, trans. E. B. Ashton (Philadelphia, 1974), p. 60.

[26] Ibid., p. 63.

[27] Ibid., p. 58.

[28] Ibid., p. 59.

[29] Kant, "On a Supposed Right to Tell Lies from Benevolent Motives," in *Critique of Practical Reason and Other Works in Moral Philosophy*, ed. and trans. T. K. Abbott (London, 1909), p. 364.

[30] Ibid., p. 365.

[31] Ibid., p. 363.

[32] Ibid.

[33] *MM*, 239, 245; see also the glossary in Ladd, p. 143.

[34] Cited in Norman E. Bowie and Robert L. Simon, *The Individual and the Political Order* (Englewood Cliffs, N.J., 1977), p. 70.

[35] John Stuart Mill, *On Liberty* (New York: Norton, 1975), p. 11.

[36] *MM*, 311; Ladd, p. 95.

[37] Ibid., 306; Ladd, p. 69.

[38] Ibid., 297; Ladd, p. 68.

[39] Ibid., 249; Ladd, p. 55.

[40] *MM*, 261; translation adapted from W. Hastie, *The Philosophy of Law* (Edinburgh, 1887), p. 86.

[41] *MM*, 311; Ladd, p. 75.

[42] Ibid., 256; Ladd, p. 65.

[43] Ibid., 257; Ladd, p. 66.

[44] Ibid., 307; Ladd, p. 71.

[45] Allen Wood has reminded me that Rousseau's view on this matter was very close to Kant's. See Jean Jacques Rousseau, *The Social Contract*, bk. 1, chap. 9.

[46] *MM*, 261; Hastie, p. 86.

[47] Ibid.

[48] *MM*, 314; Ladd, p. 78.

[49] Ashton, p. 63.

[50] *MM*, 312; Ladd, p. 76.

[51] Ashton, p. 65.

[52] *MM*, 297; Ladd, p. 68.

[53] Ibid., 226; Ladd, p. 93.

[54] Ashton, p. 67.

[55] Ibid., p. 67.

[56] Ibid., p. 65.

[57] Ibid., p. 73.

[58] *MM*, 306; Ladd, p. 71.

[59] Ibid., 312; Ladd, p. 76.

[60] See Kant, "Idea of a Universal History from a Cosmopolitan Point of View" in L. W. Beck, *Kant on History* (New York, 1963), pp. 18-21.

[61] Ashton, p. 60.

[62] Ibid.

[63] *MM*, 331; Ladd, p. 100.

[64] Ibid., 332; Ladd, p. 101.

[65] Ibid., 332; Ladd, p. 102.

[66] Ibid., 332; Ladd, p. 101.

[67] Ibid., 333; Ladd, p. 102.

[68] On this see H.L.A. Hart, *Punishment and Responsibility* (Oxford, 1968), chap. 1.

[69] *MM*, 231; Ladd, p. 36. Italics mine.

[70] Ibid., 313; Ladd, p. 77.

[71] Ibid., 235; Ladd, p. 41.

[72] Ibid., 332; Ladd, p. 101.

[73] Ashton, p. 59.

[74] *MM*, 333; Ladd, p. 102.

[75] *MM*, 460; Gregor, p. 130.

[76] Jeffrie Murphy, *Kant: The Philosophy of Right* (London, 1970), pp. 142f.

[77] *MM*, 307; Ladd, p. 72.

[78] Ashton, p. 57.

[79] Murphy, p. 134.

[80] See John Rawls, *A Theory of Justice* (Cambridge, Mass., 1971), chap. 3.

[81] *MM*, 231; Ladd, p. 36.

Chapter VI

[1] *Metaphysics of Morals*, pt. 2, 379 (hereafter cited as *MM*); trans. Mary J. Gregor, *"The Doctrine of Virtue": Part II of the "Metaphysics of Morals"* (New York, 1964), pp. 36f.

[2] Kant may have thought that *P1* and *P2* are merely equivalent formulas, expressing equivalent rather than identical intentions, but I ignore this possibility here. See chap. I, sec. 5.

[3] *MM*, 390; Gregor, p. 50.

[4] Ibid.

[5] Ibid.

[6] Ibid., 409; Gregor, p. 72.

[7] Ibid., 219; Gregor, p. 18.

[8] Ibid., 385; Gregor, p. 44.

[9] Ibid.

[10] Ibid.

[11] Ibid., 391; Gregor, p. 51.

[12] Ibid., 392; Gregor, p. 53.

[13] Ibid., 408; Gregor, p. 71.

[14] *Groundwork*, 430; trans. H. J. Paton, *Groundwork of the Metaphysic of Morals* (New York, n.d.), pp. 97f.

[15] Ibid., 423; Paton, p. 90.

[16] See my discussion of Kant's Third Example in chap. II, sec. 3.

[17] *MM*, 445; Gregor, p. 112.

[18] Ibid., 419; Gregor, p. 82.

[19] Ibid., 420; Gregor, p. 83.

[20] Ibid.

[21] Ibid., 429; Gregor, p. 93.

[22] Ibid., 387, 449; Gregor, pp. 47, 117.

[23] Ibid., 452; Gregor, p. 120.

[24] See *Groundwork*, 423; Paton, p. 91.

[25] *MM*, 392; Gregor, p. 53.

[26] Ibid., 450; Gregor, p. 118.

[27] *Groundwork*, 415; Paton, p. 83.

[28] *MM*, 453; Gregor, p. 121.

[29] Ibid., 452; Gregor, p. 121.

[30] Ibid., 449; Gregor, p. 117.

[31] Ibid., 389; Gregor, p. 49.

[32] Ibid.

[33] *Groundwork*, 415; Paton, p. 83.

[34] This claim assumes a nonintensional criterion for event identity. For a theory of events built on such an assumption, see my book, *Reason and Action* (Dordrecht, Holland, 1977), chap. 1.

[35] The notion of permissibility in principle is discussed toward the end of sec. 4, chap. II.

[36] *MM*, 223; Gregor, p. 23.

[37] Ibid.

[38] Ibid.

[39] Ibid., 425; Gregor, p. 89.

[40] Ibid., 468; Gregor, p. 139.

[41] Ibid., 216; Gregor, p. 14.

[42] Ibid., 468; Gregor, p. 139.

[43] Ibid., 223; Gregor, p. 23.

[44] In a recent book, *The Theory of Morality* (Chicago, 1977), p. 93, Alan Donagan has claimed that moral duties cannot actually conflict, because of tacit qualifications that they involve. Unfortunately, Donagan does not attempt to spell out these tacit qualifications, so his claim remains essentially conjectural.

Selected Bibliography

English Translations of Pertinent Works by Kant

Lectures on Ethics (*ca.* 1780). Translated by Louis Infield. New York, 1930.

Critique of Pure Reason (1781, 1787). Translated by Norman Kemp Smith. London, 1929.

"Idea for a Universal History from a Cosmopolitan Point of View" (1784). Translated by Lewis W. Beck in *Kant on History*, edited by Lewis W. Beck, pp. 11-26. Indianapolis, Indiana, 1963.

Groundwork of the Metaphysic of Morals (1785). Translated by H. J. Paton. New York, 1964. (This translation was originally published in London in 1948 under the title *The Moral Law*.) Another translation is *Foundations of the Metaphysics of Morals*, translated by Lewis W. Beck, New York, 1959.

Critique of Practical Reason (1788). Translated by Lewis W. Beck. New York, 1956.

Critique of Judgment (1790). Translated by J. C. Meredith. Oxford, 1952.

Religion Within the Limits of Reason Alone (1793). Translated by T. M. Greene and H. H. Hudson. New York, 1969.

On the Old Saw: That Might be Right in Theory, But It Won't Work in Practice (1793). Translated by E. B. Ashton. Philadelphia, 1974.

"The Metaphysical Elements of Justice": Part I of the "Metaphysics of Morals" (1797). Translated by John Ladd. New York, 1955. (Not a complete translation.) An older, but complete translation of this is *The Philosophy of Law*, translated by W. Hastie, Edinburgh, 1887.

"The Doctrine of Virtue": Part II of the "Metaphysics of Morals" (1797). Translated by Mary J. Gregor. New York, 1964.

Commentaries Concerned with Kant's Moral Theory

Beck, Lewis W. *A Commentary on Kant's "Critique of Practical Reason."* Chicago, 1960.

Gregor, Mary J. *Laws of Freedom.* Oxford, 1963.

Murphy, Jeffrie. *Kant: The Philosophy of Right.* New York, 1970.

Nell, Onora. *Acting on Principle: An Essay on Kantian Ethics.* New York, 1975.

Paton, H. J. *The Categorical Imperative.* London, 1947.

Wolff, Robert P. *The Autonomy of Reason: A Commentary on Kant's "Groundwork of the Metaphysics of Morals."* New York, 1973.

Wood, Allen W. *Kant's Moral Religion.* Ithaca, N.Y., 1970.

Works Cited in the Text

Anscombe, G.E.M. *Intention.* Oxford, 1959.

Aune, Bruce. "Abilities, Modalities, and Free Will," *Philosophy and Phenomenological Research* 23 (1963): 397–413.

———. *Rationalism, Empiricism, and Pragmatism.* New York, 1970.

———. *Reason and Action.* Dordrecht, Holland, 1977.

Bowie, Norman E. and Robert L. Simon. *The Individual and the Political Order.* Englewood Cliffs, N.J., 1977.

Donagan, Alan. *The Theory of Morality.* Chicago, 1977.

Glossop, Ronald J. "Is Hume a 'Classical Utilitarian'?" *Hume Studies*, 2, no. 1 (1976): 12.

Goodman, Nelson. *Fact, Fiction, and Forecast*, 3rd ed. Indianapolis, Indiana, 1973.

Hart, H.L.A. *Punishment and Responsibility.* Oxford, 1968.

MacIntyre, Alasdair. *A Short History of Ethics.* New York, 1966.

Mill, John Stuart. "Nature." In *The Philosophy of John Stuart Mill*, edited by Marshall Cohen, pp. 445–488. New York, 1961.

———. *On Liberty.* New York, 1975.

Rawls, John. *A Theory of Justice.* Cambridge, Mass., 1971.

Rescher, Nicholas. "Belief-Contravening Suppositions," *Philosophical Review* 70 (1961): 176–196.

Robinson, John M. *An Introduction to Early Greek Philosophy.* New York, 1968.

Ross, W. D. *The Right and the Good.* Oxford, 1930.

Rousseau, Jean Jacques. *The Social Contract.* Edited by Charles Frankel. New York, 1951.

Sellars, Wilfrid. "Fatalism and Determinism." In *Freedom and Determinism*, edited by Keith Lehrer, pp. 141–174. New York, 1966.

Index

Library of Congress Cataloging in Publication Data

Aune, Bruce, 1933-
  Kant's theory of morals.

  Bibliography: p.
  Includes index.
    1. Kant, Immanuel, 1724-1804—Ethics.   2. Ethics.
I. Title.
B2799.E8A95   170'.92'4   79-17938
ISBN 0-691-07238-8
ISBN 0-691-02006-X pbk.